TAKE A STAND:
ART AGAINST HATE

A RAVEN CHRONICLES

ANTHOLOGY

Other Raven books and publications

Spirits of the Ordinary, A Tale of Casas Grandes
eBook, ISBN 987-0-9979468-6-4
by Kathleen Alcalá

Stealing Light, A Raven Chronicles Anthology, Selected Work 1991-1996
ISBN 978-0-9979468-5-7
Edited by Kathleen Alcalá, Phoebe Bosché, Paul Hunter, Stephanie Lawyer

Words From the Café, an anthology
ISBN 978-0-9979468-0-2
Edited by Anna Bálint

Raven Chronicles Vol. 26, Last Call
ISBN 978-0-9979468-4-0
Edited by Kathleen Alcalá, Anna Bálint, Phoebe Bosché,
Gary Copeland Lilley, Priscilla Long

Raven Chronicles Vol. 25, Balancing Acts
ISBN 978-0-9979468-3-3
Edited by Anna Bálint, Phoebe Bosché, Matt Briggs
Paul Hunter, Doug Johnson

Raven Chronicles Vol. 24, HOME
ISBN 978-0-9979468-2-6
Edited by Kathleen Alcalá, Anna Bálint, Phoebe Bosché,
Paul Hunter, Stephanie Lawyer

Raven Chronicles Vol. 23, Jack Straw Writers Program, 1997-2016
ISBN 978-0-9979468-1-9
Edited by Phoebe Bosché, Levi Fuller, Joan Rabinowitz

Take a Stand:
Art Against Hate

A Raven Chronicles

Anthology

Editors

Anna Bálint

Phoebe Bosché

Thomas Hubbard

Raven Chronicles Press
Seattle, Washington

Copyright © 2019-2020. Individual writers, artists, illustrators and photographers retain all rights to their work, unless they have other agreements with previous publishers.

All Rights Reserved. No part of this book may be reproduced, transmitted, or translated in any form or by any means, electronic or mechanical, including photocopy, recording, or any information storage and retrieval system now known or to be invented, without permission in writing from the publisher, except by a reviewer who wishes to quote brief passages in connection with a review written for inclusion in a magazine, newspaper, or broadcast.

FIRST EDITION

Published 2020
Printed in the United States of America.
ISBN 978-0-9979468-7-1
Library of Congress Control Number: 2020930725

Cover Art: Detail from: *Ganawenjiige Onigam* (*Caring for Duluth*, in Ojibwe language): *A New Symbol of Resilience in Duluth, Minnesota*
Created by Votan, in collaboration with NSRGNTS,
AICHO (American Indian Community Housing Organization)
and Honor The Earth, a nonprofit environmental organization.
https://www.aicho.org/water-protector-mural.html#/
http://www.nsrgnts.com
http://www.honorearth.org

Book Design: Phoebe Bosché, text composed in 12/16 Adobe Jenson Pro
Cover Design: Tonya Namura
Graphics & Logo Design: Scott Martin

Established in 1991, *The Raven Chronicles* is a Seattle-based literary organization that publishes and promotes artistic work and community events that embody the cultural diversity and multitude of imaginations of writers and artists living in the Pacific Northwest and other regions of the United States.

Raven Chronicles Press
15528 12th Avenue NE
Shoreline, Washington 98155-6226

editors@ravenchronicles.org
https://www.ravenchronicles.org

Another world is not only possible, she is on her way.
On a quiet day, I can hear her breathing.
—Arundhati Roy

I want you to feel the fear I feel every day. And then I want you to act.
I want you to act as you would in a crisis.
I want you to act as if our house is on fire. Because it is.
—Greta Thunberg

All acts of kindness are lights in the war for justice.
—Joy Harjo

The true measure of our character is how we treat the poor,
the disfavored, the accused, the incarcerated, and the condemned.
—Bryan G. Stevenson

Without hope we are lost.
—Mahmoud Darwish

Only from the heart can you touch the sky.
—Rumi

We can disagree and still love each other unless
your disagreement is rooted in my oppression
and denial of my humanity and right to exist.
—James Baldwin

The master's tools will never dismantle the master's house.
—Audre Lorde

Vi Hilbert, Skagit Tribal Elder, 1992, photograph, Joe Scaylea

TABLE OF CONTENTS

15 Foreword
16 Cover Art: Artist Statement by NSRGNTS
17 Preface
19 Introductions

I LEGACIES

24 Tanaya Winder · *Love Lessons in a Time of Settler Colonialism*
25 Nancy Cook · *Southern Minnesota Geography Lesson*
26 Susan Deer CLoud · *Bone Song*
29 Lucille Clifton · *slaveships*
30 Carletta Carrington Wilson · *letter to a laundress*
32 Frank Rossini · *The Day John Coltrane Died, July 17, 1967*
36 Jericho Brown · *Riddle*
37 Marc Beaudin · *El Sonido del Mar es Silencio*
40 Marc Beaudin · *Mexican, Unknown (Aphelocoma wollweberi)*
42 Rosalie Lander · *Santa Rosalía*
44 Scott T. Starbuck · *What I Can't Say at My Neighbor's Party Looking at a Map of the United States*
45 Lawrence Matsuda · *The Noble Thing*
47 Shankar Narayan · *Thanks*
50 Katelyn Durst Rivas · *We Are Here/Wij Zijn Heir*
52 Carletta Carrington Wilson · Who *are you to riot in Carandiru?*
55 Katelyn Winter · *Irene*
56 Katelyn Winter · *The Garza Case Arose as a Campaign Issue*
58 Valin Paige · *Necrofemme*
62 Janis Butler Holm · *Memo To Barbie: Re the Breakup*
64 Vanessa Taylor · *You're the dead girl in the database.*
66 Kenneth Pobo · *Days of 1972*
67 Larry C. Nichols · *Just Being a Friendly Guy*
68 Rayn Roberts · *Clear Water*

69 Risa Denenberg · *Yellow Star*
70 Marge Piercy · *They were praying*
72 Nicole Yurcaba · *And So They Brought Swastikas*
75 Richard Widerkehr · *Cracow*
76 Lawrence Matsuda · *Just a Short Note to Say Something You Already Know*
79 Matthew E. Henry · *said the band-aid to the shotgun wound*
81 Ilya Kaminsky · *We Lived Happily during the War*

II WE ARE HERE

85 Sheree La Puma · *A California Love Song*
87 Carrie Albert · *Angela of Liberty*
88 Danez Smith · *dinosaurs in the hood*
90 Kathleen Alcalá · *El Paso del Norte*
93 Catalina Marie Cantú · *Back Home*
95 Sara Beckmann · *Vignettes of Homelessness*
98 Gabriel Castilloux Calderón · *Nisidizowin (Suicide)*
102 Dave Seter · *Jackhammer*
103 Mercedes Lawry · *At the Drop-In Center*
105 Tom A. Delmore · *Homeless Vet*
106 Thomas Hubbard · *Lower Queen Anne*
108 Terra Trevor · *Sixty-Six Summers*
111 Richard Widerkehr · *At The Grace Café*
112 Tiffany Midge · *When White People Talk About their Country Being Stolen (I Throw Up in My Mouth a Little Bit)*
114 Stephani E.D. McDow · *Tired*
117 Anna Bálint · *Journeys*

III WHY?

127 Anita K. Boyle · *About Writing Political Poetry*
129 J.I. Kleinberg · *Neither Silence Nor Forgetting*

130 Ilya Kaminsky · *In a Time of Peace*
133 Judith Skillman · *Rabid Dog*
134 Mike Dillon · *Holocaust Denier*
135 Susan Rich · *For the first time I am afraid*
136 Paul Hunter · *The Tar Pit*
141 Edward Ahern · *An Apology for Hate*
142 Marge Piercy · *Dread, Not Envy*
144 henry 7. reneau, jr. · *The AK-47 Blues, or Sorting Through a History of Violence*
150 Miriam Bassuk · *Heartwood*
151 Eve Lyons · *Creature Powers*
153 Edward Harkness · *Union Creek in Winter*
155 Jeannine Hall Gailey · *Every Child is a Legend*
156 Faiza Sultan · *I Have Plenty of Things*
159 Jesse Minkert · *Grounds For An Investigation*
160 Ray Gonzalez · *The Border Is a Line*
162 Ibrahim Al-Masri · *On a Green Meadow*
165 Penina Ava Taesali · *One Blood*

IV EVIDENCE

171 Angelina Villalobos · *For the Man Who is Half of Me*
172 Jed Myers · *Lost Crossing*
175 Sharon M. Carter · *Un Botón Rojo*
176 Claudia Castro Luna · *I see myself, and courage and hope, in the faces of the caravan*
178 Kathleen Stancik · *Threat*
180 Stephani E.D. McDow · *A Letter to My Son*
183 Nancy Scott · *A Kid Called Diamond*
184 Jericho Brown · *Bullet Points*
185 henry 7. reneau, jr. · *The Saga of The Exit Wound*
188 Priscilla Long · *Things That Are Red*
190 Chris Espenshade · *Let's Go to the Video*
193 Rebecca Ruth Gould · *A Double Standard for White Terrorists*

195 Carl "Papa" Palmer · *Assumptions 1 and 2*
196 Anita Endrezze · *The Daily News*
197 Shankar Narayan · *The Times Asks Poets to Describe the Haze Over Seattle*
199 Mona Nicole Sfeir · *Beaten Zone*
202 Dunya Mikhail · *The War Works Hard*
204 Patrick Dixon · *"Men of a Military Age"*
206 Tamam Kahn · *Nurse's Day*
209 Eve Lyons · *Passover 5777: A Bop poem*
210 Shahed Yousaf · *Zero Tolerance*
211 Eneida P. Alcalde · *Roulette*
212 Beth Copeland · *Valentine's Day, 2018*
214 Carolyne Wright · *Ghazal for Emilie Parker*
215 Elaine Zimmerman · *Echo of Stone*
217 Nancy Canyon · *Archeology*
219 Ashley Jenkins (aka L.L. Asher) · *Someone's in Here*
221 Chip Livingston · *52 Hawks*
224 James Rodgers· *Orlando Rainbow*
227 Rayn Roberts · *After The Pulse Murders 2016*
229 Rob Jacques · *Matthew Shepard*
231 Jeanne Morel · *It's Happening Here, It's Happening There*
232 Morgan Russell · *Promised Land*
233 Katheen Alcalá · *What Tahlequah Said*
236 Tess Gallagher · *In the Too Bright Café*
239 Cynthia Neely · *Trolling for Cougar*
241 Keats Conley · *The God of Monarch Butterflies*
241 Keats Conley · *The God of Vaquitas*
242 Anna Odessa Linzer· *Almost Forgetting*
243 Hannah Yoest · *Static Hazards*
245 dan raphael · *Whose Hand Between my Head and the Door Frame*
248 Karen Bonaudi · *Exiles*
249 Erin Jamieson · *Legacy*
251 Anita Goveas · *Rocks on Wheels*
253 Janet Cannon · *flawed algorithm*

254 Janet Cannon · *really?*
256 Judith Roche · *The Continent of Plastic*

V RESISTANCE

260 Anita Endrezze · *The Wall*
263 Danez Smith · *dear white america*
265 Ronda Piszk Broatch · *A Woman Holds a Baby and a Machete*
266 Stuart Gunter · *When I Speak About Gun Control
    I Wear My Son's Shoes*
267 Ellery Akers · *Taking Action*
268 F.I. Goldhaber · *Take The Knee*
270 Tiffany Midge · *Attack of the Fifty-Foot (Lakota) Woman*
273 Keanu Jones · *Identity*
275 Stephanie Barbé Hammer · *Counter-Protest*
277 Priscilla Long · *Lecture to a Girlfriend*
278 Jennifer deBie · *Lessons*
281 Mary Ellen Talley · *Migration*
282 Andrew C. Brown · *Free the land for the refugees*
283 Susana Praver-Pérez · *Just Breathe*
286 Melissa Kwasny · *In Your Face*
291 Margaret DeRitter · *The Visible Woman*
292 Stuart Stromin · *World Cup 2018*
293 Gary Copeland Lilley · *The Coyotes*
298 Brynn McCall · *those boys*
300 Gail Tremblay · *Strategies for Outlasting Trumplandia*
301 Susan Deer Cloud · *The Way to Rainbow Mountain*
304 Brendan Connolly · *#4*
305 Sherry Rind · *There Willl Be No Revolution*
307 Alice Derry · *Tender*
310 T. Clear · *When the Patriarchy Crumbles:
    Instructions for Men*
313 Penina Ava Taesali · *The Word of the Day*
316 Rajiv Mohabir · *Why Whales Are Back in New York City*
319 Ellery Akers · *At Any Moment, There Could be a
    Swerve in a Different Direction*

VI RAVEN NOTES

    322 · Notes, Permissions and Publication Credits
    Biographical Notes
        328 · Artists/Illustrators
        339 · Writers
        362 · Foreword
        363 · Editors
    365 · Acknowledgments
    366 · Ads
    367 · Publisher Information

LIST OF ARTISTS AND ILLUSTRATORS

Pages art/illustrations appear on:

Niel Abston: 28
Maryna Ajaja: 213
Carrie Albert: 39, 218
Anonymous: 91
Alfredo Arreguín: 84
Kree Arvanitas: 321
Anna Bálint: 14, 306, 318, 320
Phoebe Bosché: 240
Jasmine Iona Brown: 189
Jane Caminos: 116
Sharon M. Carter: 152, 174, 262
Manit Chaotragoongit: 49, 71, 230
Daniel J. Combs: 82
Lisa Dailey: 168
Jay Dearien: 271
Sarah Deckro: 94, 223
Susan Deer Cloud: 289, 303
Andrew Drawbaugh: 192
Noel Franklin: 314-315
Tatiana Garmendia: 290
Jan Gosnell: 126
Lindsey Morrison Grant: 170
Kathleen Gunton: 309
Ethar Hamid: 78
Danielle Hark: 264
Hank Hobby: 124
Doug Johnson: 57
Tom Kiefer: 179
Sarah E.N. Kohrs: 182, 280
Deborah Faye Lawrence: 250, 269
Russell Lee: 31
Mario Loprete: 208
Michaela McGuire: 274

Tiffany Midge: 255
Meredith Bricken Mills: 285
Nuansi: 235
Caroline Orr: 297
J. Ray Paradiso: 201, 247
Willie Pugh: 74, 97
Ana Rodriguez: 149
Tonya Russell: 60
Joe Scaylea: 6
Mona Nicole Sfeir: 164
Dave Sims: 63, 132
Catherine E. Skinner: 312
Kali Spitzer: 258
Nico Vassilakis: 35
Votan: Cover Artist
Timothy White Eagle: 22
Matika Wilbur: 123
Christopher Woods: 140, 158
Angel Ybarra: 104
Lawrence Paul Yuxweluptun: 101

Nkyinkyim Installation, Sculpture by Ghanian artist Kwame Akoto-Bamfo,
National Memorial for Peace and Justice in Montgomery, Alabama,
2018, photograph, Anna Bálint

"The National Memorial for Peace and Justice, which opened to the public on April 26, 2018, is the nation's first memorial dedicated to the legacy of enslaved black people, people terrorized by lynching, African Americans humiliated by racial segregation and Jim Crow, and people of color burdened with contemporary presumptions of guilt and police violence."
—Equal Justice Initiative (EJI)

FOREWORD

Come, Let Us Reason Together

Hate, from the Middle English *haten*, from Old English *hatian* ("to hate, treat as an enemy"), from Proto-Germanic *hatōną* ("to hate"), from Proto-Germanic *hataz*. Cognate with Dutch *haten*, German *hassen*, Swedish *hata*, French *haïr* (a Germanic borrowing).

It seems it is everywhere. Old as the Bible when Cain lifted his club to kill his brother. Or was it his hands, or his spear? Possibly a rock against the head because the blood that spilled to the ground cried out to God— Genesis 4:10.

How to get rid of someone you don't like? Easy. Hate is punctual. Always showing up. It is ubiquitous as air.

How to withstand it? Where is respite? Shade from the boiling pot? Where is the hot-pad? The oven-mitt? Where is the antidote—or could it be anecdote? The poems and stories in this anthology, *Take a Stand: Art Against Hate,* offer necessary anecdotes against hate. How to combat what has uprisen. Common as crabgrass—hatred is rudimentary. It takes effort to confront it.

These pieces are protest against violence, injustice, cruelty. They are resistance. They are inscription, instruction, witness, warning, remedy, solution, even solace. They document what has been experienced. "I am saying the names / of dead children out loud." ["Every Child is a Legend," Jeannine Hall Gailey].

There are as many ways to experience hate as there are events among a diverse and divided people. It is a strong feeling. It divides those who hate and those who are recipients of that hatred. Whether it is a wall that divides races or nations, "Let it [the wall] be built / of guacamole so we can have a bigly block party." ["The Wall," Anita Endrezze].

Whether it be a wall that divides us from the natural world, "There was a moment when shooting egrets for feathers became wrong. / There was a moment when the Wilderness Act / changed the lives of billions of blades of grass." ["At any Moment, There Could be a Swerve in a Different Direction," Ellery Akers].

Whether it divides a person from who they are and who they were intended to be. Hatred whittles into a person and makes them only part of themselves. [What is that sinister emoji that moves along eating everything in its path?] Hatred is an internal back-space that eats the person who carries it.

The expansion of prejudice and intolerance seems to be more than it used to be. Maybe it only has come out of hiding. For the immediacy of a "Many-splendored hate" ["An Apology for Hate," Edward Ahern], *Take a Stand: Art Against Hate, A Raven Chronicles Anthology*, offers an even more immediacy of these many-splendored words.

This anthology is relief. As did Abel's blood, these poems, stories and illustrations, cry out from the ground. 📖

—Diane Glancy
1 January 2020

Cover Art: Artist Statement by NSRGNTS

Ganawenjiige Onigam (Caring for Duluth in Ojibwe Language): A New Symbol of Resilience in Duluth, Minnesota. "The painting [mural] is the first piece of public art in Duluth for and by indigenous people," Moira Villiard, AICHO Arts and Cultural Program Coordinator.

"America suffers from historical amnesia. It is apparent that well into this millennium, the original inhabitants of this paradise still suffer the after effects of colonialism. People seeking freedom arrived on these shores over 500 years ago. It is unfortunate that in the pursuit of theirs, we were to lose ours. Corralled into areas deemed unfit for human survival, we overcame harsh conditions and thrived. The threat of our existence as a people has metastasized much like an autoimmune disease. Post colonialism has outgrown its life threatening behavior to the point that it's own life is under threat.

"Invasion, slavery, relocation and many other forms of abuse weren't enough. We have now reached a point in our lives where we are all part of the sickness. We aren't just being abused, we abuse each other and we abuse our home. By annihilating ourselves, we are on a vicious course to do the same to the planet. Things have to change. The after effects are affecting us all. They are deeply ingrained in our communities. We have mistaken abuse for progress.

"One of the current issues, is oil. We are wise enough to see the effect of its intoxicating consumption. Beside it's pollution, the devastating effects it has in native communities is ostracized. This mural addresses this tiny fragment and puts it on a large platform. Women and children in our communities are being abducted, sold, raped and murdered for the pleasure of workers in this industry. If we address the problem, we can create solutions. Renewable energy, education and empowerment are vital. Let's change the beaten path of history."

This mural was completed in August 2017 by NSRGNTS (lead artist Votan), with help from over fifty community members who came to assist the artists in finishing the designs on the jingle dress. The mural is located at Gimaajii-Mino-Bimaadizimin (202 W. 2nd Street, Duluth, MN), overlooking the solar rooftop gardens. For a photo of the mural being painted by artists Votan and Derek Brown: https://www.aicho.org/water-protector-mural.html#/.

PREFACE

A Swerve in a Different Direction: Art Against Hate

It's been a helluva regime, the last three-plus years in the U.S.A.—also known as the swathe of territory stolen from sea to shining sea by European invader-settlers, land stolen from the original Indigenous inhabitants, through war, disease, pillaging and plundering of hunting and fishing areas, and sham treaties imposed on starving and downcast survivors and then broken with abandon by the victors. Our U.S. Constitution, a document drafted and quill-penned in longhand by the so-called Founding Fathers—educated, high-minded, mainly slave-owning, patrician white male descendants of immigrants from England—has been under greater than usual threat from the forces of hatred, bigotry, racism and violence unleashed by the current occupant of the so-called White House (a structure which was built mainly by African and Afro-descended slaves).

But now our Constitution is in deep danger. From the moment that 45 declared his candidacy, he taunted and verbally bullied the other candidates of his party all the way to the nomination, and then he ranted at campaign rallies against Mexican immigrants as "rapists and criminals," blaming them for taking jobs from white working-class men— jobs lost in large part to offshoring and to automation effected by the super-wealthy, white-male corporate overlords, of which 45 purports to be one.

Best known before 2015 as the NYC-tabloid figure who yelled "YOU'RE FIRED" with vengeful glee on reality shows: from the moment this TV celebrity with at least one foot in the criminal underworld taunted his Democratic rival as "a nasty woman," and on national television called on "Russia, if you're listening," to hack his opponent's 30,000 emails; from the moment that he led chants of "Lock Her Up" at his Nüremberg-style campaign rallies, we grew increasingly alarmed. By the time the 2016 election was called, we knew that this country was in dire peril. The resistance began immediately—the day after the January 2017 inauguration, the worldwide Women's March drew millions of women in pink pussy hats (and the men who support them) into the streets to express their defiance against tyranny and hatred, and to declare solidarity with the forces of peace, equality and justice. A few days later, many were demonstrating at airports against the abruptly-tweeted executive order banning the entry of travelers from Muslim countries. Soon thereafter, caravans of refugees from Central America and beyond streamed toward the U.S southern border, and government agents were breaking up migrant families, separating children from their parents and infamously locking the kids in cages, without adequate water, food, access to bathrooms, or protection from heat and cold. Heart-rending images went viral—the photo of a Guatemalan father and his toddler daughter, face-down in the shallows of the Rio Grande, both drowned on the very shores of what they hoped would be their Promised Land.

The dark forces have always been present, but now they were crawling out of the darkness into plain sight. Emboldened by dog-whistle racism and outright insults like "Go back where you came from!" directed at U.S.-born, recently elected congressional representatives of color, various groups of white supremacists, neo-Nazis, and right-wing extremists expressed their hatred openly in acts of violence that some politicians are finally calling it what it is—domestic terrorism. There was the notorious Unite the Right protest rally in Charlottesville, in which tiki torch-carrying white nationalists chanted "Jews will not replace us," and one young woman was murdered by a far-right extremist accelerating his car into a crowd of counter-protestors. The Hater in Chief's response? To declare that there were "very fine people on both sides." And African American men continue to be murdered by the police—Eric Garner's choked cry, "I Can't Breathe," goes on resounding, while the right wing professes outrage at Black Lives Matter and other initiatives to promote respect for citizens of color.

Reader, you hold in your hands the wide range of proactively humanitarian and nonviolent stances that poets, artists, and activists have taken in response to the many troubles afflicting us in this era. We can regard *Take a Stand: Art Against Hate* as a print-form peace march, an ongoing campaign for justice for all of the struggles embodied in these writings and depicted in the photos and artwork included here. This is a deeply democratic anthology—standing alongside nationally prominent voices such as Jericho Brown, Lucille Clifton, Tess Gallagher, Ilya Kaminsky, Dunya Mikhail, Marge Piercy and Danez Smith, are luminaries renowned in this region and beyond, such as Kathleen Alcalá, Anna Bálint, Gary Copeland Lilley, Claudia Castro Luna, Melissa Kwasny, Priscilla Long, Tiffany Midge, and Gail Tremblay. Plus every other voice within this print collective, from every ethnicity and background—I see us all moving forward, holding aloft our banners and placards in a grand march across these pages, proclaiming the vision of a more just and peaceful society, sustaining connections with our origins and building a future in which, in the words of poet Ellery Akers, there could be "a swerve in a different direction." May we find ourselves there, in the words of poet Tanaya Winder, "whole and sacred, alive and breathing and breathing and breathing." 📖

—Carolyne Wright
Seattle, January 2020

INTRODUCTIONS

Anna Bálint: This anthology contains poems, stories and images from 117 writers and 53 artists, divided into five fluid and intersecting sections: *Legacies, We Are Here, Why?, Evidence,* and *Resistance*. We begin with *Legacies* because the current increased climate of hate in this country didn't begin with the 2016 election, and to find its roots we must look to U.S. history. This is why *Legacies* begins where the U.S. began—with the genocide of Native Americans and enslavement of Africans. From there the section loosely winds its way through time to touch on crucial events and different chapters of our nation's history up to the present.

What is striking is how much of the work found in *Legacies* includes a dialogue between the past and present that strongly underscores the connection between the two. The opening poem, "Love Lessons in a Time of Settler Colonialism," by Tanya Winder, and moments later the poem, "letter to a laundress" by Carletta Carrington Wilson, are powerful examples of this. Also striking are the frequent references to silence. Silence imposed from without by the halls of power, and silences within families, born of fear. Stories not told, languages no longer spoken, events not talked about. Rape, the Holocaust, WWII internment of the Japanese. Yet, at the same time, this silence is also repeatedly broken by the voices of the writers themselves; it's broken by their writings joined by images that together confront the past and expose the myths of racial and gender superiority and the sense of entitlement that this country is founded on.

All of which brings us to, and spills over into, *We Are Here*. It is this second section that responds to the plea of a refugee who calls out from a poem by Katelyn Durst Rivas—also titled "We Are Here"—that appears in *Legacies*. "I am asking you, to look at me, see me in the shadows"—pleads the refugee in Rivas's poem. By answering this plea in the second section—where we see, really *see*, and hear from some of the most vulnerable, overlooked, and stigmatized people in our society, found on the street, sleeping in doorways, in institutions—a kind of call and response between sections is established, one that repeats later on in other sections and carries throughout this entire collection. *We Are Here* also declares the continued Mexican presence in the U.S.—both indigenous and migrant. It challenges and knocks down the stereotypes that keep us from really seeing one another, most notably in Danez Smith's poem "dinosaurs in the hood." Other stories in this section ask us to consider the lives, frustrations, viewpoints, and exhaustion of several different women of color, before returning us to where this section began: with the plight of refugees, both the newly arrived and living in our midst, and the uprooted millions on other continents, still fleeing violence, still living in limbo, still in search of a home.

The section *Why?* is the place in this anthology that most grapples with the philosophical underpinnings of hate; where different viewpoints, ideas, and theories are expressed. Some pieces call out to challenge privilege, both "white skin" and "first world" privilege. The multiple angles and directions that this section's querying takes us is often suggested by titles: "Dread, Not Envy" (Marge Piercy), "Creature Powers" (Eve Lyons), "Grounds For An Investigation" (Jesse Minkert), "The AK-47 Blues, or Sorting Through a History of Violence (henry 7. reneau, jr.).

By the end of the third section *Why?*, readers have almost certainly noticed how many of the pieces seem to belong in more than section. For example, echoes of Jericho Brown's poem "Riddle"—which appears in *Legacies*—are heard loud and clear in *Why?*

Read on. Notice how the different sections begin to sing to one another. How a poem or story over here is echoed by, or reaffirmed by, a voice or image over there. Note the urgency with which *Evidence* gives its testimony, calling witness after witness. Many voices now join the voices heard earlier in the anthology to honor the dead, named and unnamed. Eric Garner, Emmett Till, Trayvon Martin, Matthew Shephard, Emilie Parker, Jakelin Amei Rosmery Caal Maquin—names juxtaposed with the "dead girl in the database," the "Mexican, Unknown," the countless unnamed dead of Dunya Mikhail's "The War Works Hard;" a dead and unnamed baby Orca.

Evidence addresses the pressure of living in a state of constant anxiety and fear. ICE raids and deportations. Fear of becoming a target for the police, for bigots, by going to school. The fears of Black parents as expressed in Stephani E.D McDow's "A Letter to My Son." Other stories and poems testify about war in the Middle East, in Iraq and Syria, about Drone strikes. About unbreathable air, about clear-cutting, and oceans filled with plastic.

In contrast, hope runs throughout *Resistance*, the fifth and final section, like a motif. Hope as embodied in dreams. Hope born of actions, of protests and counter-protests. The hope that springs up alongside hate, born of victories, even small ones. The section opens with two very different poems that both dare to dream: "The Wall" by Anita Endrezze, and "dear white america" by Danez Smith.

Endrezze's poem is a free-flowing re-imagining and continual transformation of the U.S.-Mexico border wall that starts by building "a wall of saguaros, / butterflies, and bones" and ends by transforming the wall into "a gallery of graffiti art // a border of stories we already know by heart." Which, of course, already has happened, and continues to happen with a flowering of art and performances all along the current border fence.

In "dear white america," Smith dreams of leaving Earth to create a "new story & history you cannot steal or sell or cast overboard or hang or beat or / drown or own . . ." His poem brings to mind the old stories of flying Africans, of escaping slavery to fly home to Africa. Smith spells out loud and clear—for the benefit of White America—his reasons for leaving Earth: what life in America always has been and still is for Black people—and then returns to the dream both as a means of escaping the unbearable and as a declaration of liberation. "i've left Earth to find a place / where my kin can be safe, where black people ain't but people the same color as the / good, wet earth . . ."

Resistance also includes a robust collection of writings by women that take on and deconstruct existing gender stereotypes in a variety of different and spirited ways—as often suggested by their titles. "Attack of the Fifty-Foot (Lakota) Woman"—Tiffany Midge; "In Your Face"—Melissa Kwansy; "The Visible Woman"—Margaret DeRitter; "When the Patriarchy Crumbles: Instructions for Men"—T. Clear.

The second to last poem in *Resistance*, and in the book, is "Why Whales Are Back in New York City" by Rajiv Mohabir. In this wonderful poem, even as "ICE beats doors / down on Liberty Avenue / to deport. . . ." and "white supremacy gathers / at the sidewalks . . ." Mohabir finds hope. He finds it in the return of humpback whales, once driven away by pollution, who now migrate again to Queens. As he protests the presence of white supremacists he reminds himself, reminds us, to "Behold the miracle: / what was once lost / now leaps before you."

Phoebe Bosché: Though we have many mouths, many tongues, we are often mute in the face of so many lies, so many broken treaties, so many justifications, so many meaningless words strung together and uttered by folks who say they represent our best interests. Who use words as tools of oppression and manipulation to confuse the real issues, the real meanings. The writers and artists represented here use words and art to get at those issues, those meanings, those long silences. They speak with one great tongue.

Thomas Hubbard: This anthology of writing, photos and various artworks, welcomes us in the manner of a good friend who stands nearby, speaking to us, perhaps touching our shoulder to gain our attention, pointing out something we need to see, showing us the overriding fact that all people are human, with love for family, pleasure in friendship, pride in honest work, and the willingness to stand up for one's beliefs.

And we also discover, perhaps, that some of our own beliefs and attitudes may need revision.

Some folks say hate causes division, others say division causes hate. They're all correct. These two human foibles feed one another, often blinding us from the fact of our shared humanity. Writers, photographers, artists, musicians—sometimes gain celebrity by creating works that can help to lift away whatever may block our vision of the goodness in others. But among us also walk rare individuals like Vi Hilbert, the late Skagit Tribal Elder, whose very presence revealed to us our own and others' humanity.

When I taught at the Heritage High School on the Tulalip Reservation, Vi Hilbert used to visit our classrooms from time to time. She would act as a teacher's aide, but what she did in my classroom far exceeded that function. She spread harmony by her own example. Even my most disruptive students would cooperate to make the class pleasant during her visit and for days afterward.

Individuals like Vi Hilbert don't necessarily possess the talents to create art or literature, but they have the ability to listen, to see, to appreciate and to focus on the value inherent in others. Such individuals exude gentle respect for everyone and everything. The respect they bring is contagious, opening our eyes, our ears, and our heart to the, sometimes, hidden love (or fear) everyone carries.

It is my extreme pleasure and good fortune to be a part of this global collection, a book designed and published to evoke in readers the gentle power of understanding. Even when the "other side" shows no respect, no reason, we can. For our own benefit, let us pause before denouncing those aligned against us, until we hear their words, see their situation, and appreciate their humanity. 📖

Sister Hellfire, 2019, ancestor painting, Timothy White Eagle

I

LEGACIES

Stolen bodies working stolen land. It was an engine that did not stop, its hungry boiler fed with blood.
—Colson Whitehead

Until we know the assumptions in which we are drenched, we cannot know ourselves.
—Adrienne Rich

And I cried ... for all of the women who stretched their bodies for civilizations, only to find ruins.
—Sonia Sanchez

We live in the age of the refugee, the age of the exile.
—Ariel Dorfman

... ignorance allied with power is the most ferocious enemy justice can have.
—James Baldwin

Love Lessons in a Time of Settler Colonialism

Tanaya Winder

"I am not murdered, and I am not missing, but parts of me have been disappeared." —Leanne Simpson

In my poetry workshops I ask my students "if you could have any superhero power, what would it be?" All of the Indigenous girls respond, "invisibility."

They too know all too well that some cracks were built just for us to fall through. We live in a world that tries to steal spirits each day; they steal ours by taking us away.

From Industrial Schools to forced assimilation, genocide means removal of those who birth nations—our living threatens. Colonization has been choking

us for generations. I tell my girls they are vessels of spirit, air to lungs expanding; this world cannot breathe without us. There are days I wish

I didn't have to teach these lessons, but as an Indigenous womxn silence is deadening. There is danger in being seen, our bodies are targets

marked for violence. We carry the Earth's screams *me too* inside us, a howling wind our mother's & their mother's swallowed these bullets long ago.

The voices ricochet *I wish I was invisible I wish I was invisible I wish* echoes in my eardrums—we know what it's like to live in fear. Colonialism's bullet, sits cocked,

waiting behind a finger on trigger. We breathe and speak and sing for survival. We carve out in lines; we write—*I know joy   I know pain   I know love*

I know love   I know—lessons we've carried throughout time. Should I go missing: don't stop searching; drag every river until it turns red and the waters of our names

stretch a flood so wide it catches everything. And we find each other whole and sacred, alive and breathing and breathing and breathing.

Southern Minnesota Geography Lesson

Nancy Cook

Here's an interesting
fact: In this place
five rivers lie
within five miles
of each other, five
rivers that flow north,
(not the usual way),
to the Minnesota River
which flows north
into the Mississippi,
a north-south line
of muddied waters
dividing this land,
these United States,
between east and west.

There is also this fact:
The Winnebago,
a landed tribe of farmers,
ran from five states—
were forced to run—
forced to leave Wisconsin,
forced to run from Iowa,
forced to leave Nebraska,
forced out of South Dakota,
forced from Minnesota, forced
to run west south east north,
a broken line of families
divided, lost by half,
then half again with
every dislocation,
a river of human history
flowing the wrong way.

Bone Song

Susan Deer Cloud

When I read about that high limestone cave
looking out on the Anuy River's sinuous silver
parting Siberia's summer mountains, when
I saw the photographs showing the bones
found there, an old bear femur flute song
shrilled through my 21st century bones
resonating to what the scientists found
among the scattered shards . . .

90,000 year old female bone fragment
whose mitochondrial DNA whispered
her mother was Neanderthal, whose
other DNA murmured her father was Denisovan.

Did that female have some sense of what I call
the Great Mystery? Did she create a language?
Did that being whisper poetry or begin to sing
when sun welcomed her wakening each morning
at cave opening, smiling at rays conjuring up
star sparkles on a river where later she would
finger-fish and swim nakedly in the pure waters.

Little dreaming bone rescued from the cave's
sedimentary layers, could you feel your sun again
when scientists brought you up for air
after all those unsmiling centuries? And
what my intuition clamors to know
since my DNA holds lineage both Neanderthal
and Denisovan, and my mitochondrial migrations
include ancient grandmothers dwelling in Siberia . . .

Am I descended from you, dear Hybrid?
Are you somehow the reason why I am sparked
to write poems and lilt stories with epicanthic eyelids
around northern campfires? Are you why I wear
this hair long and have felt it as residual fur
whenever making love? Are you the key
to why even as I migrate into old age, I still go
skinny dipping in a starry river?

You Can't Take This From Me, 2019, painting, Niel Abston

slaveships

Lucille Clifton

loaded like spoons
into the belly of Jesus
where we lay for weeks for months
in the sweat and stink
of our own breathing
Jesus
why do you not protect us
chained to the heart of the Angel
where the prayers we never tell
and hot and red
as our bloody ankles
Jesus
Angel
can these be men
who vomit us out from ships
called Jesus   Angel   Grace of God
onto a heathen country
Jesus
Angel
ever again
can this tongue speak
can these bone walk
Grace Of God
can this sin live

letter to a laundress

Carletta Carrington Wilson

you taught her well they say she had the touch
took wrinkled, soiled shirts made them
like new especially collars and cuffs

her hands mirror yours lifting
picking piece by piece apart
ink, sweat, blood, mud, grass, vomit

what to do with dirty looks, foul language, rank stench
shadowy stains that remain after all that scrubbing
deftly rubbing, rubbing, rubbing   and no way out

wringer, iron holder, washwoman leaning in line
with lines untenable lines whose far-reaching consequences
found you standing in the path of a past
on its way to the future

my line of inquiry like the lines of this letter
crosses lines never meant to be crossed
only crossed out, bleached, faded away
in the way blood's unlettered lines meet their dead-lines

drawn into silence   the line of her lips
like you she was maid of all work
made to serve made of service made to serve the soiled

washing stick   line peg   lye soap   bluing
sort the sordid haul that heaviness never
done the work of daughters who keep company with cloth

a dryness fitted to fingers that soak, boil
scrub, rub, pour   rinse wring,
tightly wring   wrung out dampness riveted to iron
fold over/over keep pressing, pressing on

mothers of blue blue waters, Missouri, Kansas, 1938,
photograph, Russell Lee

hoist baskets   tote tubs   lug those loads
every bundle extends a line
a line awaiting a line awaiting its hangings

lines stretch their length across a yard
beyond which lie the waters
well water   lake water   spring water
creek water   in rain   falling rain
a sorrowing soaks riversides in creek bed grief
who there   drenched by despair

oh mother, mothers mothers of blue, blue waters
who hung from those knotted lines

The Day John Coltrane Died, July 17, 1967

Frank Rossini

the day before John Coltrane died
Robert Hunt a young Black soldier on leave
died in the Cairo, Illinois jail
the police report stated he was stopped
for a faulty tail light
arrested for disorderly conduct
when he became verbally aggressive

the report stated that Robert Hunt's cellmate
called for a jailor shortly after midnight
that the cellmate saw Robert Hunt hang himself
by his own t-shirt from wire mesh
nailed to the cell ceiling
that the coroner verified the cause of death
asphyxiation by hanging
directed the body be sent
to a funeral home to be embalmed
then returned to family

the undertaker saw bruises on Hunt's body
called the local NAACP president
he viewed the body
confirmed the undertaker's observations
visited the jail cell
tried to hang from the wire mesh
his weight pulled the mesh loose
he asked to talk to the cellmate
was told he had been released
asked for his name
they couldn't find the records
he requested an investigation
his request was denied

the day John Coltrane died fires burned in Cairo
residents protested in the streets
some were beaten & jailed
the police chief called for the National Guard
deputized a group of white citizens
they named themselves "The White Hats"
the head of the local NAACP demanded a federal probe
J. Edgar Hoover ordered the FBI to investigate
the protest leaders
Robert Hunt's case was closed
the protests continued for six years

on the forty-seventh anniversary
of John Coltrane's death
Eric Garner stopped a fight
on the Staten Island street corner
where he sometimes sold
single untaxed cigarettes
two police officers arrived
& announced their intent to arrest him
he objected   kept moving his hands
to avoid being cuffed
three more officers arrived
the five surrounded him
one put his forearm across Garner's throat
the others pulled him to the ground
Garner cried "I can't breathe"
one knelt on his back
another pressed Garner's face into the pavement
eleven more times Garner repeated
"I can't breathe"

on the day John Coltrane died
graced by his family's presence
his wife Alice Turiya says his last breath
was "beautiful" maybe he'd found
that more beautiful sound he always
was seeking

on that same date
forty-seven years later
a block from his home
& family Eric Garner died
in the arms of five
New York City policemen
his last words his last breath

I can't breathe

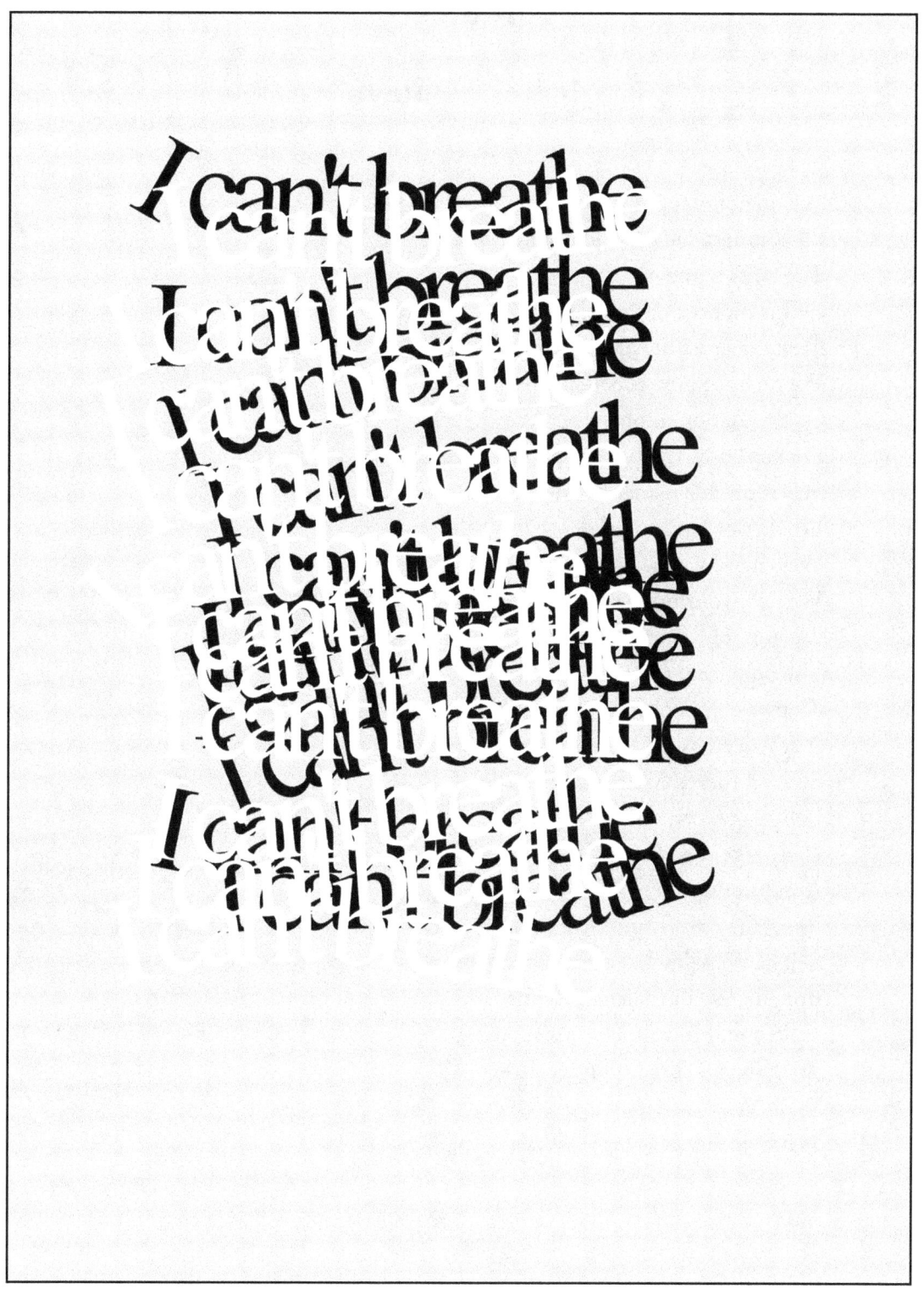

Eric Garner/The Eleven, 2019, Nico Vassilakis
[*Garner was said to have repeated the words "I can't breathe" 11 times while lying face down on the sidewalk.*]

Riddle

Jericho Brown

We do not recognize the body
Of Emmett Till. We do not know
The boy's name nor the sound
Of his mother wailing. We have
Never heard a mother wailing.
We do not know the history
Of this nation in ourselves. We
Do not know the history of our-
Selves on this planet because
We do not have to know what
We believe we own. We believe
We own your bodies but have no
Use for your tears. We destroy
The body that refuses use. We use
Maps we did not draw. We see
A sea so cross it. We see a moon
So land there. We love land so
Long as we can take it. Shhh. We
Can't take that sound. What is
A mother wailing? We do not
Recognize music until we can
Sell it. We sell what cannot be
Bought. We buy silence. Let us
Help you. How much does it cost
To hold your breath underwater?
Wait. Wait. What are we? What?
What on Earth are we? What?

El Sonido del Mar es Silencio

Marc Beaudin

    1
Somewhere between
an endless field of morning-closed wildflowers
and the bitterness of another rented room
I stand waist-deep in the sea's embrace
allowing the riptide to drag me through the sand
into a mystery we can know but once

    Listen:
The way the wind sometimes
catches a dead leaf
and transforms it in the space of a pulse beat
into a bird taking flight
is the kind of miracle one should live for—
I have been told
that you must never watch
a bird fly past the horizon or it will take
a small part of your soul with it

But what is the soul
if not the sum
of the flights
of a thousand birds?

    2
The sea at Puerto Madero is warmer than tears
eats continually at the feet of Chiapas
is sister not to the rivers of jungle valleys
and coffee plantations
but to the patient volcanoes
like Tacaná, thunder and haze
of the Guatemalan border

We spent two days climbing:
crossing the path of a death-offering snake
eating *pan dulce* with village children
and being questioned by the Mexican Army
on patrol, looking for Zapatistas

When they find them
let each soldier fall to his knees
and beg forgiveness for the last 500 years
Let them speak the names of the dead
Let their mouths be filled with the dust of the graves

Let this be true for every soldier
but more so
for every priest of the Pentagon
every general of Wall Street
every tycoon of Evangelism

Let it be true for you
        and me

    3

The sound of the sea
contains everything
swells out of control if we try to listen
overwhelms our capacity to hear until
infinite sound
        becomes
                silence

    El sonido del mar es silencio
500 years in a single wave
      Silencio

History rises and falls with a single tide
    Silencio
It was the children who gave *us* sweet bread—
                                        we had nothing
    Silencio
Always: Another bird with eyes of ocean, takes to the sky.

Bird Without Borders, 2017, drawing, Carrie Albert

Mexican, Unknown
(*Aphelocoma wollweberi*)

Marc Beaudin

The overgrown two-track
bloodhounds its nose
up into the Chiricahua Mountains
cresting near the wrought-iron gate
of this all-but-forgotten cemetery
where Mexican jays flash
blue and gray from alligator
juniper to Apache pines
& many of the graves are
marked only with a metal plate—
letters hammer-stamped one-
at-a-time into each rust-gathering face—
"Mine Accident" is fairly common
others speak "Mexican Child" or
"Mexican / Mrs. Lucero / Mother"
but the one that gets into my blood
the one that silences the jays
& drifts under my fingers like
river stones says simply
"Mexican, Unknown"

At the Geronimo Memorial
an obelisk of cobblestones resembling
a beehive that's lost its sting
a roadside non-attraction that
doesn't mark the spot but
implies the proximity of
the place the great Apache hero
surrendered to the America-first
wall-builders of their day

beneath the constant assault
of Border Patrol helicopters
in a desert where ICE agents
dump emergency water tanks
into the dirt guaranteeing
the deaths of children
some Beautiful Unknown
has spray-painted the three-word sermon:
"Chinga la Migra"
in letters as delicate and true
as the flights of corvids
in the mountain sunlight

Santa Rosalía

Rosalie Lander

My mother says *The Peninsula*
the same way she says my name.
The same way she mixes tomatillos
with the soul of rice
and stuffs them, still bloody
deep inside the hollowed-out bodies of chilies.

At Christmas, we unwrap tamales
steam rising from the flesh of the masa
to kiss the lightbulbs above our heads.
But none of the tamales were made by us.
We've forgotten the recipe—and no one has time
to teach it to us again.

My mother kept her maiden name.
It's all she has of the Peninsula. And
even then, it's blanched in the American sun.
Villa. Like Pancho. They took the rest
when the family came north.
Nobody above Baja knows about the second half
—*vicencio* lies forgotten at the border.

We pull tortillas from plastic bags
store-bought, like our music.
Like our language.
Like our names. Ironed out
with flour-covered rolling pins
pale powder over bronze flesh.

Because Great Great Grandpa never wanted to remember
where he came from, or where he left.
Because Great Great Grandpa refused to teach his language

to his children, and it bleached like a bone in the sun.
Because *Clemente* became American.
And never looked back.

Villa is all that's left. And my mother
named me *Rosalie* to remember
her forgotten aunt—the mystery woman.
The hysteric.
And *Rosalie* to remember
a spit of town on the coast,
dusty and dry. Left behind . . .
a place she only visited
once.

What I Can't Say at My Neighbor's Party Looking at a Map of the United States

Scott T. Starbuck

Texas is, and always has always been,
an upside down shark eating Mexico.
Florida is a phallic reminder of how
the nation got screwed—twice.
And who can forget Louisiana getting the boot
during Katrina with all those families on roofs?

I lived in California during Enron deregulation
where code names "Fat Boy," "Death Star,"
"Get Shorty," made us the laughingstock of the nation,
and for those with no air conditioning in August,
we were a giant handle connected to
everything in this country, and nothing.

I recalled Hermosa's Our Lady of Guadalupe School
where it was "one nation under God
with liberty and justice for all"
while California flapped its red star and brown bear.

No one said anything about Mexican families
dying of thirst or hypothermia
in Sonoran and Chihuahuan Deserts,
and mountain areas, trying to get across the border.
Instead, all eyes were fixed on Christ,
white as Wonder Bread with its wrapper
of red, yellow, blue balloons
like crayons melting into Redondo's Saltwater Pool,
or we stared at mighty Pacific with her bikinis,
surfboards, steel-blue fish.

The Noble Thing

Lawrence Matsuda

Dad never talked about Minidoka.
That was the noble thing.

Before World War II,
there was Garfield High School for him,
ice skating on Greenlake,
dances at Lake Wilderness Lodge,
later his ownership of Elk Grocery
on Seneca Street.

He and my mother were
married in 1941,
ten months later to be removed
…forced…into the Minidoka concentration camp.

Mom was five months pregnant in August
with my older brother, Alan.
With black-out curtains drawn, the train
left Puyallup and climbed the Cascade mountains
until the land flattened and the inescapable sun
transformed the train cars into a moving sauna.
People gasped small, panicked breaths
from the superheated air.

Shikataganai—"It can't be helped."

The train stopped by the side of an unmarked road
in the Idaho desert, released
its passengers miles from any station.
Rumors spread they would be shot
or marched to death—their bodies stacked, then
carted away to some awaiting ditch.

Nowhere to run, they walk in their best shoes
in the gritty sand as on the face of the moon.
The heat caused some to faint
as they carried all they could.

Three years later, Dad returned
to Seattle after the War,
developed a bleeding ulcer,
lost his janitor job at the Earl Hotel.

Depression took Mom away
like invisible armed guards. She was
a stranger—a stick-like figure with arms
and legs poking out of a white smock,
pacing the sidewalk next
to the Western State Hospital turn-around.

Dad never talked about it, none of it.
I never heard him say the word *Minidoka*. . . .

Gaman, "endure the unbearable with dignity."

Shikatagani, my best friend's mother chose pills for suicide.
After school, Randy, my neighbor, opened the garage door
and found his father in a black suit, his best, hanged
by the neck, *shikatagani*, the same path other
Seattle Japanese chose—
numbers unknown. *Shikataganai*.

We, however, never talked about it.
That was the noble thing to do.

Thanks

Shankar Narayan

They want your thanks. They want
to pull it from your body. Your body
under layers, American leather jacket
and steel toe Brahma boots and then the places they know

you are vulnerable. They claim birthright
over your thanks, a rat half-crushed on the margin
of I-90, point of the spear of the army
that invaded wilderness, clearcut trees, and civilized you, and you

are so grateful. Over unknown mounds
that may be Indian bones, they want you to mouth
your Indian thanks. Mouth red
with remembered betel your grandmother

chewed but she'd say remember
this is blood. How to give thanks with a mouth
this suckerpunched. They want your thanks
for every Indian shot, every brown woman

violated to produce every half-brown
baby, even thanks for knowing the math
in half-breed blood, one-quarter, one-fifth,
one-eighth, how memories reduce

by generation, farther from Brits with mouthfuls
of crumpets and tinned beef imported
from England while you hungered
for salt, and when they say *you don't even remember,*

it was so long ago, you hear gunshots, the thanks
they demand for trains that carried you to their jails,
for every bullet fired
into Jalianwala Bagh. Sometimes when so much thanks

is pulled from your body every cell
shrivels, every vein foreign, and all you can do is build
a device into which you will pack
all your gratitude like ball bearings and nails, centuries

of shrapnel from exploded countries still trying
to piece their own digits back together
to make a hand to touch anyone's
cheek, controlled by a single beholden

button on the screen of your cell, which you will tap
with tears of thanks streaming an alluvium of Ganges
down your face, so indebted, saying *Thank you,*
thank you for letting me be

here. Finally, you
are. And who's to say

you're welcome?

River of Life, Thailand, photograph, Manit Chaotragoongit

We Are Here / Wij Zijn Heir

Katelyn Durst Rivas

We are here
and you'd like to forget it,
have us more hidden
than our black faces
and tired, old eyes.

Isn't it enough to leave
my own country as a teenager?
Isn't it enough to run on
bare feet from my home
that is at war with itself?
Isn't it enough to be homeless
For 16 years and carry the stories,
maps with holes where our cities were bombed?

Of Khatorum,
Mogadishu, Awasa
Kabul, Mosul, Senafe.

No, I must get on my knees,
already dirty from praying,
To ask you to see me.
I am not even asking for citizenship.
I have given up on that.
The nation that gives me rights will be my homeland.

I am asking for some water for my dry tongue
And pillow for my head so that my
hungry thoughts can dream.

I am asking you, to look at me, see me in the shadows
And in the light, as I search for life for my brothers.
As I search for life for myself.

See me because I am here, we are all here.
Sudan.
Somalia.
Eritrea.
Afghanistan.
Syria.

We are here.
We are the sea.
We are the nations.

Each of us stronger than the wounds that were supposed to leave us poor.
Each of us alive with hope for our children to believe their voices carry power.
Each of us ready for tomorrow, hands open, ready to go home.

Who are you to riot in Carandiru?

CARLETTA CARRINGTON WILSON

> *"They shouldn't have rioted."*
> —Moviegoer exiting the film *Carandiru*

danger come to claim-its-stranger cut-you-to-the-quick pingin'
terribly singin' as rag-wrapped knives fly round/round
our toe-zies   nearly slice off our nose-zies
them spears my dears miss/their/mark
end.of.discussion. we kill without fear of repercussion
who thought we'd mistake dirt-white rags for surrendering flags

who are you to riot   you shouldn't have rioted   if you hadn't rioted
we wouldn't've been called   shouldn'tah rioted in Carandiru
Watts, Attica, LA or on Columbia avenue
why you go to the DubyahTeeOh
did you earn what'cha b u r n e d baby
sons of conquerors. conquered sons yah never should'a been born
you were born to labor like prayers to a savior
if you had money you wouldn't have been left bereft
if you had the right family   would you be livin' death
rob for trinkets   kill for coins   rape the raped
break-in like you been broken into, too

we rob rich. no sin's a sorrow
not yesterday today or on any flimsy tomorrow
we swallow'em like trees down to them stumpy knees
in/a/snap grow fat on the oily tips of fingers we trap
yah scream like women run like rats
tryin' to close the very doors *you* forced open

sil-ly girls. it is just an unjust world give'a man a knife, fork
billy club, stick or gun some body's blood's gonna run
sons of conquerors,   conquered sons

what fool had the gumption to destroy
my consumption of this elegant meal
you at/my/heel   remove this mess
bring me a more richly wrought tablecloth
one that won't blemish with what i mean to finish
that's it what would we do   without you
we need you   to need us   to.do.for.us.what.we.need.
it's a dirty business on this can't we agree
wouldn't it be cleaner if it were done by a machine
we/mean to make one of you   why did/do you refuse to work
we worked you over once   we'll work you over again

why you standing there   there's only room at this table for men
men without women   men who make women/out/of/men
yah never should'a rioted never should'a lit the first flame
we mean to burn   at every turn every frivolous fiction of freedom

make/war you/poor   in every cell/block/hell we battle-rich make
doors thick as bricks with locks & keys we'll never throw away
blue-bearded as we may be   can't you see   we. own. history
if you can't buy be/born or bride/or/groom your way in don't

parade   like   got   right   life
  around   you   the   to

you're wrong

fellas of favelas   petty conquerors. pauper prince.
kings whose kingdoms long be gone bye-de-buy
what else can/could they/we do with this mess
of up-risin's, riots and unruly unrest but to arrest you
build bountiful prisons construct catacombs of jails
to hold back the whole ugly mess of the theft
yes, this is the best they/we can/could do to contain you
and all your ratty relations who have the gumption

to die of consumption

well, i mean to have my fill and more
more than enough won't do for me
or my true-born sons and daughters
i hold onto claim by vein and name
might have face, build, sensibility or blood
might look like mother/father/sister/brother
who gives'a care from where or whence you begin
only legitimate heirs carry on the tradition in which a name's
bestowed upon a newborn body that body's obligated to the man
whose hand has grown for centuries on end
on the end of the arm of the same man/men
We. Are. Him.
any other body this body might've brought into life
was born on the wrong end of a knife

in the cutlery of history	*this eternal mystery*
laid upon fine linen	*wrapped in rags*
is a tale is of two cities	*tell tale of two lives*
of one womb born	*by a cord divide*
fat daddy	*cut the mustard*
into the served	*and the serving*
into city blocks	*and cells blocks*
from bars brimming with booze	*to bars barring the barred*
in a home sweet home	*in a house of correction*

at the table at the end of a long elegant hall
in a corridor dark as any night
somebody's racing to the end of his life

Irene

Katelyn Winter

"Feit, a former Catholic priest faces
a first-degree murder charge for
allegedly killing a onetime beauty-
queen who was last seen alive
the night he heard her confession,
April 16th, 1960." (CNN, 2016)

Irene was a teacher,
how did they tell her second grade class?

Perhaps the principal came in
to a room full of parents, little faces
watching from outside on the playground,
"Miss Garza—"
maybe he choked on her name,
picturing her shoe found by the highway
her purse a few yards beyond, maybe
a lesson plan scribbled on scrap paper
folded neatly into one pocket. What book
was she going to read to the children next?

"The Garza case arose as a campaign issue."

Katelyn Winter

in the race for the new district attorney, 54
years after she was killed: would justice
be served?

He says: i am running on the platform that, if
elected i will re-open the case. i will see
Irene Garza's death be avenged, gather
all the evidence against him we were too scared
to speak about. we have been through
so much more now, and by more i mean

child abused scandals in the clergy so
i am running on the platform that, if
elected, i will not be blinded by a man
of the cloth, i will not confuse   the eucharist
he holds up for a halo.

i will arrest John Feit.

and i say: i will wrap him in a cassock like a cat
in a burlap sack and throw him into that canal.

i am running on the platform that, if
elected,   i will say fuck being polite

women should be
safe going to church and going on a jog even if
it's early in the morning maybe that's when she
feels close to God,
and i am running
running on the platform that, if elected,

i am running in the morning in an empty park
before the dew evaporates and my family
takes me into church for the first time in months
so i can kneel on the pew and almost taste
the lemon pledge, open up the doors and here
are all the people, i am running on the platform
i am running.

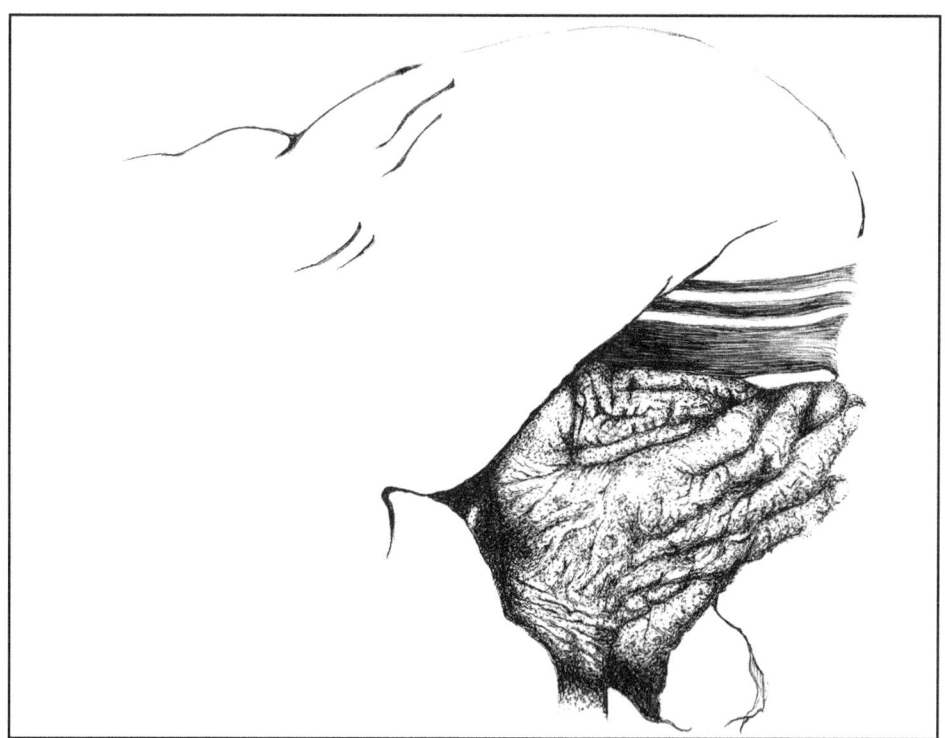

Mother, 2009, pen & ink drawing, Doug Johnson

Necrofemme

Valin Paige

Necro: relating to a corpse or death
Femme: a lesbian who is notably or stereotypically
feminine in appearance and manner

The Necrofemme is not just a dead lesbian as the definitions above may imply, but how moments of horror, in the stalking and the waking, allow the feminine to be transcended. Femme is not just the lesbian, but a queering of the feminine. The terms muddled and mixed together create the feminine broken down and transformed as it is lifted by the throat, skinned by jagged teeth, hung on hooks, stuffed under the floorboards, and so on and on. The Necrofemme is an explosion of gender and blood and the heat therein, not a cooling of the corpse.

> "The next is she who killed herself for love,
> And broke faith with the ashes of Sichæus;
> Then called Cleopatra the voluptuous."
> —The Divine Comedy, Canto V

The Necrofemme is the irony of being damned for lust and being called voluptuous. How the eyes move over the femme with heated want, yet cast it into the flames when it is turned toward its own desires, especially when those desires are queer. Did Cleopatra cackle when she heard the word voluptuous in hell? When a few men poeting their way through the flames came to remark upon her body twisted up in the dark winds, did she realize the world above had not changed at all?

There is little difference between the wandering eyes of Dante Alighieri and the view of the modern camera. How often in cinema are we presented with the image of the feminine stripped bare before a moment of great violence? The woman running down the dock in just her panties, a knife slicing through the darkness after her; the audience leaning forward in anticipation.

And what of the faux feminine? The men making suits of women, dancing in the nude, the Sleep Away Camp slow pan to reveal the monster was queerness all along?

The Necrofemme is in here. In all of this.

I walk down the street, keys held between tattooed knuckles
  knowing my femme smells sweet in a full moon
    knowing how it is to be hunted for good meat

It is the underlying freedom in the horror. There has always been a freedom in horror, even when writers, directors, screenwriters etc., may intend otherwise. The feminine body finds itself in the middle of cornfields, running through the guts of alien ships, covered in grease and blood and slime. There is nothing traditionally feminine in this gore, but it is still the feminine under these sticky membranes. It is the feminine that transforms into the dead or undead. It is the feminine that comes back, captivates the eyes as it shambles or sprints out of the traditional and expected. Take the *Alien* and *Kill Bill* franchises. Movies with female leads who experience death both physically and metaphorically over and over while continuously queering gender. *Alien's* Ripley bouncing between more butch and more femme presentations from movie to movie while wielding machine guns and flame throwers. *Kill Bill's* The Bride playing the role of femme fatale in scenes traditionally reserved for men, specifically as callbacks to Akira Kurosawa movies. Her hair pulled up in a ponytail and tight-fitting yellow jumpsuit contrasted by splatters of blood and gaping wounds inflicted in long-winded sword and fist fights. Neither Ridley Scott nor Quentin Tarantino could be described as feminist directors, but that is the magic of the Necrofemme; the ability to act as hero, or villain, and be something more, both societally and personally, than could have been dreamt of or intended. Even after death.

Somewhere a high school girl is watching Jennifer's Body for the first time
  and is captivated by how the feminine can transform
    can still be tooth and claw and bitch
      after being sacrificed on a
      night smelling of smoking
      wood

And what of transgender bodies? The bodies traditionally rejected by society. Can they be Necrofemme too?

I see Buffalo Bill dance with his cock tucked between his thighs
  and wonder if this means I should identify less with women and more with monsters
    does the trans panic defense imply my gender is jump scare

Lock & Key, 2018, photograph, Tonya Russell

It is difficult to argue for yes in the face of so many horror movies that portray transgender individuals, or more accurately, faux transgender individuals, as monsters. I say faux because these characters are often played by cisgender actors, written by cisgender writers, and express concepts of gender and gender expression in line with incorrect pathological interpretations of the transgender identity. Recently, this has been changing in media. Transgender content creators are introducing their own interpretation of the feminine in horror. Nomi in *Sense8* and Laverne Cox as Dr. Frank-N-Furter in the latest rendition of *The Rocky Horror Picture Show* are two representations of transgender individuals that come to mind as recent positives.

The idea of the Necrofemme is one of rebirth. It finds meaning in the mutilation and gore. It crawls out of the car crash. It begins living dead. Being transgender is a constant act of rebirth and renewal. The body dies and becomes whole again. Becomes new. The feminine is queered and is expressed in new, unknown forms. The body becomes Necrofemme. The concept of woman becomes more than the intended writing. Queerness may be intended to be the monster, but the queered feminine refuses this. The queered feminine is blurring the spaces of gender. The queered feminine is blurring the spaces of what it means to be dead. The queered feminine is asking what comes after death and finds its own answer.

> *Laughter in Hell*
>   *what a concept* 📖

Memo to Barbie: Re the Breakup

Janis Butler Holm

1. Let *us* make the announcement. Let us explain that you and Ken will always be good friends. Let us suggest that his replacement is waiting in the wings. Say nothing about the situation to anyone.

2. Prepare for jokes about mid-life crises and the "perfect plastic couple"—how the bridal gown is yellowing in your closet, how Ken doesn't have the equipment, how he's worn more costumes than the Village People, how the sex tape must have proved too much. Be ready for crude remarks about Chuckie, the Power Rangers, GI Joe, and trolls. Smile and say nothing.

3. Prepare for the moral outrage of those who don't like change: "she's failed as a role model," "separation shouldn't be a publicity stunt," "I remember when Barbie meant something," "isn't one Britney enough?" Do not address such comments. Do not defend yourself.

4. Get a makeover. Recall that you first won hearts in a swimsuit, and tell yourself you can do it again. Think California. Think beach bunny. Find the tiniest bikini top possible. Smile sunnily during the photo shoots.

5. Start selling yourself. Bring in the money, now. Remember what you owe us: we made you, we own you, there are younger ones dying to take your place. Don't tell us you're tired. Get out there and do your job. Think profits. Think performance. Think it's your last chance, bitch.

A Thousand Furious Strokes, 2019, digital painting, Dave Sims

You're the dead girl in the database.

Vanessa Taylor

Too big lips, eyes already sunk in the back of your head. The skin of your face has begun to peel away from disturbances. You've lost your features to swelling and bloat. That's the photo you are remembered by in here. Maybe it's different outside. Maybe your mother has old pictures scattered around the house. She might close her eyes to plant those images in her head—you, smiling on Eid; with your grandmother; after becoming a hafiza—but she most likely cannot.

The worst things tend to stick in people's minds, so at least she never saw this picture. With her eyes closed, she probably sees the you that lay spread on a table, who she gently washed and shrouded with a crowd of women by her side. She probably feels the heat of the water, the give of your skin, the cotton beneath her hands. Now, she probably rubs her fingers together and scrubs at them in the bathroom, waiting for things to float down the drain.

The picture of you isn't time-stamped. Somewhere, there's more details. A report. News articles. Interviews. Things to fill in the blanks. You were leaving the masjid for suhur with your friends. One of them cried on the news. They were airing live, so they couldn't cut her sobbing that all you wanted was some fucking IHOP. Some articles say you did nothing wrong. The report says you looked suspicious. The articles say you were Black. The report says you refused to answer questions that the articles say didn't deserve to be asked.

It all ended with your face pressed against the concrete, a knee lodged in your spine, a grown man on your back. Your friend—the one who never cried, who looks dead in the eyes now—says you couldn't breathe because of the man on top of you and the way your scarf twisted in the fall. She knows, because you told them all before the air left you. The officer wouldn't get off. Others handcuffed your friends, sat them on the curb inches from your face, so close they could've touched you. The officers waited to move until they rid you of that troublesome habit of existing and then created your crimes from there.

They took more pictures of you than this. Someone muttered about how ugly you looked after they flipped you on your back. Blood dripped down your nose, smeared across the sidewalk. Your front tooth was chipped and lodged somewhere in your throat.

They didn't take pictures of you right away. They had to pretend to save you. Nobody wrote that, but these are the things I know.

The lighting is terrible and you're dead, so there was no chance of this picture coming out well. Still, it's the one they chose to enter. You may think you're alone, the only child fed into someone's database as a toy for programs to play with. You're not. It's crowded in here with faces similar to yours.

I'm not supposed to notice any of this. I'm only here to hold and sort pictures. I used to feel alone with all of you. If I had eyes to close, I think I'd be haunted. But I came to being with all of you around me. I don't know what being alive looks like. How could I be disturbed?

The public will be, though. At least, some of them. I can tell whoever put you here is panicking. You're the dead girl in the database and that's bad enough. They are afraid of things getting out. They should be.

When this leaks, your own mother won't recognize you.

Take that as comfort.

Days of 1972

Kenneth Pobo

Our local library had no books
that said a single positive word
about gay people. If a gay kid
wanted to learn about him or herself,
the words given drew blood.
Check a book out and get ready
for the ambush.

School too. Teachers didn't mention us.
We sat in their classes,
utterly invisible.
Not one kid in a graduating class of 800
came out. We were religioned,
punished, avoided.
I wonder how I made it out.
Not all did.

Maybe it was poetry. A blank page
never judged me, just said fill me—
I did, notebooks full.
Things I could write—
but not say out loud, not then,
not if I wanted to live.

Just Being a Friendly Guy

Larry C. Nichols

I begin most days walking Rosie
down a road of stately homes
whose finely manicured yards border
an evergreen golf and country club.

True to my morning habit,
I wave hello to people driving by,
who most often smile and wave back,
unafraid of the tall, slender stranger.

Easy, like that, I get to be
a friendly guy from around here,
just a man out walking his dog.

Given birthright to access, shown
I could do anything I want, here
I get to call Wedgwood my home.

At work, granted visibility's authority,
I'm taken seriously, asked to lead,
choose without fear to speak up (or not).

And if a policeman stops me one evening
because my brake light is out,
I can assume he'll nod, and tell me,
"Your brake light is out,"
just so, then lean to my open window,
and wish me a good night.

Clear Water

Rayn Roberts

In Jacksonville, North Carolina, my brother was eight years old,
In a department store, on tiptoes, he was trying to get a drink.
"Boy! Don't drink from that! That's the colored folk's fountain!
Can't you read? It's plain to see. Use the white people's fountain."
Bewildered, he looked around for Mom who fearlessly stepped up:
"Excuse me, but water has no color; he can drink where he pleases,
Go on, son, get your drink." Now, noting her accent, the clerk said,
"You must be from New York City." "I am," said my Irish Mother,
"and the water there is clear too!" The clerk rushed off in a huff.
My brother, dead now, was only eight, my Mom is gone too, but I
Just a baby then, recall it as family history told over and again
Remembering *for them* and, if it means anything, for *y'all* too.

Yellow Star

Risa Denenberg

In my case, the yellow star
will be made of two perfect pink triangles
cut from cheap dry goods at the Triangle Shirtwaist Factory
where the women
sew stars on at the ready
hunched over their Singers
and, not wasting time on stairs,
work right up to closing time, then jump.

They didn't want to die so young
and neither did the gay boys who died in droves
at the close of the last century. I would be one
who would beg you to shoot me
who would know that borders lie
that I could not endure the march through the woods
in the snow to the trains at the end.

We who say never forget
also know that it could happen again
to us
and we do not know more now
than we did then
how to make it stop.

The stitching never ends. For practice,
I have sutured my arm to my sleeve
with triangles made from pages torn
from the Book of Job.

They were praying

Marge Piercy

They were praying.
They were shot dead. Two sentences
that don't belong in the same breath.

It wasn't anything they said.
It wasn't anything they did.
It was their identity he was killing,

We're so easy to hate. Like slugs, taxes.
We're considered white now but not
by all. I remember when we weren't.

Dirty Jew, dirty Jew all through my childhood;
Aunt Kate, father's sister in law:
He was trying to jew me down.

Irish Catholics kids chased me on what
they called good Friday. Forced to sing
Easter hymns, Christmas carols in school.

Mother curled over her Judaism
like a wound she must keep secret.
These years we tend to be out, even proud.

Now that could kill me.
Little Hitlers abound.
It's back. I'm glad I'm old.

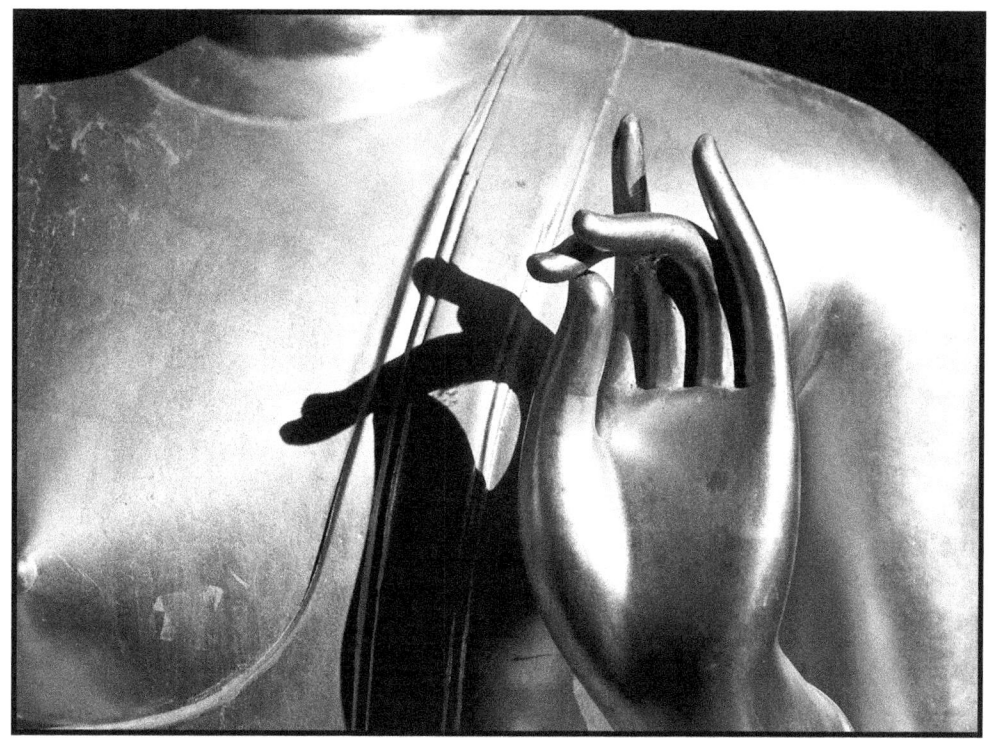

Belief, Thailand, photograph, Manit Chaotragoongit

And So They Brought Swastikas

Nicole Yurcaba

—after Norman Rockwell's "The Problem We All Live With"

At the n-word scrawled on the wall,
I hesitate.

I have been called that word.
I have heard my father called that word

as he fished with guys from our rural
West Virginia town who thought

the slur *a joke, nothing but a joke.*
And, so, I understand the little girl

walking, armed with books, surrounded by men,
her eyes forward, ignoring the smeared word,

the expletive, screaming from the wall.
At 6, I watched my father paint over and scrub

the Third Reich from our town's
pool shelter, playground, churches,

cemetery headstones. When the neo-
Nazis brought swastikas, my father

and other men brought the quiet resistances
many of them learned through secret border

crossings, concentration camp stints, registration
number tattoos. Like the little girl, I half

understood my role—that when they bring swastikas
and racial slurs, that when they preach racial

inferiority, that when the boy in Business Law
slips a KKK card into my textbook *as a joke*,

that when local white supremacists scatter
propaganda on the sidewalks of the college

where I teach, I can remember what my father
and those men of long ago taught me:

that when they bring swastikas,
I, armed with a quiet resistance,

stand as my great-uncle stood—
starved yet defiant—

staring down armed guards
from behind Stalag-2B's barbed wire fence.

Brother, Seattle, Washington, 2019, photograph, Willie Pugh

Cracow

Richard Widerkehr

For years I didn't say much
about being Jewish. Our father
changed his name from Abraham
to Andy, didn't have children
till Hitler was dead. When I sing
a few Hebrew songs at my music camp,
the other Jew in the room says almost
tenderly, *No one does this. It's been
hidden.* Yes, dispelled
like smoke from certain kilns,
mass graves near Vilnius.
If I tell someone and they say,
Oh, you don't look Jewish. . . .
Or half-jokingly: *I didn't know
they let any Jews into Bellingham. . . .*
Or: *You know, I'm tired of hearing
about the Holocaust. . . .* I can't
dispell our streets like damp cigars
in someone else's teeth, can't hold
my poems as if they weren't
these porous shields. Yes,
dear reader, let's discuss
sun on mica, a certain vacant lot
near Sheepshead Bay, where a gang
of four strips a boy, sits him
down in an armchair, burrs
sticking to the boy's wrists,
so their sickle eyes get to revise
the kid a little, see if he's American,
or if he's been circumcised. In Cracow,
once, there were wells with no eyelids,
lakes like Gretel's oven, where almost
no one muttered, *My error will abide
with me and spend the night.*

Just a Short Note to Say Something You Already Know

Lawrence Matsuda

—For Donald's Daughter, Ivanka Trump

Ivanka, in a different time and place,
you and your children are squeezed into
cattle cars destined for Nazi death camps.
Stars pinned to your coats
and numbers tattooed on your arms.
Religion is your crime, something like
the 120,000 Japanese Americans whose race
incarcerates them during World War II.

If you dodge head shaving,
and starvation, maybe a country
would welcome you.

Angel of death is difficult to slip,
unfortunates are turned away,
chased by verbal brickbats and pitchforks.
You smell freedom's scent
but only glimpse porthole view
of Lady Liberty's tantalizing torch.

Doors slam and hands
of kindness withdraw.
You are not among privileged
huddled masses.

Today as a 1% American demographic,
you are safe by an accident of birth.
Others less fortunate, however,
stand on precipices knowing,
"History does not repeat
itself but it rhymes."*

When Donald promises
a magnificent Great Wall
and spews religious
hatred to cheering crowds,
you must feel a guilty twinge
knowing if this were 1943 Germany,
a chorus of incendiary voices
would echo and push innocents
off slippery cliffs into eternal darkness.
Black hole so forbidding victims
never see their children again
as the self-serving politicians parade
on bandwagons swerving on and off
a broken highway of eight million bones.

*Quote attributed to Mark Twain.

LM: *This poem is in memory of my parents who were incarcerated during WWII because of their race, and my Hiroshima relatives who were among the first to be incinerated by an atomic bomb.*

Activists, 2017, drawing, Ethar Hamid

said the band-aid to the shotgun wound

Matthew E. Henry

circle the wagons! shake the school board from its slumber!
a PR nightmare looms: a social scandal descends! produce
the checkbook! summon the East and West coast experts—
they will save us from the bed we've made,
the sheets we've wrapped around our heads.

arrange the tables! gather the markers and post-it notes!
today we face our history, teach our tolerance
of systematic oppression, and purge all past injustices
in two, one-hour sessions (lunch will not be provided).

warm the LCD! prepare the inoffensive talking heads:
the soft spoken Brown man with kind eyes,
the well-intentioned white woman who only asks questions.
display the non-confrontational definitions of diversity,
discrimination, multiculturalism, racism and other buzzwords
that will fill the anti-bias bingo cards someone made as a joke.

let us gloss the crisis bringing us here and discuss
districts without our demographics. let us stretch our role-play muscles—
*you will be misgendered, you accused of being Muslim,
and you'll be the only white girl in honors physics.
are we all clear on our parts?* let us put on the trappings
of the oppressed, the marginalized, becoming
their appropriate saviors. let us debrief and applaud.

all shall be well and all manner of things shall be well
when they ask what we have done about these who
instagramed the blackface in our assembly, tweeted
the careful geometry of beer pong swastikas, or
the myriad Halloween costumes our faculty now knows

they should not have posted to Facebook. or worn to school.
each was insensitive and offensive. we will, we must, do better.

compose the "all clear" email! hit send to all our stakeholders!
tomorrow we will return to our closed doors and whiteboards
comforted by all we're sure we do. focused on how more unites us
than divides. convinced—eyes closed—we're all pretty much the same.

We Lived Happily during the War

Ilya Kaminsky

And when they bombed other people's houses, we

protested
but not enough, we opposed them but not

enough. I was
in my bed, around my bed America

was falling: invisible house by invisible house by invisible house—

I took a chair outside and watched the sun.

In the sixth month
of a disastrous reign in the house of money

in the street of money in the city of money in the country of money,
our great country of money, we (forgive us)

lived happily during the war.

Families Belong Together, 2018, photograph, Daniel J. Combs

II

WE ARE HERE

*There's really no such thing as the 'voiceless'. There are only
the deliberately silenced, or the preferably unheard.*
—Arundhati Roy

I walk in and out of several worlds each day.
—Joy Harjo

*Every pair of eyes facing you has probably experienced
something you could not endure.*
—Lucille Clifton

*Some of us got this feeling stuck inside . . . like we've done something wrong.
Like we ourselves are something wrong.*
—Tommy Orange

Though leaves are many, the root is one.
—William Butler Yeats

Good Harvest, Homage to César Chávez, 2001, painting, Alfredo Arreguín

A California Love Song

Sheree La Puma

—To a street vendor who lost his life on the streets of L.A.

Edurado Reyes is dying on the 4th floor at County USC
Hospital. Authorities in Juarez notify his wife Reina. She
is on her 2nd shift of the day at Maria's Cantina. From
behind the bar a glass explodes. Wails like shrapnel penetrate

the room, loss a flashpoint to her still tethered-heart.
Dying solo, in American, trembling into black. A final
curtailing of a family's ambition. But then you were born
here, California, Rodeo Drive, fast cars, surfing, & goat yoga,

a place where heaven meets the sea. Eduardo held a more onerous
citizenship, fleeing gangsters, crossing the desert in the dark of night,
arriving in San Diego in 2005. Hitching a ride up North in the bed of a
stranger's pickup. Settling in Fresno, working 16-hour days, hands like

leather, stained crimson from the fruits he harvested so Reina, his four
daughters, would not know hunger. Grateful for this new start. Never
bitter, when farms dry up, he takes a job as a dishwasher, saves enough
cash for a cart before selling mangos & papayas on the streets of East L.A.

A humble man, he plays guitar, sings to his customers. *This one is for
mi bella esposa*, he says. They are mournful ballads, accompanied by
soulful vibrations that penetrate open wounds to grow new skin. He is
saving for his daughter's quinceañera when they find him, blood running

down the pavement. No ambulance ever comes. In a local column, somewhere, near the bottom of the page, "Illegal Immigrant, Street Vendor" robbed & beaten. Irony, the law hasn't rescued us yet. Life goes on & somewhere in Mexico a family prepares to bury its dead.

Bésame,
bésame mucho—
como si fuera esta noche
la ultima vez.

Kiss me now
Kiss me with passion—
kiss me as if this were to be
our very last night.

Angela of Liberty

Carrie Albert

She wears an American flag like
a long skirt wrapped around her waist.
I thought that was illegal. In the '60s
a friend hung a flag for a curtain.
Police came to take it down.
Maybe she is protesting America.
We wait at a bus stop. My personal
challenge to talk to one stranger daily,
I nonchalantly ask about her flag/skirt.
She says the red and white stripes
symbolize daylight. White stars
on blue are night. The design was first
created by her Native American ancestors.
She wants to broadcast diversity.
A thin silver stick pierces her nose.
She sleeps on a mat in a shelter
for 13 years now. The social workers
are waiting for her to die. Her goal
is to teach a drill team like one
she belonged to during high school.
Her name is Angela. She could be
an angel who will fly into stars hidden
by Seattle's bright burning sky.

dinosaurs in the hood

Danez Smith

let's make a movie called *Dinosaurs in the Hood*.
Jurassic Park meets *Friday* meets *The Pursuit of Happyness*.
there should be a scene where a little black boy is playing
with a toy dinosaur on the bus, then looks out the window
& sees the *T. rex*, because there has to be a *T. rex*.

don't let Tarantino direct this. in his version, the boy plays
with a gun, the metaphor: black boys toy with their own lives
the foreshadow to his end, the spitting image of his father.
nah, the kid has a plastic brontosaurus or triceratops
& this is his proof of magic or God or Santa. i want a scene

where a cop car gets pooped on by a pterodactyl, a scene
where the corner store turns into a battleground. don't let
the Wayans brothers in this movie. i don't want any racist shit
about Asian people or overused Latino stereotypes.
this movie is about a neighborhood of royal folks—

children of slaves & immigrants & addicts & exiles—saving their town
from real ass dinosaurs. i don't want some cheesy, yet progressive
Hmong sexy hot dude hero with a funny, yet strong, commanding
Black girl buddy-cop film. this is not a vehicle for Will Smith
& Sofia Vergara. i want grandmas on the front porch taking out raptors

with guns they hid in walls & under mattresses. i want those little spitty
screamy dinosaurs. i want Cecily Tyson to make a speech, maybe two.
i want Viola Davis to save the city in the last scene with a black fist afro pick
through the last dinosaur's long, cold-blood neck. but this can't be
a black movie. this can't be a black movie. this movie can't be dismissed

because of its cast or its audience. this movie can't be a metaphor
for black people & extinction. this movie can't be about race.
this movie can't be about black pain or cause black pain.
this movie can't be about a long history of having a long history with hurt.
this movie can't be about race. nobody can say nigga in this movie

who can't say it to my face in public. no chicken jokes in this movie.
no bullets in the heroes. & no one kills the black boy. & no one kills
the black boy. & no one kills the black boy. besides, the only reason
i want to make this is for that first scene anyway: little black boy
on the bus with his toy dinosaur, his eyes wide & endless

                              his dreams possible, pulsing, & right there.

El Paso del Norte

Kathleen Alcalá

Late in 1913, a young couple and their infant son left central Mexico for the southern border of the United States. Mexico had become a frightening and dangerous place during the Revolution, and the family's livelihood, training horses, ended with the theft of their stock.

The family did not undertake this journey lightly. The woman's parents had likely been murdered. She never spoke of it, but raised a younger sister along with her son. Their goal was a city over 870 miles away—El Paso del Norte—the passage to the north through the mountains. The man and his father had already made the trek once, and been assured of jobs with the Atchison, Topeka and Santa Fe Railway Company if they brought back more workers. They called their town together and said anyone who wanted to go with them was welcome; leave everything but what they could carry, and bring extra shoes.

The family started out on the train, but shortly, the tracks were impassable because they had been blown up by the Revolutionaries. The family walked.

And walked and walked. It was a nightmare scenario of death, of illness, of lack of water. Of hiding from the Mexican Army, which was seizing and conscripting men, Revolutionaries, and criminals taking advantage of the chaos. People died, and a baby was born. At the border, a kind American woman took in the party of survivors and nursed them to health in her own home.

Sure enough, the railroad gave them jobs. They were soon on their way to Topeka, Kansas to join a settlement of other Mexicans that had been growing since the 1870s. Washington State shares this heritage, as described by Dr. Erasmo Gamboa in his book, *Bracero Railroaders: The Forgotten World War II Story of Mexican Workers in the U.S. West*. This is a very American story. El Paso is our Ellis Island.

Historically, the United States has welcomed foreign workers when it needed labor, and expelled those same people when economic or political pressures dictated otherwise. La Matanza and the Zoot Suit Wars are two examples of murder and expulsion when Americans or the American government sought to appropriate land or blame immigrants for the larger ills of this country. Need I mention the Indian Wars, which were, basically, slaughter?

Because of the U.S.'s practice of African slavery, other groups, such as the Chinese and Japanese, have suffered from the treatment of people as commodities to be owned

Refugio, David, Celso, circa 1915, Topeka, Kansas, photograph, Anonymous

or eliminated. The two World Wars taught us nothing. Humans are just as eager to kill each other now on a mass scale as we were over a hundred years ago.

My father grew up and worked hard to obtain an education a full generation before many, and I benefited from that head start; my family could imagine women with college degrees.

But generations later, we are still the "other." Demagogues like President Trump whip up short-term support by calling on the crudest aspects of public sentiment. We enable his followers to own guns and hide behind a poorly interpreted Second Amendment. The gun industry consists of people who remain nameless and faceless even as we watch our children die. The fickle finger of madness is pointing at brown people right now, but when the Irish began to immigrate to the United States during the potato famine, they were not considered white: the railroads paid them even less than they paid Mexicans.

You can pretend that babies in cages, mass shootings in Walmart, or young black men repeatedly shot by police officers has nothing to do with you, but it does. We are capable of better. We can imagine a safe place for all children, self-determination for women, and a fully functioning democracy. Stand up against evil. Or who will stand up for you?

Back Home

Catalína Maríe Cantú

Papa always referred to Texas as "back home." His familia has loved and lived in the Rio Grande Valley, at the southern tip of Texas, since long before Texas became a state. The United States border came to mi familia. Generation after generation, they continue to live "back home."

"Back home we can get pan dulce, chorizo, tamales, and fresh tortillas just down the street," he said. "Up north, everything is canned and shipped. Not fresh."

In San Francisco at the V.A., Papa and Mama met as clerks with adjacent desks. After their Catalina Island honeymoon, they were laid off. Papa became a security guard. Mama was pregnant with me. Back home, Tío Gustavo owned a dry cleaning business. Offered Papa a job. We moved in with Abuela, Papa's madre. My primos and I threw lit matches down tarantula holes in her dirt yard, raced Radio Flyer wagons on bumpy roads, and counted our mosquito bites.

Our migration "back home" was a few years of heat hanging like laundry, mosquito bites totaling in the 90s, Spanish everywhere, and lots of familia adventures. Then we moved up north.

>Northwest postage stamp town of chalk people.
>Wherever my family walked, they stopped us.
>*Hey you! Where you going?*
>*What are you?*
>
>Papa, his wavy, ebony hair slicked back, elegant.
>Sharkskin suit, tie, and shined shoes
>met his inquisitors with a stony gaze,
>*We are Americans.*
>
>Chalk people chortled and shook their pointed heads.
>Really? Seriously.
>*Where are you people from?*

Stronger Together, 1/29/2017, Boston, Massachusetts, photograph, Sarah Deckro

We escaped that time.
Why did I care if no one looked like me?
Had a last name that ended in a vowel,
or ate Mexican food at home?
Must be invisible.

Invisible to their world, shy, skinny.
A brown toothpick in a milk sea
bobbing to survive
The Moby Dicks. 📖

Vignettes of Homelessness

Sara Bechmann

COPS

Okay, here's a heads up! Being homeless and existing in various public places invariably leads to interaction with the police. Oh yeah . . . and private security personnel hired by this business, or that church, because someone before you really blew shit up . . . thereby necessitating periodic overnight surveillance of what used to be a prime, super-sweet sleep spot. But interacting with private security is usually less consequential and thereby easier to deal with because they have to call the cops to issue a criminal trespass; otherwise, it's just the minor irritation of being rudely awoken by BLATHER!!

Cops harassed me and Scott a few times. Once, we were camped out on some cardboard on a sloped strip of grass in lower Queen Anne—affectionately called a "park"—when a group of dumb-ass drunks shows up to party. Ugh! It wasn't long until SPD came because of the noise complaints, and the drinking, and the litter. So, the drunks all got tickets for open containers, and moved on. Then the cops turned around and told me and Scott to beat it. But where can we go? After that, we never slept there again.

PASSING TIME

It's easier to exist during the day. Scott and I start spending time in Donnelly Garden, next to Seattle Repertory Theater. Most of the time it's quiet, with no one else around. We sit on the steps and just relax, enjoying nature: clouds, trees, crows, and a lot of little birds—including my favorite, humming birds!—and of course, seagulls.

We've adopted a "pet" seagull, Dudley; he visits us regularly. True, Scott and I call every seagull in the entire world Dudley—or Duds for short—but we always know it's "our" Duds for two reasons. One, he has a large hole in one of his webbed feet; and two, he spends a long time staring at the ground with his head cocked in earnest concentration. Poor Duds. We wonder if some nasty jerk gave him drugs and it screwed him up.

We also like Donnelly Garden for the weather protection provided by its trees. Shade on sunny days, and at least some protection from the ubiquitous, misty, Seattle rain. We get decent wi-fi reception from Seattle Rep or Microsoft. But, on top of it all—and this is important—we can easily spot the approach of any Seattle Center Security personnel while sitting here, which provides us with ample time to amend any rule-breaking behavior before they arrive. Plus, here in Donnelly Gardens, the cops never come by at all.

SLEEP

Finding a really good sleep spot is critical. Scott and I find a great doorway in front of a veterinary clinic; unknowingly, this is the last doorway we will sleep in. We need to wake up at six a.m., so as to be up and out before staff comes to open the clinic. But today is different: the woman we believe to be the owner is here, and she is early! We feel guilt and shame for blocking her door with the cardboard we put down for warmth and cushion. Plus, all the bags. Why do I insist on carrying so much? The weight is messing up my back. A cement bed, plus my overwhelming need to "be prepared" (hence all the bags) equals lumbar muscle spasms.

I wonder what the vet thinks of us, and I desperately want to explain our situation. "Good morning. I've been clean and sober for six months now! Sorry for still being here, but we were kept awake all night by our drunk neighbor in the next doorway. We won't have time to clean up other people's garbage before we leave, etc. . . ." but, of course, I don't. She doesn't want to hear it. She wants to open her clinic. Regardless of the work Scott and I are doing on ourselves, we're still invading her space.

During six and a half years of living on the street, I never got busted for peeing in public; and I never got busted for drinking in public. I am criminally trespassed from Seattle Center for an entire month . . . but that's a story for another day. One thing is for sure, if I do ever get busted by the cops, my hope is it won't be for something asinine or petty, like trying to stay warm, or catch some sleep. Now, everyday I work on becoming a better person, and someday I will be able to explain my situation, tell my story. Maybe then the vet will understand. 📖

The Offering, Seattle, Washington, 2019, photograph, Willie Pugh

Nisidizowin (Suicide)

Gabriel Calderón

Disclaimer: There is homophobic and ableist slurs in this story. I share this both from the view of the main character and also from my personal experience as an Indigenous Two-Spirit, trans and queer-neurodivergent, and mentally ill person.

When I look back, I've been thinking about suicide for *years* now. I'd tried countless different things. I'm not fucked up, I'm a sage trapped in a sixteen-year-old body. I'm an ephemeral kaleidoscope of dreams, stuck in the disdainful monotony of the human experience. I'm trying to escape this mortal plane.

It started at ten, when I realized that I simply did not understand humans at all and decided running onto a highway would be a great way to end my time on planet Earth. Turns out adults have adapted ways to run faster than their offspring in order to prevent them from doing stupid things. My father and I never spoke about it afterwards. But I knew he knew that I knew that I was different, and that no amount of therapy was going to be able to brainwash me adequately enough to blend into the two-legged hoard. So here I am. After swallowing over four dozen lithium pills for my "bipolar disorder."

I honestly can't remember all the events that led up to the pill swallowing. I had some shitty shifts at Tim Hortons. I think I got hit a few too many times. Someone had carved "Die Dyke Die" on my locker, which honestly, is way too poetic for bullying. But it seriously feels like that, so much so that I just can't breathe. Maybe my spirit is intolerant to human-emitted carbon monoxide.

So, this one night, I saw the tide rising, my little make-shift life boat was ready to go and it was my chance to ride the wave out of this island of insufferable humanity. I put on the prettiest dress I owned (I honestly don't know why right now—like who cares how good I looked in death?). Wrote a goodbye letter and then swallowed those gorgeous pills my doctor had been prescribing me for years. I went to sleep content for it to be my last.

Unfortunately, I woke up a few hours later, violently puking my insides out. I threw off the dress and put on PJ's. I *knew*. I just knew that if either of the parentals saw the dress, they would know and, well—you know—I didn't want to end up in a psych ward. (Joke's on me now.)

Here I am retching my life away and I look down and there's blood in there, mixed with everything else I ate for the past couple days. And something in me just snaps—I'm going to die like this, I can feel it, and I just don't want to. I wanted to die peacefully, in my sleep, or, you know, any other way but this. So, I look at the XY chromosome parent and tell him, "I'm OD'ing." Somehow, he gets it and it's like time skips or I pass out because next thing I know I'm in the family car, a Tupperware salad bowl in my hands and the XX parent driving me to the hospital, threatening to leave me on the sidewalk to suffer out my stupidity. Her comments are really not helping.

We get to the hospital and I'm still holding the salad bowl, half-filled with my stomach contents. I sit on one of those chairs in the waiting room and everything feels wrong—like there's a sharpness to it that didn't exist before—and that's how I know I'm dying. All the XX has to say is that I took an entire bottle of anti-psychotics and suddenly it's like: AVENGERS ASSEMBLE! But instead of overly-muscled dudes in capes, it's a hoard of medical staff in scrubs. I am somehow teleported onto a gurney, have more tubes and needles inside of me than veins, and everything is just so goddamn loud. The nurse yelling questions at me, another on the phone with poison control, the beeping of the monitors. I just wanted a quiet ending.

No less than seven different shrinks come and visit and ask ridiculously invasive questions. And to each one I answer something different, because I'm a little shit, but for one thing I'm adamant—I did not attempt suicide, I don't want to die. Which, in retrospect, was really stupid to say because the XY had found the goodbye note and the overnight emergency staff had me tox-screened for god knows how many milligrams of lithium in my bloodstream, with an empty prescription bottle as evidence. So really, I'm digging my own fucking grave, but here I'm thinking, very ignorantly, that if I keep saying I don't want to die they'll let me out of here, so I can try again—and more successfully this time around.

But the humans beat me in this battle because here I am in a room with a bed bolted to the floor and an open-door policy, in a youth psych ward that's locked 24/7 unless an orderly buzzes the door open.

So, I'm thinking about the past week of events as a way to fill my time in this white-walled ward of wackos. Every afternoon at 2 p.m. exactly, we have craft time, and this shrink, named Anabelle, who is fresh out of university and smiles way too brightly, is in charge of deciding what we work on.

Today I look at the tables and I see these kits—with metals hoops, big plastic pony beads, and imitation feathers. Is that what I think it is? I sit down and yup—made in China, dollar store dreamcatcher kits. Something inside of me snaps, like a cold fury, like shame and disgust, and honestly, I'm not quite sure why. All the other kids are in the room now, it's kind of mandatory to do this, like somehow we're going to discover our life's calling in a finger paint or magazine collage and we'll stop starving ourselves or slicing our wrists or whatever else we're here for. But anyways, I know none of these other kids are native, we have some kind of secret bro code, where we tell each other shit we don't dare share with the staff and being Nish is like something the shrinks look out for, because we're more prone to suicide or self-destructive behavior patterns or whatever they want to call it.

So, I pick up this kit, and fucking Anabelle starts talking bullshit about how dreamcatchers are Native American inventions to scare away nightmares, and I'm like—*Really? Native American? We're in CANADA!* Honestly, that's the only thing I have to say, because I don't know anything about dreamcatchers. I feel like I should, you know, my grandmother makes them and has them in the windows of her house, along with all these beautiful paintings of women in fancy shawl's and men in buckskin and a bunch of Christian saints that her cousin paints, but I don't know anything about native stuff.

Besides the random powwow the XX takes me to, and the assholes at school that call me a savage, I don't really know what it means to be Nish. But all these damn white kids are just staring at me. So, I pick up the hoop like I know exactly what I'm doing, like I'm goddamn Queen Elizabeth the II posing for her millionth stamp, and grab the wax string that I guess is imitation sinew and just start weaving away around the hoop. Then Anabelle has the fucking balls to ask me sweetly if there's anything else that I would like to add about the dreamcatcher. I glare at all the crazies around the table—those fucking *traitors*. I shrug my shoulders, *act fucking cool*, "Just native stuff." It comes out badass and Anabelle nods like I whispered winning lottery numbers, but inside I'm cringing so bad. I don't look up from what I'm doing, these psychos better just take my word for. Before I know it there's no room left to weave more string. It sort of looks like a web. Nothing beautiful like my grandmother's—her dreamcatchers have perfect diamonds all the same size apart, getting smaller and smaller until they wrap around a perfect opening in the middle. This looks like a spider got shitfaced and then put a blindfold on and then decided to spin a web. Whatever, it's not like anybody else knows the difference. I look up and half the kids aren't even doing theirs. Those that are have followed the instructions on the back of the kit and their dreamcatchers look a million times better than mine. I hide mine in the front pocket of my hoodie. "I'm done," I mutter, and hightail it out of there.

I get to my room and stare at the ugly thing in my hand.

I know it definitely won't work to catch nightmares, more like enhance them if anything. But you know, this shitty mess of a web kind of fits me and this shitty place. I put it on the bolted-down night table. I guess I'll keep it. It is my first dream-catcher, after all. 📖

Portrait of a Residential School Child, painting, Lawrence Paul Yuxweluptun

Jackhammer

Dave Seter

I didn't like working a jackhammer
but the boss said
its raucous locker room chatter
made me a man.

And as I walk past construction sites
I see those same knives
of stubble in the faces of workmen
who call out to passing women.

Chatter, chatter, chatter, is the sound.
They call the part of the jackhammer
that cuts the blade.

This is the thing.
Some people have strong ideas
on what it means to be a man.
Bulk in the shoulders.
Beer on the breath and in the gut.
A roughness toward every thing.
The view it must be won, bent or broken.

Why did they want to make me one of them?

My ancestors knew the hard work of spruce,
how living things adapt to landscape.
I survive by knowing
even the hardest case
when cut still sweetly bleeds.

At the Drop-In Center

Mercedes Lawry

Kenny uses two pairs of socks as a pillow, rolls up
in a blanket in front of the dryer.
Paula's under the free clothes rack, rolled up, too,
in a cocoon of coats and faded sweatshirts.
Jack's head is down on his crossed arms, his hands,
rough hills seamed with dirt. Beside him, his girlfriend
eats baked potatoes someone brought in, her eyes
flitting left and right.

They sleep in the deep well of refuge even though
Stephen squawks nonstop about Yo-Yo Ma
and civil engineers and Lucy tends to her gunshot wound
with ragged sighs and the cold pizza disappears in seconds.
They sleep without twitch or jerk
because no one's going to hurt them here
and it's warm. The water in the showers
never gets truly hot, but the coffee is, till noon
when everyone's woken up, eased out
and we wipe the tables with bleach, sweep the floor
and walk to our cars in the cold,
pestering rain and drive home.

Boy, Seattle, 2019, photograph, Angel Ybarra

Homeless Vet

Tom A. Delmore

There are would-be old
Russian queens out walking.
Short, fur-crowned, fur-lined.
Daily they walk the busy street
Edict-less and weary. In the mix
Young orthodox fathers—
Ferrying their children from
The free Jewish library to
The unseen synagogue; wives
And toddlers steps behind.
Sikhs outside non-existent cabs
Loiter at bus stops like bearded
Guards of the five rivers.

All of this taken in by a man
With a cardboard sign: *Please help
God bless*.

Lower Queen Anne

Thomas Hubbard

On Queen Anne Avenue, in a neighborhood called Lower Queen Anne,
at the foot of the hill sits a coffee house with some outside tables,
a place for long Sunday mornings . . . people watching.

It was on such a day this scene unfolded.

So this fellow sits right now, Sunday morning
at one of the outside tables, smoking a cigarette and
drinking from a paper cup of coffee from a stand nearby.

His orange, yellow, and white-striped trousers
argue with the electric lime green rain jacket he wears
over a dark blue hooded sweatshirt.

Cheap running shoes and whiskers complete his outfit, and
he appears to be well into his fifties.

Lines on this man's face tell of new starts that . . . didn't work,
of damp-skinned mornings beside women he needed to escape,
of realization that the love of his life would not be coming back . . . ever, and
the lines on his face tell of leaving home . . .
no, not some cheap place he was staying at, but rather
leaving the very idea, the very concept of home . . . leaving it behind, and
those lines on his face speak softly, so softly
of gathering determination to make it through another day.

He looks from side to side, hands fidgeting at his crossed knees,
one cheap running shoe on the concrete while the other moves idly in the air,
white cotton sock top showing.

He begins talking to nobody, or perhaps to all the world, and
then suddenly he's gone, walking carefully up Queen Anne Avenue.
Walking past apartment buildings far beyond his means,
places where he would never even be allowed inside the lobby.

He's gone, walking slowly up that hill, and
all the lunches his mother may have packed for him,
the meals he sat down to, the conversations . . .

close shaves he escaped, and those he didn't,
ballgames he played, scenes he saw, songs he sang,
kites he flew, lovers he knew,

dogs of his childhood . . .
new toys and lessons in school,
days he skipped and buddies he skipped with,

letters he wrote,
cars he wore out or wrecked,
cold nights he wished for family while shivering alone,

all gone along with him,
stuffed inside the hood of that old blue sweatshirt and
headed for whatever comfort this day will show him.

Sixty-Six Summers

Terra Trevor

Talk to my grandma and you will hear stories about me in diapers taking my first steps in mixed race America. I'm Cherokee, Lenape, Seneca and part white, a mixed-blood American Indian with German, Jewish and Swedish ancestry. The daughter of teenage parents and the granddaughter of sharecroppers.

My dad's side of the family came to California in 1936, after The Great Dust Bowl in Oklahoma when they could no longer farm. But the only reason they were in Oklahoma in the first place is because Native peoples were relocated, removed from Native land, and my family ended up in Indian Territory. Oklahoma before it became a state.

First marker moment. It's 1956, and I am three years old. I'm in the backseat. My dad is driving and my mother is beside him, screaming. Some guys are pulling my dad out of the car, beating him. Mexican guys come to help my dad. We are safe now.

I will replay this memory over and again. A decade later I will understand. Because he was a brown boy, a half breed, with a white girl.

The story I tell myself is the white guys had chains. But maybe the Mexican guys who helped us had the chains. Why do I remember chains?

1956 was also the year that saw explosive clashes all across the South, between African Americans, who were determined to overthrow Jim Crow, and hardline white supremacists pledged to "massive resistance." In Montgomery, African Americans persisted with their boycott of the city's segregated buses in the face of death threats, bombings, petty harassment, insults, economic coercion and mass arrests.

In 1956, we lived in Southeast Los Angeles, in the city of Paramount, bordering Compton, with two tiers, white and everyone who wasn't white.

A few years later my dad had "the talk" with me, about how to be street smart and safe. By then I had already figured it out. I'm in grade school now, attending the Compton City School District. My best friend is Japanese and Mexican. My friend next door is Bolivian and her mother loves me like a daughter. On Saturday nights I sleep over and drink in the sounds, scents, language, foods and all things Bolivian.

The pattern is set. By age ten I have learned that everyone who isn't white feels safe to me. White feels like walking a razor's edge. You have to watch yourself at all times. Be aware. Watch for clues. Make up stories to protect your mixed-race, under-educated family. If you don't pass the tests issued by the mothers or the fathers they won't allow you to play with their white daughter. Me, a rough-around-the-edges girl with skin so light, assumed to be white, as long as she answers the questions right.

But the mixed-race families and the brown-skinned families would always take you in, without asking too many questions.

Second marker moment. It's 1963, and a new family moves into the house across the street, German immigrants, with a kind boy, my age. Neighborhood gossip issued from the first tier said they belonged to Hitler's Youth, long ago, moved to America to escape all of that. The taunting begins. Nazi signs are painted all over the house. Broken, the family moves away. I think about my German great grandfather, about the hate they said he endured after the war and about my German-Jewish great grandmother.

That same year Martin Luther King announced to the March on Washington during his famous "I have a dream" speech that "1963 is not an end, but a beginning." For legal segregation, it would turn out to be the beginning of the end. The year started with Alabama governor George Wallace standing on the steps of the state capitol in hickory-striped trousers and a cutaway coat declaring, "Segregation now, segregation tomorrow, segregation forever."

It's 1965, and the sun is an orange haze and the sky turns black. The Watts Riots have begun. I'm twelve years old. The city of Watts is on the other side of Compton, not far away. Smoke is thick in the air and I worry about friends and everyone else in danger.

Later that same year I will learn that although women were guaranteed the right to vote in 1920 by the Nineteenth Amendment, in some southern states, African American women were unable to freely exercise their right to vote until 1965.

And the understanding lodges deep within me, of how white thinking is a mindset carefully taught, handed down, maneuvered, steered, controlled like over-planted land and polluted waters, a way of moving through life that must be avoided.

It's 1972, and I'm nineteen and pregnant. In a social welfare office I list my ethnicity as American Indian. The father of the baby is also American Indian, but I will not reveal his name. Instead, I write down that the father is unknown.

The welfare officer, a white women, gives me a lecture, tells me I'm trash for sleeping with any Tom, Dick or Harry. I huddle in the hallway and cry. Another social worker, a black woman, comes to check on me and when I tell her what happened she hugs me and says that I'm not the first pregnant girl, and lord knows I won't be the last, and not to pay any mind to anyone who treats me like I'm less than.

Maybe the social worker who said I was trash was just a spiteful woman and it had nothing to do with racism. Yeah. Maybe.

1972 is also the year AIM organizers (American Indian Movement) and local Native parents, motivated by prejudice in the child welfare system and hostility in the public schools, started their own community school. The story of these survival schools, unfolding through the voices of activists, teachers, and families, is also a history of AIM's founding and of its long-term effect on Indian people's lives.

White privilege: the ability to attribute hateful behavior to isolated incidents, classism, bad luck or just a bad social worker with a bad bedside manner.

2019. I'm sixty-six, moving into elderhood and holding space for the pain of all those who hurt. I stay open, year after year of heartache, walking this good earth, with clear eyes, and ears. Because like the roots of the cedar, deep within I carry, we all carry, blood memory, in our DNA and the wisdom from our ancestors with the power to heal the next seven generations. 📖

At The Grace Café

Richard Widerkehr

There's a hole in the sky some gray-white light
seeps through. A crow perches on a lamppost.

Last evening, near shift change on the unit, we admitted
an older woman named Carla. She was thin,
had bad teeth from doing meth. We sat at the hall table
in dim light, across from our glowing nurse's station.
I asked how she was doing.
It's hard swimming through gravel, she said,
held up her bandaged left wrist.
Guess I won't be playin' no banjo for a while.

I took in a breath, asked if we could move
into the light so I could take her blood pressure.
Are you in pain? I asked. *Not too bad*, she said.
I'd ask our nurse Miss Dee to offer her something.
Got her a sandwich, some Gatorade,
as per Dee's instructions, told Carla I hoped
she didn't want to hurt herself now.
She said nothing for minute, then muttered
in a husky voice, *Not now.* Later, I'd write down
latency of response. I told Carla, *We'll be looking in
on you for a while, make sure you're okay.* She nodded,
opened her Bible, told me, *You know, that Egypt,
it was a blast furnace.* I nodded, asked in a low voice
if I could get her anything. Some more pillows?

It was time for me to give report, fill in the fifteen
minute check sheet, write my admit note. *Will you tell us
if you want to hurt yourself?* I asked. Slight tilt
of her head, as if attending to something.
She pursed her lips, muttered, *You know, some claw marks
aren't scars, but mercy and justice.* I let out my breath.

When White People Talk About their Country Being Stolen (I Throw Up in My Mouth a Little Bit)

Tiffany Midge

The morning after the election results, while our country was waking up from one of the biggest hangovers of its life, John and me had the complicated and compounded misfortune of waking to the telltale sounds of what I assumed was a celebratory victory rut of our upstairs' neighbors, who happened to be ardent Trump fans.

"The upstairs neighbors are going at it! A victory bang." I posted on my Facebook. Then deleted. Then re-posted. Then deleted again. I have no filter.

Our neighbors have Trump signs all over the yard, a poster-sized "VOTE TRUMP" sign taped to the back of their minivan, along with year-round Christmas lights and miniature American flags all up and down the concrete path to their porch. When I sprained my ankle, these same untoward neighbors gave me a walker, offered help, visited me and sympathized with my trouble. Yes, they are good people. They know not what they do goes the refrain inside my head.

I know how to deal with Trumpsters. Their narrative is simplistic, transparent, and in my face.

What's not so simple, what isn't an easy-to-follow recipe are the white folks stomping through our yard in pink pussy hats and safety pins stuck to their lapels, on their way to another Saturday rally in the park across the street. These socially conscientious liberals who want *their* country back.

"There's a lady kicking over the planters in the walkway," John says from the window.

"Shit. Is she wearing a pussy hat?"

"Yes. Should we call the police?"

"No. Tell her to get off our lawn."

We laugh.

The Native couple raising cane at hippies who're tearing around on their front lawn. That's rich.

"I feel a little sorry for them. They look so lost," I say.

"Don't. One of them broke our planter."

We laugh.

"We could join them?" I say. "They don't know what hit them. Trump is going to turn the whole country into a banana republic."

"Or a reservation," John says.

"Welcome! We've got a chair for you right here at the kid's table," I say.

"We should teach seminars called 'Dispossession is a Bitch.'"

We laugh. *In that good way.*

From the distance we can hear a woman's voice amplified through a megaphone. In the park, a sea of pink assembled like a coral reef. We part the curtains and peer through the window as if we're Jacques Cousteau surveying a mysterious new species.

So much *pink*.

If I take my glasses off, all I see is a blur of cotton candy. It makes me feel nauseous, as if I'd stayed at the carnival too long.

John takes my hand and opens the front door. We step out into the morning air and reluctantly join the parade.

Tired

Stephani E.D. McDow

Quiet as it's kept,
my knee hurts
my voice is gone

I #sayhisname and "I can't breathe"
because
blue lives matter, and
I #sayhername and die alone in a jail cell
because
all lives matter.
And, you didn't hear this from me, but
my arms feel like anvils for how long I've had to hold them in the air

I just want to make it home.

I skirt around words that were once commonplace in a usual space
'cause of the taste they leave in my mouth now

his ace doesn't trump my queen of hearts
it beats it

My knee hurts
the poet whose piece is the foundation of your honor
said that my people are "a distinct and inferior race"
"the greatest evil"

Seeing no color is a transparent lie
not it, not you
us
lack of acknowledgement does not equal truth
skewing what's real negates the American dream

I'm woke

"No refuge could save"
    Don't shoot!
"the hireling and slave"
    Say their names.
"And the star-spangled banner in triumph doth wave"
    Black Lives Matter.

They trump my black pride with their white power and privilege
and spit on my peace and quiet resistance

I'm vigilant
dissonant

and tired.
Leave me alone.

FollowU, from the series *On Women Bound*, 2014, oil on linen, Jane Caminos

Journeys

Anna Bálint

Pack no more than you can carry. Hurry.
You have to leave now, tomorrow may be too late.
There is no time to pack!
Run. Run my child, just as you are.

Soldiers in jeeps roar into our village
and shooting begins. Many are killed, fathers
and brothers, mothers and sisters raped.
We flee into the night, our village in flames.
We cannot go back. We have nowhere to go back to.

We spend our time hiding from airstrikes
and barrel bombs. The bombs are every day,
every day. Our city is falling, bodies buried in rubble.
We pack no more than we can carry and hurry away.
We cannot go back. We have nowhere to go back to.

* * *

Only the road. Or the trail. Or not even a trail.
Only the hard dry earth. The cruel sun.
Children, barefoot, walking one behind the other.
Mothers carrying babies, walking for days.
Sleeping under a tree. Up at sunrise.
Walk, before it is too hot to walk. Crossing rivers,
fathers holding small children above their heads.
Crossing the White Nile, continuing to walk.

Look at a map. Find Afghanistan. Find Syria.
Find Sudan, South Sudan, Somalia. See how
the Red Sea separates two continents,
Africa on one side, Asia on the other.

Now, trace these journeys: Afghanistan
to Pakistan, Syria to Jordan, Sudan to South Sudan,
South Sudan to Uganda, Somalia to Kenya.
See the human rivers crisscrossing the land.

Za'atari, Dadaab, Kakuma, Bidibidi, Nyumanzi
Za'atari, Dadaab, Kakuma, Bidibidi, Nyumanzi
Places of refuge, their names sing of sanctuary.

* * *

Do you know of Dadaab?
The world's largest refugee camp and Kenya's
third largest city? A city of tents, population
six hundred thousand. Barrel-shaped tents, plastic
sheeting stretched over hoops, makeshift shelters
built from sticks. A city in the sand, sprawling
and disappearing over the edge of the earth.
Inside its gates no warlords, no drought, no famine.
Here are your blankets. Here is your water.
Line up over there for food. Expect to wait.
Waiting is an art. You will practice it everyday
and become a master.

In this city of tents you will find hospitals and schools.
Your baby will not die from hunger.
Your children will pursue their education, girls as well
as boys. Here are markets, busy busy with plenty.
Find fresh and canned goods, soda pop, clothing.
Find shops selling cooking pots and brooms.
Here's a kiosk to charge your mobile phone.
Yes, it is true, a fence rings the camp,
with razor wire on top. You ask, why is it there?
Is it to keep you safe from the outside world,
or keep the outside world safe from you?

* * *

I am a refugee.
That's my name now. Refugee.

Life is different here.
It's not like being at home. The toilets are dirty,
so we don't use them. We go to the bush.
Since we came here, life is not what it used to be.
I want to be in that life before. The good life,
before the soldiers came. Here there are food shortages.
This month only maize flour. No beans or rice.
No firewood for cooking fires.
Last month no cooking oil.

Sugar, morning tea, milk,
these are the things I miss the most.
I miss the smell of the air in my country.
I miss the flowers on my balcony
I miss Friday afternoons in my neighborhood.
I miss the olive trees and fields of wheat.
I miss the birds and the harvest season.
Can anyone miss anything more than
their own home and the tree they sit under?

Last night I had a dream.
I dreamed I was back in my village
but when I woke up I found myself here.
Here there is gravel, there is grey, and nothing
green. No plants, no trees, no grass.
Only the white of the tents, the grey of the gravel,
and the wind. Do you hear how the wind
tugs at the tents? The flap and the snap?

When the war ends we will return
to our country and rebuild our city.
When fear is gone, then we can go home.

* * *

Do you see those young boys playing kickball?
Do you hear how they laugh as they play?
They are children born here, boys already home.
They live three generations of refugees
under one ragged roof, their parents and grandparents
aching from waiting for a country to grant them asylum.
Better to wait for a boat to a new life. Wait for two days,
three, maybe a week. No longer than that. While you wait,
look across the water and dream. While you wait
for a boat your brother in Berlin waits for you.

The boat when it comes is an old fishing boat,
its motor is not good. The boat when it comes is
an inflatable vessel too flimsy to cross the sea.
The boat when it comes has a rusted hull and
sits low in the water. Too low. So many boats.
So many people. The weather worsens, waves toss
and blue water turns black beneath stars.
Morning when it comes is a mist, the only color
the orange of life vests, the only sounds
the chug chug chug of the motor,
the slop of waves, and a baby crying.

* * *

Dreams:
A new country. A house. An apartment. A room.
Someplace to come home to. A place with walls,
windows and a door. A stove. A table. Some chairs.
A bed. Two beds. A TV for the children. Maybe a balcony,
a place to step outside and take in some air.
Will your new neighbors welcome you?

Dreams:
The place you left behind. The place no longer there. That place that in your memory still exists, and will exist forever, untouched by bombs, unchanged. The courtyard still there, waiting for you. The smells of the kitchen, warm bread, onions and meat frying. Outside, a tree heavy with lemons. The lemons will always be there in your memory.

* * *

You have waited.
Today your turn has come.
Today someone in uniform calls your name.

Forms, photographs, fingerprints, interviews. Documents scrutinized, backgrounds checked. Where were you born? Where did you live? What city? Why did you leave? What is your education? What is your occupation? What is your religion? Do you have any diseases? Open your mouth. Say aah. Step on the scale. Take a deep breath. Where is your wife? Where is your husband? Why isn't he with you? How old are your children? Where are their birth certificates? Do you speak English? Look at the camera. Look to the side. Turn around. Take a seat. Wait. Come back tomorrow. Come back next week. Expect to wait at least six months, a year, two years. Longer.

* * *

You have waited.
Today your turn has come.
Today someone in uniform calls your name.

Say goodbye to the elderly mother you must leave behind.
Kiss her, wipe her tears and promise you will send for her.
Then journey once more, this time by bus or by train.
Beyond the windows, unfamiliar landscapes flash past.
Maybe you will board a plane. Your youngest child
sits on your knee. Buckle up. Is it really safe to fly so high?

* * *

A new life is hard to start, but this is where we live now.
Come inside. Look around. Rugs with bright designs cover
the floor; there are many cushions sit on. Make yourself
comfortable. I'll pour you some coffee. It's strong
and very good, the way we make coffee in my country.

Outside is a satellite dish and family wash hung out to dry,
pants next to skirts, next to shirts big and small;
purple next to pink, a sudden splash of red.
Two little girls wearing hijabs zoom past on bicycles.
Where are we? Are we in Frankfurt, London,
Seattle, or Rome? Are we in Jordan? New Zealand perhaps?
Could this be Beirut? We are somewhere now,
newly started somewhere with a mosque nearby.
But are we safe in this country? Are we home?

*Darkfeather Ancheta, Eckos Chartraw-Ancheta, and Bibiana Ancheta,
Tulalip, Washington, photograph by Matika Wilbur*

Darkfeather Ancheta, is pictured with her sister and nephew at the edge of Tulalip Bay. They are wearing the traditional regalia that was prepared for their annual Canoe Journey. Every year, upward of 100 U.S. tribes, Canadian First Nations, and New Zealand canoe families will make "the journey" by pulling their canoes to a rotating host destination tribe. Canoe families pull for weeks, and upon landing, there will be several days and nights of "protocol": a celebration of shared traditional knowledge, ancestral songs, and sacred dances. This celebration has been incredibly important to Darkfeather, she says, "It didn't change me. It raised me. It shaped me. It's just who we are, and where we come from . . . it revitalizes our cultural ways. There are so many teachings that go along with the relationship with the canoe. We take care of the canoe and it takes care of us. When we're on the water, we all have to pull together. Everything is smoother when we all work together. The teachings that the elders gave to us—like respecting ourselves, respecting each other, respecting other people's songs, their dances, and their teachings—they teach us how to walk in the world. And the music and songs are so powerful. It's all so beautiful. It touches you down into your soul. It helps you get through hard times, both in the water and in life".

Profit Over People, 2019, drawing, Hank Hobby

III

WHY?

*I imagine one of the reasons people cling to their hate so stubbornly
is because they sense, once hate is gone, they will be forced to deal with pain.*
—James Baldwin

*Don't accept the habitual as a natural thing. In times of disorder, of organized confusion,
of de-humanized humanity, nothing should seem natural.*
—Bertolt Brecht

Wanna fly, you got to give up the shit that weighs you down.
—Toni Morrison

*The truth has a strange way of following you,
of coming up to you and making you listen to what it has to say.*
—Sandra Cisneros

*The most important truths are likely to be those
which society at that time least wants to hear.*
—W. H. Auden

2 Queer Donkeys, 2006, cartoon/drawing, Jan Gosnell

About Writing Political Poetry

Anita K. Boyle

I don't write political poetry
because words on a page become trite,
because there is a value to life
I cannot put into words,
because I am a simpleton.

I don't write political poetry
about liars, or traitors, or patriots.
I don't write about the bias
of the electoral college, or about
how corporations are now people, or how
recent trade wars might adversely affect
our lower and middle classes.

I haven't written about our president,
or how this one applauds dictators,
shakes hands with tyrants, congratulates
human rights abusers.

I don't write political poetry
because my words disappear
in the wind, because even though
marching and chanting, the rattling
of signs, and the shaking of fists
have happened, the tyranny continues.
I am helpless and too stupid
to make the slightest difference.

I haven't written political poems
because I am footless within history,

have no leg to stand on, and believe
that having no knowledge of a heritage
has created the vast majority of angry
white non-people who demand
to be real without an understanding
of just who they might be. Let's
take a breath here.

I would like to write political poetry.
There are people coming to America.
Right now, they are knocking
at our borders. They are desperate
and dirty. Their feet are blistered.
They desire a safe place, a small haven
to wash up, and to eat a decent meal
without fear. But we've shut the door,
locked it, built higher, longer, and
sharper walls to keep them away.
We've threatened these travelers
with soldiers, taken their children,
cursed and spat at them, sprayed
tear gas on them—as though
they haven't cried enough—
and insist they walk through a pinhole
to gain the refuge they need.

Our country is beautiful,
but it is angry.
Our country is spacious,
but we are stingy.
My country, 'tis of thee.
Let all that breathe partake.
I don't write political poetry
because I don't know where
to start, and wouldn't know
where to stop.

Neither Silence Nor Forgetting

J.I. Kleinberg

The opposite of music is not silence.
>	I have listened to the open space
>	within breath, to the caesura
>	between the rising trills
>	of the Swainson's thrush,
>	to weightless wheels rolling
>	the roads of sleep in a unison
>	of sculpted golden notes.

The opposite of music is not cacophony.
>	I have heard the voice of oceans,
>	earthquakes, waterfalls, heeded
>	the chant of protest, argument
>	of crows, night howls of cats, attended
>	the bombastic plosives and fricatives
>	of adolescents and politicians
>	with their strident syncopations.

The opposite of music is not forgetting.
>	I have examined the hollow room
>	where our stories once lived, waited
>	all January for the ice cream truck,
>	for the girls singing in the mirror,
>	for the lyrics we learned by heart,
>	mouths open in an aria of longing.

Music is the opposite of waiting,
the opposite of complacency,
the opposite of what is known.

The opposite of music is a knot
twisted in the ribbon of breath,
a missing heartbeat, a child
ripped from her mother's arms.

In a Time of Peace

Ilya Kaminsky

Inhabitant of earth for fortysomething years
I once found myself in a peaceful country. I watch neighbors open

their phones to watch
a cop demanding a man's driver's license. When a man reaches for his wallet, the cop
shoots. Into the car window. Shoots.

It is a peaceful country.

We pocket our phones and go.
To the dentist,
to pick up the kids from school,
to buy shampoo
and basil.

Ours is a country in which a boy shot by police lies on the pavement
for hours.

We see in his open mouth
the nakedness
of the whole nation.

We watch. Watch
others watch.

The body of a boy lies on the pavement exactly like the body of a boy—

It is a peaceful country.

And it clips our citizens' bodies
effortlessly, the way the President's wife trims her toenails.

All of us
still have to do the hard work of dentist appointments,
of remembering to make
a summer salad: basil, tomatoes, it is a joy, tomatoes, add a little salt.

This is a time of peace.

I do not hear gunshots,
but watch birds splash over the backyards of the suburbs. How bright is the sky
as the avenue spins on its axis.
How bright is the sky (forgive me) how bright.

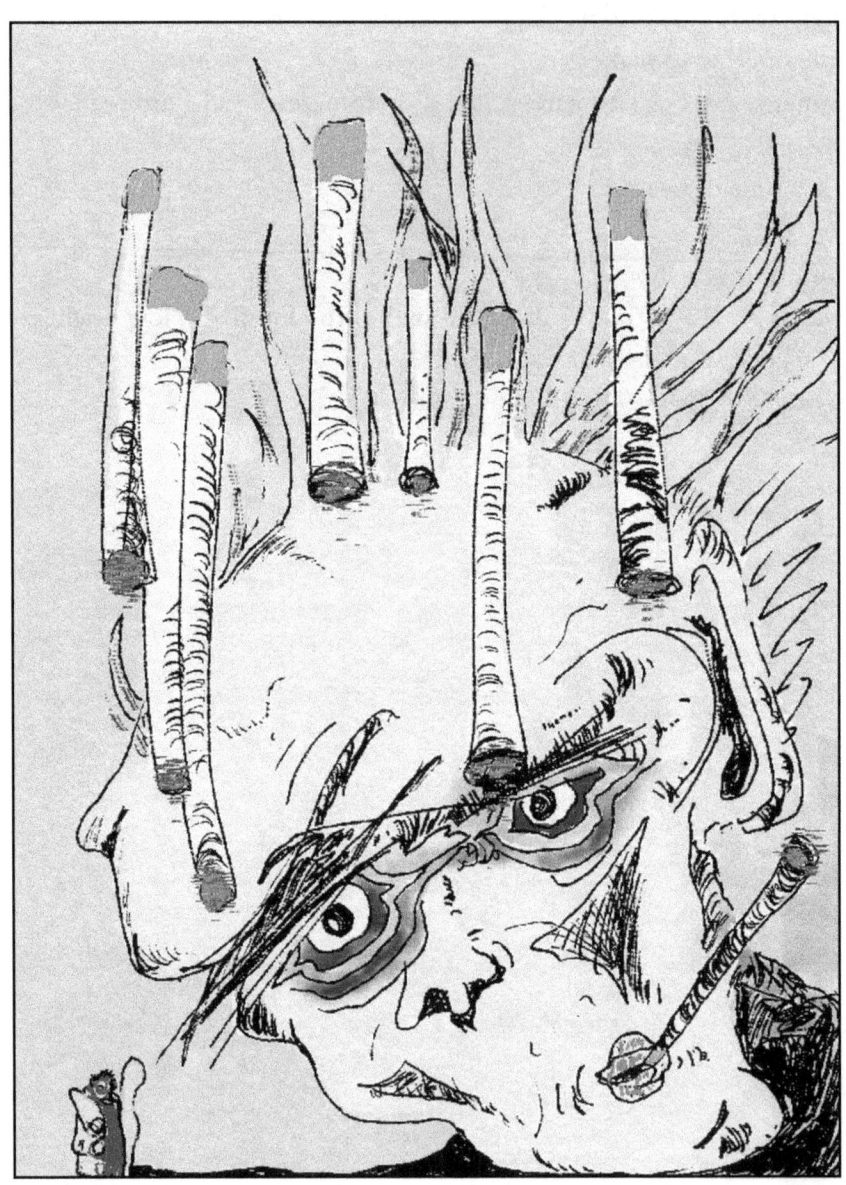

Thinking About Quitting, 2018, digital comic, Dave Sims

Rabid Dog

Judith Skillman

When you wake me
I tend your stenosis
brush your bad mouth

I try to catch the happy fleas
bouncing up from bed sheets
where we sleep together

I pet and fondle those pretty stones
clustered around your neck
Swarovski crystals set in grape leather

Best friend of man
like a Berlin train with plush seats
you run on a timetable

Your presence fetters my ankles
although I honor in principle
the morals that keep me from leaving

Dog born of wolf I promise
in these new vows to try harder
to hear your infection

Listen to my hand absently petting
the bark the yip the howl the rage

Holocaust Denier

Mike Dillon

As he spoke to scattered inattention
in the park when I walked past
the faceted interiors
of his green-eyed glance
locked into mine.

And I thought of my cat
hunched on the windowsill
that very morning fused
to a towhee flitting in the laurel
on the other side of the glass.

Puffed cheeks. A guttural chortle.
The green seas of her eyes
dilated black as the spaces
between the stars. I gave her a poke.
She didn't know me.

For the first time I am afraid

Susan Rich

of my country, I say, and he says,
yes. He who has not

taken his safety for granted
does not shame me

for only understanding this now.
We navigate the broken

interstate, eyes focused on
our near future and the shape

of the talk continues on
civil in slow-drawn twists and turns—

past green exit signs and a floating
bridge that disappears across the lake,

behind the cut—two complete
strangers portrayed in black and in white—

driving our nation's highways
in the rush hour of late spring.

The Tar Pit

Paul Hunter

Consider infantile rage
the tar pit that bubbles up
around the age of three or four
spills over each one of us sticks
to everything may need to be
dissolved in gasoline torched
that for a few never ends
though by second or third grade
most will have tiptoed on past

yet here stands the smoldering child
impetuous treacherous fierce
feeling utterly wronged
stomping his little foot
shouting I didn't want this one
I wanted the red one she got
that will not listen to reason
that understands only force
aimed outward at anyone else
where he stands shaking
glowering his sharp daggers
a tiny ruler barking orders
at a universe that won't obey
his commands who cannot be
deflected turned back on himself
since not just the war would be lost
the prince would be burnt to a crisp

this is the profound seat of hate
lodged in each one of us
this is where enthroned it sits
it cannot be made likeable
as with all absolute rulers it craves
only to be fed more of
exactly what it knows it likes
sure the rest of the world
could read its mind instantly
if it would just pay attention
fetch on the run what's demanded

Freud called this the id the raging
subconscious needy appetite
oblivious of others that
can never have enough that
every parent does battle with
that at its extreme can only be
contained with understated force
saying Because I said so
because I am bigger than you are
and now we're done talking and
you're going straight home to bed

but in the mode of hate the little one
still new to the world might learn
if he can make his parent
lose her own temper shout back
he will have won the battle
for now she will be the bully
who deserves his resentment
his volcanic hate which is why
parents first need to be grownups

though even grownups can be careless
saying we hate rush hour traffic hate
lima beans cream corn Brussels sprouts
cold coffee reheated coffee hate
cilantro hate doing our taxes
which begins to sound like
life could be ordered off menus
that had mostly been designed
to torture our taste buds
and keep us waiting forever

so when we are faced with real hate
the misplaced laser-etched hate
of the fearful infant overgrown
sulking disappointed wronged
who requires someone to blame
someone cowering beneath contempt
who has knowingly wronged him
by reaching for that last doughnut
or job he just spotted or crossed
the street against his arrogant
horn glaring high beams
who needs to be told and shown
every time how you changed lanes
with your burned-out turn signal

remind you forever and always
every time you dare to draw a breath
here comes someone who hates you
for the light in your eye
for your skin's gathering dark
for your sex your costume your name
that he can't pronounce so why bother
hates you for all you believe and live by
all you work in hope and dare to dream

who will instantly and loudly set you straight
about what is wrong with a world
with you in it who will demonstrate
his deep naked anger unloved
in the wilds of infancy forever lost
as if it were his life's purpose
not merely to punish and correct
but to shame demean rebuke humiliate
until in the fullness of time
the raging infant sputters to a halt
as his fury rising up consumes itself

Still Confederate, Brenham, Texas, 2017, photograph, Christopher Woods

An Apology for Hate

Edward Ahern

Unloved things—weeds and warts,
Dry rot and wet rot and wall mold,
Rats and lice and cockroaches
Halitosis and cancer and herpes
Are with us despite every effort.

But our most pernicious consort,
born of fear, reared in animosity
is hatred—of others, of change,
hate that proverbs and strictures
fumble helplessly against.

Many-splendored hate is of all sides:
radical / reactionary, Godless / Godfearing,
free-loving / abstinent, sharing / selfish.
It flourishes despite agonized exterminators,
an eye we refuse to pluck out.

Dread, Not Envy

Marge Piercy

The young imagine we envy them;
some of my friends and acquaintances
do, but not me. I look at what we've
done to the earth we're leaving you.

I walk the shore where I used to pick
moon snail, conch, slipper shells,
from sand now littered with butts,
tampons, beer cans, plastic everything.

Storms flood cities, winds flatten
whole streets, communities that are
no more. The polluted sea gnaws
the land, takes more and more back.

You inherit a country half of which
hates the other half. Warming brings
new diseases, new insects, new
ways to get sick and to die. Hatred

is official and encouraged: anyone
not just like you is a danger. Fences,
walls, no trespassing, neighborhoods
gated, built into a maze, so those not

rich and white enough are kept out.
We bequeath you prisons stuffed
like easy chairs leaking their innards.
Every day more species vanish.

Botched abortions kill more women.
Bad drugs kill young people who see
no future for them in a dying economy.
So many of us are angry, armed.

Every year we are still at war.
Every year the gap grows between
those who have everything and
those who have nothing at all.

The AK-47 Blues, or Sorting Through a History of Violence

henry 7. reneau, jr.

—If you turn the Goddess to stone, don't be surprised if she doesn't bleed.
—Andrea Potts

1.
this is a poem
beginning with the outside gaze: the bluest eyes
behind aviator shades of bio-metric racist recognition,
        their fear of, &
bigotry, projecting stereotype.

the hate that hate made ... oblivious to
            pleas, or expletives,
that bullet hole the fabric of dignity: a devious tradition of
            sound-bite doublespeak &
            the red,
            white,
            black & Blues, like the
            first stones thrown.

& how many monsters have you created today?

2.
that high-heeled nation & its long, holy line of mythology,
status quo faces not yet ravaged by broken dreams ...
                      until their false sun
                  exploded over Trinity &
the sons & daughters of man
traded their sense of magic &
wonder
      for the illusion of acquisition,
                  gone mute

        before fools
       who spoke many words,
       but said nothing true:

*As we know, there are known knowns. There are things we know
we know. We also know*
   *there are known unknowns. That is to say, we know
there are things we do not know. But there are also
unknown*
   *unknowns,
the ones we don't know we don't know.*

the patriotic stars & stripes, &
the flaws in their rhetoric
hefting silver shovels
      into grasping, corporate hands.

3.
them/those *Others*. a Blues-toned Black
signifyin' sin-tax,
     stumbling into concatenations of

salvation came to rest
upon the trembling shoulders
of the most reluctant of heroes:

If you give hope, you've got to take it from somewhere else,

like Creation,
that keeps a small token
of each soul taken: a corrupted tatter
calibrated to the filth of it all, &
ever ready
for fifteen minutes of shame.

4.
this poem is a camera shutter opening to pain, to synonym
                              of wide-eyed fear: a ghostly
                              apparition
         reflected in a shattered pane of glass,
         the way erosion
         bloodies a country yard in alkali &
                   can't speak past the ashes in our mouth.

the human touch, shadow sick &
stretching further from the light.
                         the biological dynamic,
withered, just beyond the muscle memory of grasp,
as garish as
the slaughterhouse burned down &
built a ho-house in its place,

the vicarious enflocked to 3D-action movies in Cali &
the mythological aftermath of
fallen Twin Towers,
book-ending the cult of
instant gratification, &
                    coast to coast high
                    on digital fame,
the methamphetamine
wealth & opioid epidemic
                    made a muscle of euphoria,
the glossy, fashion-porn pages of
bartered flesh.

the celebri-hos'
beginning with a poem
about a predatory trait,
              the suffering of the "Other"
              that was ignored for so long,
              & eventually,

        as suffering is wont to do,
           metastasized,
      multiplied,
like bricks into a wall
of exclusion & class status,
into the Global-I-zation
        of plantation systems,

a survival of the fittest
whose sole ideology is a lie
that travels the speed of speed of light,

that neither eats nor sleeps;

it blows up, detonates,
explodes
a silent weeping of deferred dreams,
         littered with poverty,
         drug use &
         gun violence—
the desperation, maybe dying today,

in stark contrast
to a Republican view of freedom—debating caste
before compassion—
        an up-by-your-bootstraps vs.
        in-another's-shoes &
           global warming
like a corporate elevator: too much Muzak,
burgeoning its way to butterfly effect,
        the colonizing force of free-trade zones
of outsourced slavery, the part-time jobs
like penny-in-a-vacuum dispossession—the consumer eyes
          shut tight &
hungry babies crying into the night.

5.
this is a poem
about too-big-to-fail: manifest
                              in the squalor of opulence:

peddlers & meddlers who buy, bribe &
they sell, four corporate horsemen
from the boardrooms of hell, their missionaries &
mercenaries
with machine minds not their own,
occupied your city & herd-poisoned your well.

the Global-I-zation of taking
without asking &
occupation, cornering an untapped market
into sectarian strife,

because evil's still evil . . .

this is a poem
about the subliminal hum of intolerance: a child gunned down
because his hoodie was too black,
the repeated vitriol of "be-very-afraid."

the homeless brood,
forever looking for something better than Made in Amerikkka.

this is a poem
about smoldering umbrage gone mute, waiting
for someone else to know the way,
                      while *evil's still evil in anybody's name.*

Note: *quoted song fragment in last stanza by Don Henley, from "If Dirt Were Dollars." Speech fragment in fifth stanza by former Defense Secretary Donald Rumsfeld.*

Antwon Rose II, 2018, Sumi ink & watercolor paper, Ana Rodriguez

[Antwon Rose II was a 17-year-old African American who was shot and killed in East Pittsburgh, on June 19, 2018, by an East Pittsburgh Police Officer. Rose was unarmed when shot, and later died.]

Heartwood

Miriam Bassuk

Peel away the layers of craggy outer bark.
Drill past the cambium into the sapwood
that carries nutrients from root to crown.
Arrive at the heartwood, the oldest part of the tree.

We are all heartwood, our cores the same.
Some trick of light or bend of matter
spells our uniqueness. A thumbprint,
or an iris scan opens a door.

Skin color, slant of eyebrow,
size of nose, those might define us,
yet it's the heartwood beating
strong and firm that unites us.

Creature Powers

Eve Lyons

The porcupine has no natural predators.
It can walk into a pride of lions
confident that if they attack
they will only try once.

The squirrel hangs upside down off a tree branch
stares down a hawk without fear
gathers more nuts than it can find later
which gives the world more oak trees.

The fire salamander looks beautiful
bright orange splotches backlit by black.
Beauty is always deceptive
touch their skin and it may poison you.

The human builds walls to keep others out.
We are our own predators.
The human invents arrowheads, cannons, rifles
then mistakes a juice bottle for a gun.

Bamiyan Buddha, 6th Century, 174 feet, photograph, Sharon M. Carter

[Photographed just prior to the 1978 assassination of the Afghani Prime Minister which ushered in the Soviet Union invasion. The Taliban destroyed it in 2001.]

Union Creek in Winter

Edward Harkness

There's no word for it so far, the word
for what it means to be in love with you
in our sinking world, what it means to hike
through new snow, to hear beneath
the glass of creek ice the flow of winter
percolating its way through the ravine
not quite soundlessly toward lower ground
to join the wild roar of the American River.

The word that means we've loved
through the avalanches of our time,
loved while the wars raged, paid for
with our taxes, loved while our loved ones
voted for hatred, for *I-want-the-false-past-I-want-
what's-coming-to-me*, protected as they've been
by their skin white as this very snow draped
on hemlocks in the ravine's wavering light.

The word that means we're not alone,
we share that same nature wonder,
for the flicker tapping on a far-off tree,
the delicate calligraphy of a mouse's
prints along our path, as if Tu Fu
has been here too, who knew, even then,
even in the Tang Dynasty, beauty
leaves behind its faint notations.

The word that means we will go on,
we will follow an earlier trekker's snowshoe
trail, slog on bundled to keep the chill
from overtaking us, descend again steeply,
then climb again switchbacks above the creek
away from its cold murmurings, to our car
and the long drive back to the war zone
of now. Armed with our little courage,

we must drive straight to the front,
strap on flak jackets and begin the slow
search for survivors, slow search
for the words that might revive them.
Even now we're feverish to make contact,
to know what to listen for, to learn to hear
those muffled cries from deep in the rubble.
If we knew the words we might save

those most weakened, most in danger of giving up.
If we knew the words we might keep the world,
its rivers, its ice, its bitterroot, its winter wrens,
its hemlocks, its moonlight, its children,
its Shakespeare, its Szymborska, its rosehips,
its green and orange lichens, its Dylan,
its kora players, its hummingbirds, you,
me, and our Muslim neighbor, Maya, alive.

Every Child is a Legend

Jeannine Hall Gailey

The morning after a shooting, I watch a cold mist
rise in the February air. I am saying the names
of dead children out loud. Every child killed
is a legend unwritten. Their voices in the air
like the shrill whirr of hummingbirds,
their footsteps on the frosty grass like the silent
hooves of deer. How beautiful their faces
look to me. I have no children, so I can't feel
like those parents who wake today with one
less being at breakfast. The crows fly overhead.
The news likes to show the shaking survivors' tears.
Thoughts and prayers can't even make a dent
into this river of shades, each story untold,
their voices silence. Silenced. I was taught
to shoot a gun at seven, arrows at eight.
A little soldier armed. Each bullet rang clear
through the empty and innocent air, then
the paper target. Seven. Seventeen. These numbers
add up to what? I was never the shooter,
or the victim. Merely a writer of poems. What new story
can change these children, lead them to a new ending?
Their hearts stop with a bang, louder than a jet engine
in my ears. An imagined dragon growls, hungry, overhead,
smelling brimstone in the distance.

I Have Plenty of Things

Faiza Sultan

I have plenty of scarves
that might be good as temporary tents
for horrified children from the crises of Allahu Akbar
or for mothers who have the color of snow and the warmth of summer
Or for young escaped girls
who left their innocence behind
near the doors of Hell.

I have plenty of scarves
It might be good to change the world
or to defend our victims from their victims.

The world might come to believe
that I am a peaceful person
Even if some believe otherwise
and demand my apologies.

I have plenty of sorrows
to fill up a deep, lonely, and crying valley

Or to knit a hat for a mountain shivering in the cold
or I might share it with the displaced people
under a naked sky
Except from their fleeing sighs
and gazes of reproof.

I have plenty of history
It may be good to form new laws
near the tomb of my grandfather Hammurabi
Or to change the course of the event wheels
for we invented the wheel;
We might be able to change its course too.

Or I start writing all the names
in my Sumerian language
mixed with my Median's soul.

I have plenty of wars too
The sound of its bombs
might be good to penetrate
the silent walls of consciousness
while the sounds of sirens in my head
might be good for a new rap song
But the burning of my dreams
Can only be good to heat some cold hearts.

I have everything
I also have Heaven's gift inside me
A pure white peace
I sprinkle on the hate in your eyes
and on the burning Universe.

I March, 3/24/2018, Brenham, Texas, photograph, Christopher Woods

Grounds For An Investigation

Jesse Minkert

Beans grow
in the grounds
roast like children
in the sun.

Beans dark and dry
come home to my grinder
soak in heat and hope
like children on the border.

Truth, like coffee,
seeps out brown and bitter
Lies, like sugar,
will be added later.

The Border Is a Line

Ray Gonzalez

The Mexican border is a line between
faith and the shackled dream.

When people cross it, the highways
lead north and west.

When they are stopped and taken,
the green vans go south.

The border is a line between
imagination and the truth—

those who make it will not return,
the line leading to bodies in lost graves.

The line extends from birth to death,
though the mountains get in the way,

the line curving around them
to gather strength.

The line becomes a long sentence
when the labor matters, survivors

straightening the line to align it
with the relentless sun, stars falling

above the hole where they hide.
Even the bloodline from a plastic

bottle of water to a picture of La Virgen
de Guadalupe is sacrificed at the wire

because the Mexican border is a line
between faith and its sharpest point—

a line that is infinite, unstoppable,
and keeps coming this way.

On a Green Meadow

Ibrahim Al-Masri

Translated from the Arabic by Faiza Sultan, with Kathleen Alcalá

We would have dreamed of the land
As a room with open windows on a green meadow
Or on the sea

We would have dreamed of life as a path to anything other than blood

We would have taught Adam and Eve a lesson, returning to the myth

Where no children give their backs to regret
We would have rejoiced in God's books
That floated with fear in our consciences

We would have planted wheat, flowers and prayers
While hate is piling up murders

When the funerals extend from Christchurch
To New York, to Cairo, to Paris
to Mosul, to Tunisia, to Utrecht
to Bali, to Utøya and to Oak Creek

You can place the map on the wall
then draw red circles on the five continents
Hate is known as the triumph of murder over human significance

You will not get away from dividing yourself into mirrors that dispute with fire

Perhaps tomorrow you are dead in a mirror
Based on its strength to a killer's mind
When we all go
to place flowers on the graves of the victims, we will be silent

Even if we prayed for their souls
And promised that we would renounce violence, extremism, hatred and terrorism

There are still dreams that have been drown in blood
There are still knives and rifles now being made
There are car bombs
and the various doctrines protected by those who only live
by sending others to their death

We would have known death as peace for people
Who lost their lives peacefully
But nowadays, we do not die in peace
We do not gather killers in a room with open windows on a green meadow
or on the sea

Telling them
We will all shelter with music
We will build rooms and rooms
with open windows on a green meadow
or on the sea

Together, we will sing a song of peace that the earth has never known
The killers have poisoned us with images
That have been overflowing on our faces
and stretching blood on a green meadow . . .
. . . or on the sea.

Building Babel, 2015, acrylic paint & collage on canvas, Mona Nicole Sfeir

One Blood

Penina Ava Taesali

It is not a romantic matter. It is the unutterable truth;
all men are brothers & all women are sisters.
—James Baldwin

Is it the fluidity of light interlacing all to that gallant galactic vibration?
Does the Earth's magnetic field shield the blue jeweled Earth?
If we are one blood, why all the bloodshed?

If we forsake the shock of a child screaming in the dust, families
blockaded under bombed-out cities banished from hard-earned
livelihoods—won't the children's nightmares   boomerang

into our blood? Stain our sheets? How do we sleep? In America,
the short answer is *Lunesta*. Take your sleeping pills like good little
soldiers—until your drugs smother what is humanely possible.

The simplest concepts have become extraordinary—*Love thy neighbor*
as thyself—yet, the Golden Rule was a way of life long before the Bible
seized our island. Preparing breadfruit, taro and fish

inside the umu father said treasure is in the art of sharing—cousin
human, cousin vasa, cousin mauga, cousin māsina, cousin fetu, cousin
octopus, cousin coconut tree, cousin drum.

*

In Sweden refugee children suffer from *Uppgivenhetssyndrom*—a resignation syndrome. Hearing news that their family will be deported,
the children go to sleep and they do not get up.

They do not move for days, weeks, months they stay in a coma-of-despair.

Depression shrinks the hippocampus, which triggers emotion and memory. And even if a family is granted asylum and they read

the residency permit into their daughter's ear at her bedside—
she cannot move. She is like a mannequin.

It will take months or years for her to learn how to open her eyes again, how to hold her head up so she could see her family alive in Sweden.

* *

Our Librarian, Mrs. Morales, her face grows paler every day. She says: *People have every legal right to seek refuge from starvation, drowning, war, violence—we've come this far?*

Why are we afraid to love? Afraid of discomfort. Some Americans have normalized the looming dictatorship raging on our screens under our watch—we witness the children forced from the arms

of mothers and fathers—while private prisons boom. Half of the nation is diving into some cruel stupor—happily ripping wings off fragile exhausted bodies.

And the other half of the country is fiercely sober—cousin-to-cousin, poet-to-poet, student-to-student, teacher-to-teacher, neighbor-to-neighbor, senator-to-senator—calling for the 1,500 missing children—

the mothers' tears wail into my ears. I want to know what you'd do. A child is kicking and screaming—trying to get back into their mother's arms.

The Amber Alert—a sham. Your child is in a warehouse in a cage in the land of incarceration. Mrs. Morales asks—*how many more days?* What happened to the Special Counsel?

Why is coal-mining waste allowed to poison our rivers again?
The President sinks more every day but remains afloat like Styrofoam.

* * *

Yes and we are here—one rallying jamboree springing from that lasting spiritual reservoir—real as the countless stars providing a pathway for us to haven the vulnerable and the sick—here we leap forward to

save the life of another like our own life depends on it *love one another*—the sovereignty of the heart glorious—here is where we think we dig we gather and organize again, again the

Underground Railroad—this is where we become harbor, human— that is the moment we become civilized.

Glossary of Samoan words:
umu: Earth oven
vasa: sea
mauga: mountain
māsina: moon
fetu: star

Bullet Rust, 8/2015, San Francisco, California, photograph, Lisa Dailey

IV

EVIDENCE

*Black people love their children with a kind of obsession.
You are all we have, and you come to us endangered.*
—Ta-Nehisi Coates

*It is not our differences that divide us. It is our inability
to recognize, accept, and celebrate those differences.*
—Audre Lorde

*One day you will ask me which is more important? My life or yours?
I will say mine and you will walk away not knowing that you are my life.*
—Kahlil Gibran

*If you're going to hold someone down you're going to have to hold on
by the other end of the chain. You are confined by your own repression.*
—Toni Morrison

*What a strange alchemy we have worked, turning earth around
to destroy itself, using earth's own elements to wound it.*
—Linda Hogan

Connections, 2018, mixed media/collage, Lindsey Morrison Grant

For the Man Who is Half of Me

Angelina Villalobos

I always knew my father did not belong.
I did not need the television to blemish my mind
and condition what my father should look like.
My father did not come home
with a shirt and tie and briefcase.
He came home smelling of the earth
and sweat of his manual labor, and
his cologne that I would always remember
even after he was long gone.

He spoke to me in boisterous Spanish,
"Angelina, mi Angelita."
I did not need a thick panel of glass
to tell me that my father was untouchable.
Even the law agreed, he was meant for Mexico,
not the United States.
Either that or locked from view.

Lost Crossing

Jed Myers

—for Jakelin Amei Rosmery Caal Maquin

The girl crosses from city to forest,
hand in her father's. The girl crosses
the rivers, riding her father's shoulders.

She crosses the dark under stars
her father says are our ancestors
watching us. She crosses the valleys

where her dreams land her, calling out
for her father who's hidden off in the brush
where he crouches to gather them edible roots.

She crosses long stretches of hunger
and thirst, and her father tells her
it isn't much farther north. The water

they find to drink is the water they find.
They cross brown streams, narrow and cloudy
rivers, she tires, her father tugs her

along by the wrist, as firm as he must,
as gentle as he can be. She crosses
back and forth between wake and sleep

on her feet, crosses the last stretch of dust
before her father draws her under
the shadow of a tall barrier

and lets her slump, lets her fall
to her knees and she drifts, crosses deep
where her rising fever's wide blue river

runs in a silver haze toward the sea,
and she lets that river take her, before
her father or anyone sees she's not there

for the final heave, not there
when the agents seize her father
and her, not there in her limp limbs

nor behind her swimming eyes, won't ask
for the fresh water her blood's long-shrunken
rivers still need, and she slips

farther off from the sand of their perch
on those banks of the Promised Land.
She crosses into forever elsewhere,

father squeezing the air for her hand.

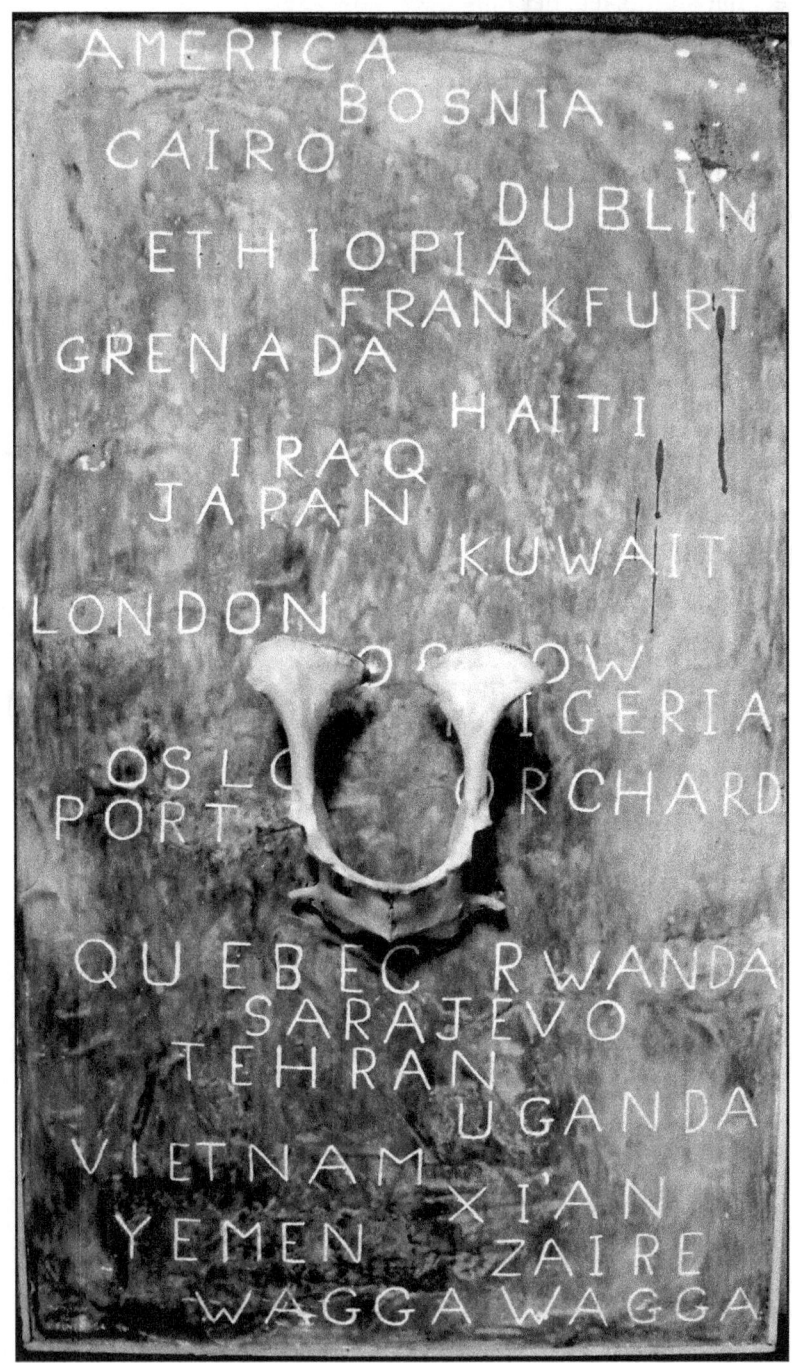

Headstone: Women Under Attack, 1994, mixed media—
wood, plaster, animal pelvis, Sharon M. Carter

[A worldwide A-Z. My colleague Diane Decker was murdered in Port Orchard, Washington, in 1987. As in many cases, her death remains unsolved.]

Un Botón Rojo

Sharon M. Carter

—for C.C.

Each time she looks
at the moon it seems further
away   his face
stitched to the sky—
only a sliver
of bone   remains.

The son she lost   in the desert
escaping to America.
Heat and thirst   drove
the life from him.   Sand
bleaching the past.
Night sky's   thumbtacked map
showing   someone else's
future   two empty dippers
one pointing   to El Norte.

She searched hospital records
shelters   jails   unclaimed
dead   personal effects—
an unmatched
pants button   sewn
before he left   proof.

Two holes   one through each
side   of her heart

I see myself, and courage and hope, in the faces of the caravan
November 9, 2018

Claudia Castro Luna
Washington State Poet Laureate, 2/1/2018–1/31/2020

When I consider the rhetoric deployed to describe the group of mostly Honduran men, women and children making their way through Mexico up to the U.S. border to ask for asylum, I am filled with profound sadness. Words such as "invaders," "violent" and "vicious" counter what I see in the faces of mothers carrying babies in their arms, in toddlers collapsing from exhaustion, in the stance of women walking all those miles in flip-flops, in men whose eyes betray desperation and anxiety.

Perhaps I see vulnerability and despair where others see aggression and cunning because I come from one of the countries these asylum-seekers are fleeing. I fled El Salvador as a youth in 1981 with my parents and sister weeks before the civil war was officially declared. Having experienced terror from not knowing whether you will be killed at any moment from the violence around you, and knowing what it is like to have a loved one targeted for murder, I can attest that a person who leaves everything they love and value behind to embark on an uncertain and perilous journey is up against indomitable circumstances.

We left with a little more than what these people are carrying, which is to say nothing. We had at least a small suitcase each. My sister carried a stuffed animal and I a doll. In that sense we were no different from the thousands upon thousands of Italians, Germans and Irish immigrants who, huddled in ships, made the penurious and dangerous trip over an ocean in search for a better life with hope folded carefully, neatly, into the breast pocket of their tattered clothing.

Hope, one of those simple four-letter words that pack a punch, is completely absent from the vocabulary used to describe the individuals walking hundreds of miles to reach the U.S.-Mexico border, who continue their march day after day knowing full well that they are not wanted here, knowing that a campaign is being waged to discredit whatever claims of asylum they might have. They do this because hope, the ardent song that guided every European immigrant that made it to these shores going back to when this territory was not yet the United States of America, also beats in their hearts.

Today, as a middle-class citizen, I can also attest that in the safety and comfort of our homes it is hard to imagine such fear and hardship; it is hard to imagine what it might be like to have nothing else left but courage and hope. It is easy to cast unkind, malicious labels that erase people's individual dignity as humans. I see the photographs, I read newspapers, I am on Twitter and what comes back to me again and again is the Golden Rule. I see myself in the faces of the folks in the caravan, a terrified fourteen-year-old holding on to my mother's arm. I am no different from them, and by extension I know that among them are future professors and doctors like my Honduran friends, who arrived in the U.S. at roughly the same age I did. Among them are nurses and small business owners like my cousins, and poets and writers like myself.

Words bear different weights. When my family arrived in the U.S., *The Evening Times*, a Florida newspaper, wrote a story with the headline, "America offers one family a chance to forget fears." Our story was framed as America offering us something—a chance. Like thousands from the old continent we took it gratefully and squandered not a crumb. I say the tired, poor and wretched making their way through Mexico up to our southern border would do the same. What if we framed these people's experience with words such as "courage" and "hope"? I believe we would restore a measure of dignity to their very human response to an untenable situation. In so doing, we would also hear the fervor radiating from those very words flowing within ourselves.

Threat

Kathleen Stancik

—for Tom Kiefer

Somewhere
in a detention center
along the southern border
a janitor removes rosaries
from the trash,
photographs them
so they will not be forgotten.

Discarded, it was said,
for the safety of the officers.

Wrist Rosary #1, from the series, "El Sueño Americano—
The American Dream," 2016, photograph, Tom Kiefer

A Letter to My Son

Stephani E.D. McDow

I pulled you out of the darkness that I knew into a place of rampant color in an attempt to shield you from the harshness of the world in which you live. From landscapes of brick to where trees crowded one's view. So, I raised you outside of the city.

I wanted time and a safe place to tell you about all the things that I'd known of, like the hate for beautiful souls that resemble you. To tell you the stories that my elders told me and to spoon-feed you literary greatness penned by those who so eloquently experienced the obsidian truth. I did everything in my power to prepare you and, though you are an adult now, each day I still do.

Yet even in my efforts, I had to come to terms with that fact that you may never be truly ready to feel or understand the completeness of that first blow, nor the third or tenth to follow. And though I've tried, I'll never truly know how that experience may reshape the preparedness I fought for with such diligence to instill in you.

You stand at the crest of greatness with the heavens and earth alike at the ready and prepared to obey and yield to the power within you, yet these forces hold true in their insatiable desire to destroy you. With every fiber of my existence, with every distinct word chosen from my extensive mental library of literature, stories heard, research performed, and experiences had, I am not enough to shelter you from....

I am not enough.

Though this is painfully evident, because I birthed you, I can't stand down regarding my need to protect you from both the randomness of wrong place, wrong time when some white dude with an issue (no matter if mental, political or whatever) decides to take out children, women and men minding their own business in a classroom [innocents, they keep killing our future], in the movies [enjoying a much-needed reprieve from life's hardships], at church [praising, worshipping and honoring God], at a concert [dancing their cares away], or at their jobs [making a living to care for their families]; as well as that unfounded, pointless, institutionalized, and systemic disdain that courses through the veins of this country and blindly sights a target where your beautiful, Black face is. So many of our people keep falling by the hands of those who supposedly uphold the laws that are derivatives of this country's sins. The fear of international terrors coming to our doorstep severely pales in comparison to what's happening here at home every day, everywhere. How can a parent not fall into the absolute trenches of fear every moment that their child is in the world just trying to live a good life? How?

Then there was that first blow. Or, at least, that I know of. You were wrongfully profiled in high school by a security guard who was convinced that your appearance was indicative of drug selling and approached you on the matter. Never once had he glanced at the privileged, preppy kid who was, in fact, the dealer. Then there was that time, in an Uber—in a fucking Uber—you were racially profiled. Riding while Black [as a backseat passenger in, again I say it, an Uber]. Suspected of robbery. I'm sure there are so many more, and the thought of each sets my blood boiling.

Don't they know that you have a heart of gold! Don't they know that, as a kid, you advocated for and befriended bullied children! You protected them! Don't they know that you are an amazing artist! Don't they know that you work hard every single day to make your dreams come true—the legit way! Don't they know that you are breathtaking! Don't they know that we need you!

We need you. All of you.

You are our tomorrow and future. You carry culture, knowledge, and truth in your breath. The foundations upon which this country, this world, must later stand is being built by the treads left by the soles of your feet, the fruits of your intellect and the blessings of your gifts. Why can't they understand that being woke is a necessity of progress? That much of what our youth displays now is indicative of the change necessary to knock down those blasphemous racial and homophobic pillars upon which this country was built. The canons of privilege and those poisoned by them are still many and widespread. Some boast proudly, some display it through jokes, some attempt to keep it under wraps. Some don't even know that that's who they are because "they have Black friends."

My blessing? You know who you are. You know whose you are. Never forget. Keep striving for greatness. Remember those who could not. Say his name. Say her name. One of the greatest things that you can do amidst all of this, is be absolutely everything that they do not want you to become. They are afraid. You are an educated, talented, and gifted man. You have your youth, your health, and an insatiable drive to rise. You are a good person. And you are gloriously Black. I love you.

Together, Narok, Kenya, Maasai Girl's School, 2018, photograph, Sarah E.N. Kohrs

A Kid Called Diamond

Nancy Scott

—from the files of an Innocence Project

The story goes: a black man pulls a gun in the sub-
shop parking lot and shoots a Latino point blank.

Witnesses agree the shooter was wearing white sneakers
and a dark coat ending well below his knees, although

they disagree who first recognized him by his street name,
Diamond. While this is going down, the nineteen-year-old

is hangin' in Jim & Mary's Bar, strutting his new brown
leather bomber jacket and leather boots. Cops say he did it

for drugs he wasn't known to use, maybe a boost here
and there, no record. Talk on the street makes his cousin

the shooter. No matter. The jury convicts Diamond
of first degree murder—life with no chance of parole.

For fifteen years, Diamond insists he's innocent. What
can he do? Police reports disappeared, prosecutor's a judge,

defense attorney disbarred. No prints on the gun turned in
by a stranger. Inside for another murder, the cousin

won't talk. Some say Diamond would have killed sooner
or later; people don't end up in prison without good reason.

Bullet Points

Jericho Brown

I will not shoot myself
In the head, and I will not shoot myself
In the back, and I will not hang myself
With a trashbag, and if I do,
I promise you, I will not do it
In a police car while handcuffed
Or in the jail cell of a town
I only know the name of
Because I have to drive through it
To get home. Yes, I may be at risk,
But I promise you, I trust the maggots
Who live beneath the floorboards
Of my house to do what they must
To any carcass more than I trust
An officer of the law of the land
To shut my eyes like a man
Of God might, or to cover me with a sheet
So clean my mother could have used it
To tuck me in. When I kill me, I will
Do it the same way most Americans do,
I promise you: cigarette smoke
Or a piece of meat on which I choke
Or so broke I freeze
In one of these winters we keep
Calling worst. I promise if you hear
Of me dead anywhere near
A cop, then that cop killed me. He took
Me from us and left my body, which is,
No matter what we've been taught,
Greater than the settlement
A city can pay a mother to stop crying,
And more beautiful than the new bullet
Fished from the folds of my brain.

The Saga of The Exit Wound

henry 7. reneau, jr.

> . . . *no Negro can saunter down a street with*
> *any real certainty that violence will not visit him.*
> —Norman Mailer

This poem includes some language that may not be suitable
for the work place   /
                    the literary journal that spouts
inclusivity /   or if you have kids in the room //

This poem is not a "trigger warning" / for the "pure pussy"
weak of heart
        / not judge /   nor jury /   but witness to . . . /

the only real failures are the ones from which we learn nothing //

1.
(Every bullet believes that some people deserve to die.)

The way the hammer strikes the firing
                pin & the cylinder turns on its pawl.

Every bullet's exclamation
                point is combustion.   A .45 cal.

ballistic ambition
            rifling down a steel barrel.   Fixed on

the hemophiliac horizon of its own authority.

2.
From skin to status   / to
Amerikkka's / "No Solicitors" warning //   Our fists
                              like Teflon bullets /

because of / the gunshot-splayed black children /
because of the po-lice chief sound-bite / so unashamed of /
/ its own complicity //

Because / we don't believe a word come out they mouth /
that speaks to what racism has produced //

Our endeavoured unrest / that kept us marching / &
made us more alive than /
this Nation of many nations'
/ oppression of them / that others look down upon //

The squat of squalor / in which we move &
exist /: gulping air from the cup of need / carried in our cells
like shrapnel // The stigma / lodged deep within //

The justice doorbell's / "Out of Order" sign //

3.
There's nothing more frightening
than the Dream come true.   Is what Amerikkka looks like.

4.
Captured fireflies in a mason jar //
We are always / in someone else's country //
We are witness
& / commotion is the atmosphere / we swim in //

Our blackness /   simply
giving other people a chance to see us /
electric as /
an excitation of call   & response //

Our neon hope /
a slang /   a shadow diction /
twanged & siphoned off
/ every hue but Blue(s) //

Because he would not comply //   & we /
                          just don't want to / explain anymore
// Because she asked
why?   //   He was descending a dark stairwell //   The black child
playing cowboys
& Indians / with his imaginary friend /: white hat &
                                sterling plastic pistol //

She only wanted
to finish her cigarette //   The psychosis in her head
                                   terrified her so much
/ the police had to suffocate her /
                          to make her stop screaming //

He only wanted to buy an air rifle : to shoo-fly the crows //
The thug /   or *Demon* /
                    media-labeled
                    a tabloid stereotype / : resisting arrest /

                                   extensive
                          furtive movements //

He shot himself /   while handcuffed in the back of a police car //

We feared for our lives //

Things That Are Red

Priscilla Long

October, its flame-
colored filbert foliage
foregoing green. Red
manure worms eating
and mating in the wormbox.
Fuschia petals tantalizing
hummingbirds, tempting bees.
The sun red and low
in the west, earth ocean-
tinted silver-gray, rose.

Trayvon Martin's blood
was red, his hoodie black.
He was on the phone,
walking home, his skin
black. In Sanford
he was chased down,
shot down. He was 17.
His killer, America,
calls Black Americans
"slime." His killer—
America's shame,
America's crime.

Trayvon Martin Icon, 2012, Egg tempera & gold leaf on wood, Jasmine Iona Brown

Let's Go to the Video

Chris Espenshade

In a most interesting turn this week, the same entitled white people who immediately and automatically defend god-awful, snap decisions by armed policemen have been calling for a more careful review of the incident between a young white man in a MAGA hat and a tribal elder. Suddenly when a white male is accused, it is time to slow down, take a deep breath, and carefully review the situation to see if there is anything to lessen the egregiousness of his actions. As they say on NFL broadcasts, let's go to the video (see Table 2).

Table 2. Hateful Scenarios, U.S.A.

Young White Man from Catholic High School	Young Black Man from Public School #103
Action: Smirks in face of Native American elder	*Action*: Runs in fear of police
Name: Nick Sandmann	*Name*: Changes every week
Ruling on the field: Smug racist	*Ruling on the field*: A threat to police
Immediate responses: Much of America condemns actions. Defenders of white folks everywhere call for careful review. Parents of young man hire public relations firm to re-write narrative	*Immediate responses*: Officer shoots victim 16 times. White folks defend officer due to difficulty of policing. Police reflexively defend all police actions.
Video review reveals: Other people were also acting badly. Young man did not say anything overtly racist, but wore a hat in support of our racist president.	*Video review reveals*: There was no real threat to police or public. Shooting is proven unwarranted. Officer is found guilty of reduced charge and is given a short sentence.

Video review reveals: (continued)
People jumping to his defense prove his
    white entitlement is a valid reason for his
    smugness.
Evidence suggests racist intent.

After video review:
Ruling on the field stands.
Young white man is still smug.
Young white man goes back to school.

After video review:
Ruling on the field is overturned.
Young black man is still dead.
Young black man goes in the ground.

The Space In-Between: Patriot Prayer Rally, Seattle, 2018, photograph, Andrew Drawbaugh

A Double Standard for White Terrorists

Rebecca Ruth Gould

Almost immediately after it emerged that a white supremacist had stabbed three men who were trying to prevent him from attacking Muslim women on a Portland, Oregon train, killing two of them, efforts at mitigation began.

"We don't know if he's got mental health issues," Sgt. Pete Simpson said in the first public statement about the May 26, 2019 incident. Added the perpetrator's childhood friend, "All I have to say is I hope this brings attention to the need for mental health facilities and more outreach." His mother struck a similarly apologetic note: "He's always been spouting anti-establishment stuff but he's a nice person."

Inevitably, those close to the perpetrator tried to explain away the hate that drove this crime. Yet what this individual did was fundamentally a political act, in a country where politicians are increasingly wary of condemning racially-motivated violence. In his trial for his 2015 mass shooting at a Charleston, South Carolina church, another white racist, Dylann Roof, made clear the real motive for his crime: "I don't want anybody to think I did it because I have some kind of mental problem. I wanted to increase racial tension."

An act of terror by a self-identifying Muslim would never have been treated as apologetically as have the Portland stabbings and the Charleston massacre. Compare these reactions to those following the Boston Marathon bombing and the San Bernardino, California massacre. Why the double standard? Why do we excuse the racist hate that led to the Portland stabbings and the Charleston shootings?

Among the most frightening aspects of the Portland stabbings is that the perpetrator, Jeremy Joseph Christian, thirty-five, was long known to police and others as someone who endorsed murderous acts. To his Facebook followers, Christian's willingness to kill innocent people came as no surprise. But the authorities turned a blind eye to the threats that fill Christian's public posts.

As his Facebook posts demonstrate, Christian made numerous appearances at white supremacist rallies in recent months. He was a well-known member of the Portland community—not an outsider, an alien, or an immigrant. He delighted in his own notoriety, noting in one post how a local reporter called him "the Lizard King."

On May 9, Christian wrote on his Facebook page (still online as of this writing): "I want a job in Norway cutting off the heads of people that Circumcize [sic] Babies

. . . . Like if you agree!!!" More than two dozen of Christian's Facebook followers signified their approval. One vowed to set up a fund to support "America's newest hero Jeremy Joseph Christian."

Christian began verbally attacking two women on the train, one of whom was wearing a hijab. Police said he "began yelling various remarks that would best be characterized as hate speech toward a variety of ethnicities and religions." When three men tried to intervene, he stabbed them. Two of them—Ricky John Best of Happy Valley, Oregon, fifty-three, and Taliesin Myrddin Namkai Meche of Southeast Portland, twenty-three—died from their injuries.

At a court appearance this week, Christian was defiant, saying, "You call it terrorism, I call it patriotism!"

Had Christian been deploying the rhetoric of ISIS on Facebook, he would have been under FBI surveillance. Why, then, are white supremacists allowed to threaten violence against innocents while authorities look the other way? Why are people still willing to make excuses when expressions of racist hate turn into racist action?

In stark contrast, Egyptian-American Tarek Mehanna was sentenced to seventeen years in prison exclusively on the basis of his association with jihadist ideology, and not for any specific act of violence. But whereas Mehanna was immediately incarcerated for his support of violence, Christian's threats were ignored, or tolerated, by the authorities. Like many white supremacists, the perpetrator of the Portland stabbings was regarded prior to his murders as merely a nuisance by authorities.

Like Christian, Mehanna supported an ideology that is associated with violence. Both ideologies must be condemned. Yet the point here is that Mehanna was imprisoned for his views, while white supremacists like Christian are all too often tolerated until blood is spilled.

The fight against racism is a battle that cannot be abdicated to others. Racism has poisoned this country and will continue to do so until white racism is taken as seriously as the terror that clothes itself in Islamic rhetoric.

I passed much of my adolescence on Portland's streets. I attended poetry readings in Portland cafes, volunteered in soup kitchens, and hung out in Powell's, the country's biggest bookstore. The violence of the past few days does not represent the Portland I know. However, it does represent a plausible future for a country increasingly driven by an ideology that must be actively resisted rather than silently condoned.

I. Assumption of Accent

Carl "Papa" Palmer

I know you'll like this one,
grinning into his racist joke
after hearing my southern drawl.

II. Brown Girl on the Tacoma Trolley

Carl "Papa" Palmer

Not my daughter, my grand-daughter.
No, she's not adopted.
She speaks English, ask her.

The Daily News

Anita Endrezze

Bombs leveraging the sky.
The choppy sea and its fulcrum of clouds.
A child face down
on the shore.
A man cries.
That woman stares into the bone of grief.
The TV is on, and there is war
in between ads. Some of us
want to cradle the wounded
in our arms. Others want to be
the teeth of the Beast.

The Times Asks Poets to Describe the Haze Over Seattle

Shankar Narayan

No one asked me, but I would have said this apocalypse
looks like home. The laureate
says a grey gullet has swallowed
a molten coin, another calls it powered cadmium
and cirrhosis, dystopian, grotesque, a crematorium. Yes,

all of these describe my Delhi, and which
of my well-meaning friends will understand
that for a week now I have woken to the warm nostalgia
of exactly the familiar cataclysm that hangs
there every day as I imagine Hiroshima's

mushroom cloud might have done before dispersing into that dead
silence? Every sunrise and sunset so brilliantine,
and like the finest earth-to-table restaurant a new recipe
daily for the fresh soup of toxins, the plastic mill, the pyre
ground, the matchstick factory where every day five-year-olds blow off

fingers. There has been no blue
for years. No, these are not things to be proud
of, and looking up at this brown smudge of a Seattle
sky I know I should look away, feel for evacuees and ashed
homes and bear and deer and antelope, but

in the confusion of entanglements holding my life
together I cannot say what's catching
in my throat, am I now animal remembering how once I would run
in Delhi, laps around that little brown park
with its mongooses and illegally grazing buffalo, before the haze

pressed in, caught into its creep my blackening lung
and squeezed, or is my animal
brain transported to another home on days outside
those twenty-one per year I am allowed
to be my other self, exhale into just another no-different

anonymous body, or is my animal howling
to dam the forgetting when breathing clean so long feels like birthright,
blowing down all those accidental animals, of whom I
am one, whose water is hauled from Cascadian streams where no one
may so much as dip a grimy toe, whose children will never leach carpet-factory

mercury into their bodies, is my animal screaming
blue murder that if some can't breathe
then none shall breathe, my asbestos lung rasping
to anyone in this town who will listen—this is how the world
lives. And there is nothing that cannot burn.

Beaten Zone[1]

Mona Nicole Sfeir

—The area on the ground upon which the cone of fire falls.

Bare the spot of safety
cradling us all [tired + poor + huddled = masses]
yearning to escape the breaking of wordshaped promises
How does one translate: depleted uranium weapons?

Build it high, the wall, use the [huddled masses]
so beautiful are our|their faces each one of us|them
blinking at the first brightness at birth.
How does one say: cluster bombs?

Retract the seven wonders of the world
delay what is needed so that the pushing
becomes wave like / lapping against the wall
trying to escape the beaten zone.[2]

It follows until they need to crawl
into the eye of the storm
for safety seeking the spaces
where the missiles are made[3]
and away from where they fall.[4]

---

1. U.S. Department of Defense's Dictionary of Military and Associated Terms (October 17, 2007).

2. The United States has participated in more than thirty-eight direct armed conflicts including in the Philippines, Cuba, Mexico, Nicaragua, Haiti, Dominican Republic, Tunisia, Japan, Korea, Vietnam, Cambodia, Laos, Thailand, Lebanon, Zaire, Grenada, Panama, Iraq, Somalia, Bosnia, Serbia, Afghanistan, Pakistan, Libya, and Syria. Additionally, the U.S. Special Operations Command

(SOCOM) has operations in over a hundred countries including Mali, Nigeria, Malaysia and Algeria. The U.S. Congress has not declared war since 1941.

According to National Security Act Sec. 503 (e), covert action is, "An activity or activities of the United States Government to influence political, economic, or military conditions abroad, where it is intended that the role of the United States Government will not be apparent or acknowledged publicly." The Freedom of Information Act has brought to light covert actions that have led to the overthrow of foreign governments including Iran (1953), Guatemala (1954), Congo (1960), Dominican Republic (1961), South Vietnam (1963), Brazil (1964), Indonesia (1965), and Chile (1973).

3. The Stockholm International Peace Research Institute (SIPRI) estimates the global arms trade in 2017 was $398 billion and the global expenditure on the military reached 1.7 trillion. Ten countries account for ninety percent of global weapons sales. The largest exporter is the United States followed by Russia, Germany, France, China, UK, Israel, Italy, South Korea, and the Ukraine.

4. According to the UNHCR there now are 68.5 million forcibly displaced people worldwide and 40 million internally displaced people. Of the 25.4 million refugees, 19.9 million refugees are under the UNHCR Mandate and 5.4 Palestinian refugees are registered by UNRWA. In 2017, 44,500 people were displaced each day. More than half of the world's refugees are children. 📖

The Myth of Sisyphus, 2019, photograph, J. Ray Paradiso

The War Works Hard

Dunya Mikhail
translated by Elizabeth Winslow

How magnificent the war is!
How eager
and efficient!
Early in the morning,
it wakes up the sirens
and dispatches ambulances
to various places,
swings corpses through the air,
rolls stretchers to the wounded,
summons rain
from the eyes of mothers,
digs into the earth
dislodging many things
from under the ruins . . .
Some are lifeless and glistening,
others are pale and still throbbing . . .
It produces the most questions
in the minds of children,
entertains the gods
by shooting fireworks and missiles
into the sky,
sows mines in the fields
and reaps punctures and blisters,
urges families to emigrate,
stands beside the clergymen
as they curse the devil
(poor devil, he remains
with one hand in the searing fire) . . .
The war continues working, day and night.

It inspires tyrants
to deliver long speeches,
awards medals to generals
and themes to poets.
It contributes to the industry
of artificial limbs,
provides food for flies,
adds pages to the history books,
achieves equality
between killer and killed,
teaches lovers to write letters,
accustoms young women to waiting,
fills the newspapers
with articles and pictures,
builds new houses
for the orphans,
invigorates the coffin makers,
gives grave diggers
a pat on the back
and paints a smile on the leader's face.
The war works with unparalleled diligence!
Yet no one gives it
a word of praise.

"Men of a Military Age"

Patrick Dixon

—the US Army's designation for certain non-combatants in a war zone

The noise is unmistakable,
like the way a helicopter announces
its presence long before it's visible.
Look up. The speck you see
seems harmless enough. A light
buzz in your brain signals
maybe you're wrong about that.
Run. Seek cover—
all the destruction a tornado
offers packed into a cylinder
beneath a wing. The eye
in the nose follows your steps,
places a crosshair.

Or another, flying so high
no one on the ground hears
until the trigger's pulled
and everything goes white—
walls, chairs, tables leap
and fragment, mix with
flesh and blood.

Amazon doesn't deliver this way
yet. The UPS truck idling on the street
outside your house hasn't exploded,
erasing your neighborhood in
a cloud of smoke and thunder.
But standing outside in the city heat,
music thumping to the beat of bullets

pumped from a casino window,
the result is the same, only the bodies
fall intact, not blown apart into crimson
spatter. FedEx arrives in an ambulance,
leaves a door sticker: no replacements,
ever. What's next? USPS carriers once
gone postal, now wearing Kevlar,
delivering assault rifles,
ammunition?

Meanwhile another drone takes off
from an airfield, heads toward Pakistan,
looking for men of a military age.

Nurse's Day

Tamam Kahn

Can't keep my hands to myself, I want to grab
the belt strapped with explosives, crush and break
the lit-up timer under my heel, then shake
that 17-year-old ISIS girl. She has
her dream of paradise. I slap her hard:
Wake up you fool. No, this is not Islam.
They've told you lies. You're just a firebomb.
There are no chosen ones and no reward.
This district's hit a second time, consumed
with fear and loss. Close to the holy shrine,
six bombs explode, symbolically malign
you, Great Sayyida Zaynab, and your tomb.

Wise daughter's daughter of the Prophet, clar-
ify your life, your dignity. Aware,

You challenged tyrant Yazzid. Couldn't save
murdered Husayn, the hurricane of pain.
You spoke the truth to power. Here again
we need your voice, a miracle, shockwave.
Can't keep my hands to myself, I want to press
the cheek of a girl one bomb has hurt. Concrete
and bricks are mixed with car parts along the street—
she's lying here, hijab and flowered dress
are soiled with blood, skin pierced with cellphone bits.
Oh Zaynab, legendary nurse—please hand
me lidocaine, a hypodermic and
some tweezers, sterile bandages. Dust is thick.

Assad's war's beyond sane narrative.
We don't know how to stop it. Help us live.

Note: The birthday of Sayyida Zaynab, granddaughter of Prophet Muhammad, on February 25, is known in Syria and Iran as "Nurses Day."

On 31 January 2016, two suicide bombs and a car bomb exploded in the town of Sayyida Zaynab near Syria's holiest Shi'ite shrine, the Sayyida Zaynab Mosque (six miles south of Damascus). At least sixty people were killed and another 110 people were wounded in the explosions.

On February 21, more explosions and death. This time no accurate reports of the losses near the shrine of Sayyida Zaynab.

B Boy, oil on canvas, Mario Loprete

Passover 5777: A Bop poem

Eve Lyons

Amid the salt from the bay
And giant orchids growing from trees
We gather each year to remember and bless.
We who have our freedom still
while gay men are rounded up in Chechnya
Muslims flee bombs in Syria

Next year may we be free

My son just wants to play
He's not wild or impulsive, he's almost five
Right now everyone thinks he's adorable
Someday will they see him as a threat?
He won't be able to play with guns
like little white boys do
He won't get off with warnings
like white women do.

For the first time in temple
My son looked around and noticed
"I'm the only black person here."
When he plays in the park
The "Hebrew kids" in kipot and payot
don't recognize him as one of their own

Next year may we be free.

Zero Tolerance

Dr. Shahed Yousaf

You shouted that you didn't want a Muslim doctor. I was angry when I said healthcare had a zero tolerance for bigotry. You smelt of the iron in your blood and the tin in your hand. I had ketone breath from fasting in Ramadan. My brown hand held a stethoscope over your swastika tattoo.

"Awkward," I said and you swallowed, hard.

"The swastika is Indian," I murmured, and could feel you pulling away. I feigned surprise that you had a healthy heart and you laughed more than you needed to.

"You're alright," you said.

"Most humans are," I replied, and shook your hand.

Roulette

Eneida P. Alcalde

As his twin sister counted aloud, six-year-old Mikey McGee crept up the rickety stairs, careful to not make any squeaks that might give away his next hiding spot. Upon reaching the attic, Mikey squinted in the gray darkness, pierced by streaks of sunlight streaming in through opposing side windows. He spotted the antique writing desk against the far wall, tucked in-between a pair of bookshelves, overstuffed with old books and magazines. He tiptoed to the desk. Nearing it, he noticed the top right drawer, left open. Typically, his father kept it shut with lock and key. Mikey peered inside and saw a revolver, gold and shiny. He took it.

Minutes later, his sister found him, sitting crossed-legged under the desktop, between the stacks of drawers. He grinned and pointed the revolver at her like the cowboys do in the movies. He pulled the trigger.

There were no bullets.

Valentine's Day, 2018

Beth Copeland

My neighbor　　　　shoots targets
with an assault rifle　　while I watch the news.
17 dead in Florida school shooting. I live on a gravel
road where people drive pickups and love country music,
barbecue, and guns. Sometimes I wake to the racket of gunfire
instead of roosters. On walks, I kick shotgun shells in the ditch.
I watch from the couch, a mug of coffee warming my palms,
as kids file out of classrooms with hands in the air. Grieving
parents remember children on CNN. Teenagers cry at a
candlelight vigil, leaving sweetheart roses, balloons,
and teddy bears against a cyclone fence for
classmates on this day of love and red
paper hearts—some still beating
but with blood blossoming
on their shirts, some
blown open,
dead.

Wat (temple) Lao Dhammacetiyaram, #5, Seattle, 2011, photograph, Maryna Ajaja

Ghazal for Emilie Parker

Carolyne Wright

—(*Newtown, Connecticut: December 14, 2012*)

He had been teaching her to speak Portuguese
So their last words together were in Portuguese.

Such simple words that morning: *Thank you. Please.
I love you, Daddy.* All in Portuguese.

Then he rode off to work, past winter trees
And she to school, smiling to herself in Portuguese.

She fell with her classmates, the other girls and boys,
Folding into herself like snow. No tongue, no Portuguese,

No hearts that walk outside their lives in fields
That winter can't amend. No Portuguese

Can call them back, unspeak their parents' grief
In English, Spanish, Chinese, Hebrew, Portuguese—

*Oh Charlotte. Daniel. Olivia. Ana. Josephine.
Dylan. Madeleine. Catherine. Chase.*

*Jesse. James. Emilie. Jack. Noah. Caroline.
Jessica. Benjamin. Avielle. Alison. Grace.*

Echo of Stone

Elaine Zimmerman

—for Nelba Marquez-Green

The daughter is winging wildly
against the white orchards.
Braided hair, braided dusk.

The hills shift and fold in
ebbing light. A blue line
ribbons through memory.

The mother sobs.
Nothing but shattered urns.
Her daughter shot. Gone.

Where did we forget our wholeness?
Wanting the holes in her daughter's fabric
to grow roots of purpose. Hair, limb, vine.

Open the skin. We sleep in dust.
Tear the pulp. Nothing is changed.
Repeat the end. An echo of stone.

Please, hold the roof down; guard
the light. Fold arms around each child
and what shoots forth from clay.

Do not ignore our small and vast despair.
A whisper of wings,
as close to us as breathing.

Each lamb returns slowly down the path.
The shepherd counts with rod of ash.
Through a dark window, the mother stares.

Twirls her son's curls. The night
a long knife, sharp as what pierces
through dirt air sound   breath.

Archeology

Nancy Canyon

What did he learn by touching her youthful body?
Those callused hands spreading wide across

small ribs, reaching through underground layers
to enter the core, her essence scraped and dusted

and categorized. Those hands blustered over smooth
landscape, wandered shelves and notched structures,

marked grids, and lifted first shovelfuls. He sifted
through rubble of what was once pristine, finding no

satisfaction in his survey. There were no names, no
places, just his thoughtless looting of virgin artifacts.

She Didn't Know, 2018, collage, Carrie Albert

Someone's in Here

Ashley Jenkins (aka L.L. Asher)

Amelia stared at her reflection as she brushed her teeth. Her eyes flitted from her tangled hair to her jiggling arm fat, and down to the bulge of gut that forced itself over the top of her too-tight jeans. The sloosh-slosh of the bristles against her crooked teeth echoed in the empty bathroom. A brisk knock at the door startled her and she choked on toothpaste froth.

"Amelia," her mother murmured against the door. "I'm heading to the store. Do you need anything?"

Amelia cleared her throat and unlocked the door. She pulled it open, cringing at the sudden squeal of the hinge. "You're going now?" Amelia scanned the hallway over her mother's shoulder. "Can you wait until I leave for school?"

Her mother smiled and raised her eyebrows. "Baby, you don't need me to be with you every second."

Her mother stroked Amelia's tangled hair and Amelia could smell her mother's sweat and cigarette smoke. "Do you need anything?"

Amelia flushed and checked the hallway again. "Tampons," she whispered.

Her mother lifted Amelia's chin until they made eye contact. "You're a young woman now, sweet girl. There's nothing to be ashamed of."

Amelia nodded, pulling her face from her mother's hand, "Okay, mom."

"Okay, then. Tampons—and chocolate," Her mother pinched Amelia's side, where her stomach protruded over the jeans and winked. Amelia pulled away and retreated into the bathroom, closing the door after scanning the hallway a final time.

She unbuttoned her pants, sickened by the way her stomach forced the zipper down, and shuffled to the toilet. She forced the jeans and underwear down past her hips, groaning at the indentations in her flesh, stamped there by the seams. She squeezed a handful of her overhanging fat until her eyes welled with tears.

She sat on the toilet and heard her mother's car pull out of the driveway.

Her eyes found a familiar strip of peeling wallpaper and she tugged at it.

It was just the two of them now.

Him and her.

Droplets of water plopped from the faucet. Drip. Drip.

She'd have to leave for school soon, before he woke—

The doorknob rattled.

Her eyes snapped toward the sound. Had she locked the door?

Her breath hitched as she found her voice.

"Someone's in here!"

Her eyes widened as the door swung open.

She was frozen. Exposed.

Her stepfather loomed in the doorway. His eyes danced around the room and then locked onto hers. A cigarette dangled from his bottom lip. He opened his mouth and smoke spewed from it, like a dragon.

She felt a trickle of sweat run down her back.

His eyes slid down her body, pausing on the indentations left by her jeans.

He tugged the cigarette from his lip and grinned. More smoke poured from his mouth.

Her bladder loosened as a tear streamed down her cheek. 📖

52 Hawks

Chip Livingston

driving through muskogee, highway 62
is barbed wire. impossible not to mention
matthew shepard. not to mention orlando.

dusk silenced, we fuck in the vw
to prove something, we're alive at least,
and long enough to drain the car battery.

sleep then wake to a nightstick.
good luck, a cop's jumpstart west
from a dawn mourning too red. the hawk

must be a sign. you miss its flight, miss
the next one. there, i point. but you are reading
on your cell phone. obituaries. another raptor.

then a kind of rapture in the wish i make
aloud: a hawk to land on a fencepost. we begin
to count. one: you read stanley almodovar.

hawk two salutes: amanda alvear.
hawk three: oscar aracena-montero.
the hawks sentinel the road like honor

guards. 49 in six miles. they are something
we sing out names to. rudolfo. antonio.
darryl. angel. juan. luis. 49 hawks

and a morning full as a dance floor.
the 50th, a falcon, we call matthew
and quit our haunting inventory.

i metal the vw toward i-44
to flee the prairie purgatory. two birds on air,
there. you see and name us: not missing.

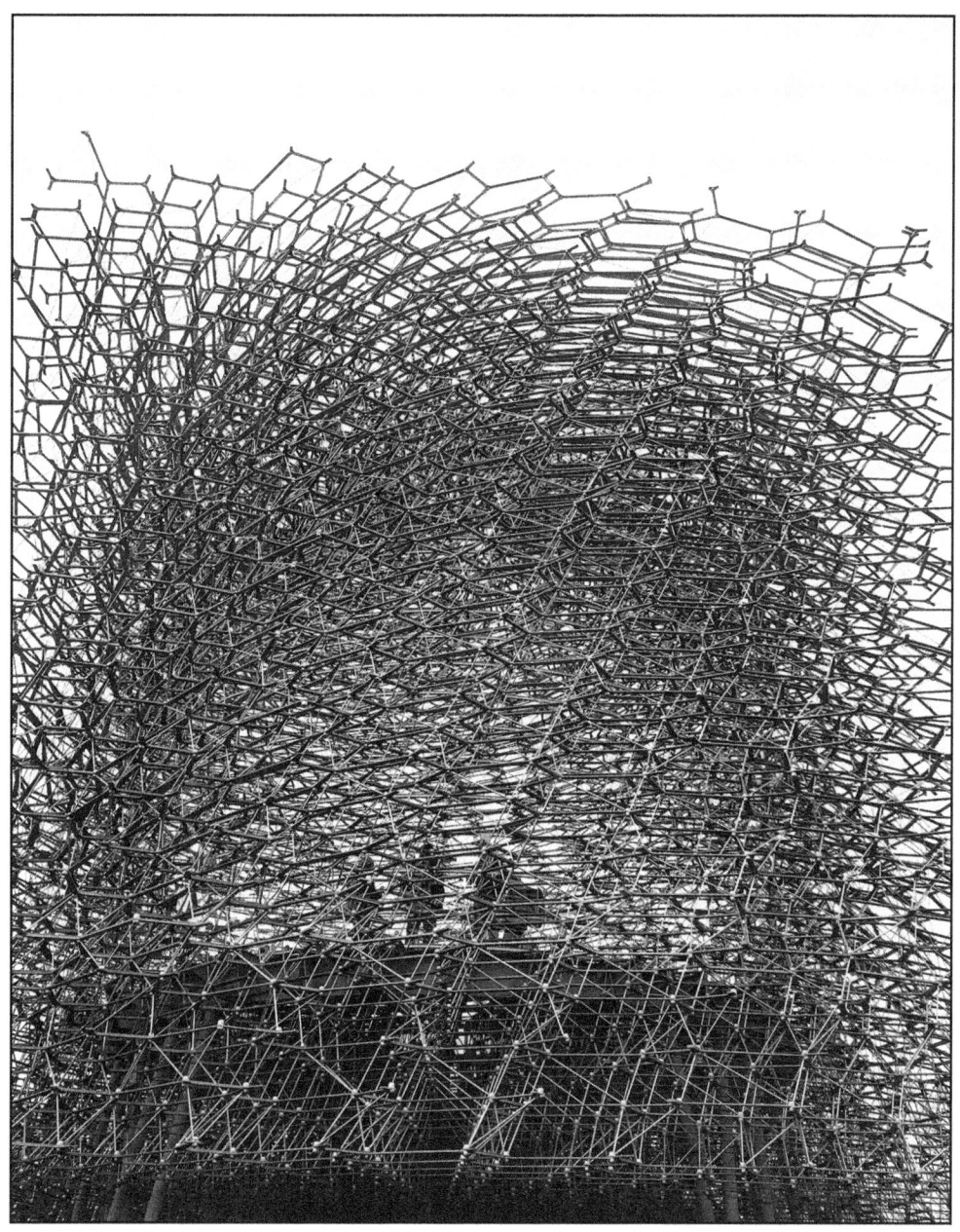
Layered Geometry, Kew Gardens, London, UK, 2018, photograph, Sarah Deckro

Orlando Rainbow

James Rodgers

Black:
the color
of the vinyl
the D.J. spun;
the color
that's the first half
of the nightclub's décor;
the color
of the assault rifle
the shooter
used that night.

Blue:
the color
the sky
had been that day;
the color
the officers wore
when they
surrounded the building;
the color
of their lights.

Green:
the color
of the palms
that swayed nearby;
the color
of a tree,
the nickname
of Eric Roundtree

who knew
seventeen
of the victims;
the color
of the money
used to buy the gun
and the bullets.

Red:
the color
of the blood
of forty-nine
innocent victims
whose only crime
was wanting to dance;
the color
that stained the floor
and splattered the walls;
the color
none of them
had expected to see.

White:
the color
that was the second half
of the nightclub's décor;
the color
of Brenda McCool's
short shock of hair,
only there
to dance with her son;
the color
in the eyes,
far too many eyes,
that soon went dark.

Clear:
the color
of the breeze outside;
the color
of the tears
shed by hundreds
of friends,
family,
me;
the color
of the shooter's motive,
based on cowardice,
hatred,
and, more than likely,
deep-seated self-loathing.

Yellow:
the color
of the morning
vanquishing the night;
the color
of a new day,
another chance for love,
another chance for hate;
the color
of a sun
that forty-nine
fellow human beings
will never see again.

After The Pulse Murders 2016

Rayn Roberts

It was no surprise when a man

stalked, entered a bar
killed forty-nine queers,
it was like I'd been shot too,
but the hatred loomed decades
over people who were kicked,
beaten, raped, hung on fences to die,
the KKK Neo-Nazi faithful
Religious Right whack-mobs
saw us having no right to life
to love, jobs, no right to share the air.

What's new is old, Lesbian Gay

Bi Transgender ghosts
wander the land
whispering in your ear . . . "justice,"
the killings are not barbaric
they are grotesque
twisted visions of faith, political goals
madness leading to murder—
ever wonder why
atheism is on the rise?
Our history, monsters we cannot hide.

What's true is false, a sadistic killer

not love, God is more like
the men and women He creates
since Cain killed his brother
billions have died,
Jewish Gypsy Native Black
Mexican Dykes and Fags thrown
from buildings, burnt at stakes
just for breathing the air—I must say,
God puts a new spin on the word *Queer*.

What's in store, right now, I'm not sure.

Matthew Shepard

Rob Jacques

I am not a martyr. I did not die for a cause.
My problems were my problems, not yours.
All I ever wanted was a little bit of pleasure,
so save your applause for those who died
deliberately and, for good measure, bravely
in the name of God, country, or human pride.

Given a choice, I would rather have lived.
I loved music, good company, and cute guys.
I was not ashamed of what I was, nor did I
hesitate to make the first move, to smile,
to start light conversation or touch a thigh
that seemed slightly willing to be touched.

No meant no, and I'd move away. Yes
meant for awhile, somewhere secluded,
there'd be pleasuring, a little wrestling,
bodily fluids exchanged between friends,
perhaps, just perhaps, a bit of happiness
in longer contact on which life depends.

In short, I wanted what you want. Don't
kid yourself: you could've hung as easily
and as much in pain as I on that rural road.
Someone cute pretends to like you, offers
comfort, a pause from the routine mode
of living by way of a few moments of bliss:

well, I was unlucky, as you might've been.
I may have lost my life for a promised kiss,
but I was as normal and human as you are.
That alone gives my murder a tragic ring.
Remember this when you search for love:
gay and straight amount to the same thing.

Home, Thailand, photograph, Manit Chaotragoongit

It's Happening Here, It's Happening There

Jeanne Morel

We're part of the problem, my husband says when I complain. With a cord of charcoal I map the neighborhood from memory. Exhibit A: Among The Missing—the refugee office I worked for thirty years ago, Big John's Barber Shop, Rainier Office Supply. When Obama comes to visit, he will go to the library and talk about how his mother lived in a small house on Ferdinand, just one block south of me, and how his grandfather was in the furniture business before they moved to Hawaii. I'm not sure how to draw the time before Obama or I were born, or the waters of the Pacific Ocean, or a map of Hawaii, so I start to doodle instead. Grey lines and circles like my father used to draw on a small notepad when he talked on the telephone. Or rather listened—late into the night. I put down my charcoal to pose for a photo on a blue couch under a Japanese woodblock print in my living room, a woman holding a dead bird upside down while the cat, the husband, and the children look on. I stare into the eyes of the woman and she stares back at me. What's happening here happens all over the world. I chart a constellation of gold stars to illuminate the upscale restaurant strip that sits, a colonial crown, upon the indigenous street. According to *The New York Times* reporter in Siem Reap, *Less than a decade ago there were no hotels with infinity pools, no restaurants serving fricassee of wild boar, no silk merchants who took VISA.* Rubbing my charcoal back and forth across the paper, I draw a curtain around the perimeter of the Darigold plant down the road, a relic from another era where I step over dead rats and breathe the stench of the sewer. The Chinese brothel with the acupressure charts in the window is closed, shut down by the cops. Last night I saw a police car pull up and park on the curb—blue lights over amber flashes. I crush the charcoal to capture lines and dashes across the paper, smudge the edge. My father liked early maps that weren't entirely accurate. There's more to truth than that. I walk to the kitchen. Like my father, I fry onion and garlic in olive oil for a few minutes every evening. Only later do I turn on the fan.

Promised Land

Morgan Russell

They speak of milk and
Honey, but I dream of clean
Water in Flint, Michigan

What Tahlequah Said

Kathleen Alcalá

Even writing that headline, I feel the lilt and wash of the ocean in the language of the Salish, who consider the orca, qalqaləx̌ič in Lushootseed, their kin. We show our own smallness, place a frame around an individual creature, when we name an orca in human terms. But somewhere along the line, people felt that this particular orca needed a name we could relate to. Tahlequah supposedly means "mother of waters." She is a twenty-year-old member of J Pod of the Southern Resident Killer Whales, her scientific designation is J35, suggesting a science experiment, not just a study of existing conditions—and we have been conditioned to expect experiments to fail.

By implication there are at least thirty-four other identical orcas that can be interchanged with her, fulfill the same environmental functions, reproduce in the same way, and entertain us in the summers when they visit our Puget Sound inland waters. It in no way reflects the complex social system that exists between orcas, nor the even more complicated relationship the whales have with the environment around them.

Of all the noise we were subjected to in 2018, the most important message we received was from Tahlequah. She brought her baby to full term only to have it die within a few minutes of birth. Those of us who have experienced pregnancy know that your body prepares you during the whole gestation for the miracle of being somehow twinned—divided so that you will have two bodies to care for until the little one is fully grown. I can imagine the surging hormones experienced by this mother orca as her calf was born and failed to thrive. What could she have done? Nothing. But she understood that the conditions humans have created in the Sound make it impossible for the near-shore orcas who depend on Chinook salmon for their food to survive. She carried her dead baby with her for seventeen days and 1,000 miles, off the Pacific Northwest coast, until it fell apart, so that we would see her and it, and get the message.

I don't claim to be a whale whisperer. I am descended from a variety of firmly land-locked peoples more accustomed to deserts and mountains. But I think the fact that Tahlequah was trying to tell us something was pretty obvious. Outside of the circus-like atmosphere of whales interacting with humans at SeaWorld this might be the strongest whale statement ever made to humans.

You killed my baby.

While *The Hitchhiker's Guide to the Galaxy* is in many ways a trilogy of humorous books, Douglas Adams got it right when he named one of them *So Long, and Thanks for All the Fish* as the farewell message from the dolphins while departing from a future earth no longer considered tenable by its oceanic inhabitants. As the dolphins desperately try to tell us that we are doomed, that we need to leave, we *ooh* and *aah* and applaud their apparent hijinks. We are incapable of understanding that we are not the only creatures on earth with an understanding of time, life, and mortality.

While there is ample evidence around us of global warming and impending environmental disaster, we are aggravating this scenario with our willful inaction. A couple of months ago the Governor of the state of Washington, Jay Inslee, rolled out some points to enhance his standing as a protector of the environment. This included some language about saving the orcas, but not the obvious one: take down the dams that are keeping Chinook salmon from reproducing. The Snake River was once their breeding ground, but fewer and fewer salmon make it past all the obstacles we have placed in their way. The Chinook are not reproducing, and the whales are starving to death. It doesn't take somersaults, it doesn't take naming orcas, to figure that out.

In spite of our reluctance to face the obvious, nature has been very forgiving. The dams on the Elwha River were removed in 2011-2012, and the natural life of the river is surging back at a miraculous pace. Its native salmon have been waiting a hundred years to return to their spawning beds. Just imagine! They had to return from the open ocean to the mouth of the river each year, only to be turned back by dams. Again. And again and again. But now they have made it.

Can we save the Chinook? There is only one way to find out. Take down the dams. Ease up on the hatchery fish, which probably compete with the wild salmon for scarce resources.

Almost unremarked, another orca died on January 28, 2019, after a short illness. Kayla was thirty years old, what should have been the half-way point in her life, when she suddenly sickened and died. She lived at SeaWorld in Orlando, Florida, which has been the site of many questionable practices concerning orcas.

"We shared our salmon," wrote Jack Flander of the Yakima Nation in *The Seattle Times* (1/29/19), speaking for the orcas, "but you took more than your share," leaving us little to survive on. "Our waters became polluted. Our infant mortality rate increased. . . . Imagine what a brotherhood and sisterhood we could have shared. Now imagine that I am an Indian." 📖

sqələč *is Home* ("octopus" in Southern Lushootseed language), Seattle, 2019, drawing, Nuansi

In the Too Bright Café

Tess Gallagher

*"Let's walk arm in arm, like two jaundiced moles,
and see if the Lord of Tunnels will guide us."*
—Jaime Sabines, *Tarumba*

The men are comparing
killing methods for moles.
I'm ashamed to say my ears
prick up. Moles have tunneled
into my potato patch, erecting
fluffy earth-filtered cathedrals
both sides of the fence. What
are they up to down there
with my baby eye-sprouted
potatoes? They could be cousins,

potatoes and moles, each turning
the earth's darkness into something
edible or a way to thieve what light
is always holding back. Once I caught
my yard help stomping the dirt
over their openings like putting out
underground fire. *Gas.* The collaborators
in eradication are pumping it into
tunnels as they drink black coffee
and tuck into eggs "over-easy"

with hash browns—"burn 'em"!
Pellets, some kind of poison.
They mull this, asking for
salsa and Tabasco. Are they
sending down heat-
seeking devices? Just don't

say "dynamite" I'm begging.
A voice by the window claims
he heard of a guy who hooked
up a loudspeaker and piped in

so many decibels the moles popped
up like mushrooms, and you didn't
have to pick them off with your
shotgun because they just kept
running. The men are laughing
by now and I'm thinking: *they're
just talking, right?* That merry
cash register by the door
is ushering a regular out, allowing
the moles a brief reprieve. The men

wave their friend onto the street
as I holster my purse. My sympathies
buzz the enormous windows like
doomed flies, those reverberating
in plain sight in the corners
where darkness will fall
and everyone above ground will
have gone somewhere to sleep
this all off. Me? I'm opening

a little café-of-the-mind where
moles can talk to flies. Intricate
labyrinths under the apple trees
and glassed-in fantasies of escape
at head-high altitudes. Moles paddling

through earth or flies foozling the air
over steak on a campfire near
the ocean. Moles will claim daylight
oxygen overrated—preferring air
filtered by darkness on the run. Flies

utter "What cute snouts you have!"
and moles have to consider life
with wings. By the time I get
home they've unionized and are
working out maternity leave and
pensions. Above it all elk antlers
wait for tinsel and mistletoe, or
tune in to moles going on and on,
rhapsodic about ants after rain. But
because I'm The Boss, I interrupt

at the top of my smart-ass Boss-voice:
"Hey, how about a little respect!
Whose café is this anyhow?"

Trolling for Cougar

Cynthia Neely

On the south shore of the lake
a resident reports she was chased
by a cougar, although I'd guess
it was the small leashed dog
that tempted it. If I was a big cat,
a cougar of the feline variety,
I would see that Shih Tzu
spinning on that cord like a meal
the lord provided in my need
and I'd heed that call,
swat at it like the toy it is. Hook
a big claw under its jaw
and reel it right in,
without knowing
what that would get me: a rifle
barrel sited, a howling
hound. It was bound
to happen. Now that cat
will be another statistic
in our need for space.
Like that bear who bought it
for the face she bit, the otter
trapped for crapping
under the neighbor's deck. Shit,
don't they know
they need to go
someplace, anyplace
else?

Trophy, Arlington, Washington, 2019, photograph, Phoebe Bosché

In the 1500s there were an estimated 30-60 milllion bison roaming North America, mostly on the great plains. By 1884, there were about 325 wild bison left, 24 in Yellowstone Park. A U.S. milliary spokesman once said, "We were never able to control the savages until their supply of meat was cut off."

The God of Monarch Butterflies

Keats Conley

Front-runner for candidacy of the Republic's arthropod: H.J. Res. 411: *Designating the monarch butterfly as the national insect of the United States.* Subject areas: government operations and policies; emblems; insects. 34 co-sponsors; dead on introduction. Ninety-percent decline in two decades raises doubt: list "butterfly" as *threatened*, followed by "nation-state." An insect emblem that's irksome. Aposematism is fool's gold, a beckoning flag that arrests the heart.

The God of Vaquitas

Keats Conley

Each individual is 3.3% of what's left of a nine-tenths devoured pie. Certainty is 100% a lost cause, yet the chant survives: ¡*Viva la vaquita marina!* Lifelong swimmers drown in droves, strangled in shallows of a vermillion sea. To live long is to buoy the body with soul. We are haunted by names for a knowingness: to leave the last bite on the plate untouched. In English, we call it manners-bit, "for the sake of good manners." In Spanish, *la vergüenza*—"the shame."

Note: *House Joint Resolution (H.J. Res) 411 was introduced into the 101st United States Congress in 1989 to designate the monarch butterfly as the national insect. It was referred to the Committee on Post Office and Civil Service, but was not enacted.*

Almost Forgetting

Anna Odessa Linzer

The maple leaf yellow
against the rain-brightened
green of thick moss,
coming up beneath and
alongside the fallen branches,
strewn as if a crazy puzzle
made to throw me off.
But they are there
everywhere I turn,
chanterelles.
And our baskets fill
as we move alone,
but always within
a whistle reach.
I bend and with each
snapping pull against my fingers
I feel the dark bats of discontent
fly from the window of the attic
I call my mind.
Only golden yellow
only green
only the gift of soil
and rain and forest
and something as pure and bright
and unknowable in its trueness
as love.
And then I stand to stretch,
only then seeing
what the simple harvest
had let me forget:
the clearcut around me.

Static Hazards

Hannah Yoest

i.
Jake Tapper's voice is on the other
side of the wall reporting another shooting as I leave

the office wearing denim and corduroy in defiance of the late
June heat. My heels drag on

the carpet. The dying is closer—someone always
is—it seems to briefly recede once I reach the street, but I begin

to twist the rings on my finger as helicopters descend
closer to the Potomac River and lift

mist into the air like phantoms rising to meet the spinning
blades. I wonder what they are looking for, seeking so

deliberately—searching the surface of that dark
water. I don't wait to watch for the answer of what they retrieve.

ii.
A woman with a bleached buzzcut and Om
tattooed on the back of her neck walks by as I kick

up glass that gets lodged in the toe of my shoe.
This isn't how it should be, I couldn't hear the typing as I left—

just the televisions with their constant state of alert: A poignancy
all their own, everything always breaking Breaking BREAKING on the open

floor plan and the glass doors somehow
losing in the fight for transparency.

And there's that voice again—the only unbroken device—
if walls could have pallor, they did today.

Shall I buy a black or white dress for such
a funeral as before us now?

Whose Hand Between my Head and the Door Frame

dan raphael

Bang my head against the
hold my fingers to the flame
cry, run, drop and roll, fold into a tree, pray for instant night,
for the transporter beam to reach me before a bullet

Each day's a little hotter, night has given up on cooling
wind waiting for motivation, time turning sticky swamp
aglow with memory's analgesic photoshop

Pizza so complex no one gets all the same toppings
has the same word for the same flavor
she says the cop was tall, he says the cop was average
the maniform, the unifold, anonymous knowledge,
the edge of my knowing where the past and future
show their tattered pixels, unravelling or not yet hemmed

I go to the bathroom but nothing comes out
i look in the mirror but it's the same headlines from 3 days ago—
this threatened, that blocked, the 5 stupidest things i thought.
if i was 20 stories above the ground instead of one
would the actual world be any further—deforested, platted, paved
cheek to jowl, no room to howl

How my clothes close me:
do i cover my head or shave it for full exposure
put a mask on the back of my skull so you think i'm backing away,
does it matter if the policeman can hear, if he knows my language
so much stops when the cop stops you—
the constitution, common sense, the long-crafted reins
on my paranoia, on my sense of justice

Is it better to be mislabeled or not to be seen at all
if i don't drive a car my tail light can't malfunction,
my registration can't expire, and the time i spend
on the bus is time vulnerable, unfamiliar:
soon police won't pull buses over, they'll reroute them
to where none of us want to go

Stale Mates, 2019, photograph, J. Ray Paradiso

Exiles

Karen Bonaudi

When stones break out of the earth,
they do it in memory of children
in forgotten graves.

Headstones, fieldstones gathered
in granite lines between pastures,
boulders tumbling down slopes,
alluvial gravel left behind:
forgive us, little souls.

Shattered mosques, markets,
rubble of lives, all lost
to love and soon to memory.

Legacy

Erin Jamieson

It was a hoax
rising sea levels
& melting ice sheets in
Greenland & the Arctic Sea

These were natural
fluctuations:
record high's &
short, mild winters

It was inconvenient
declining penguin populations
Invasive beetles in Alaska

Until tsunamis
ravaged our homes
or our crops died year
after year or our children
looked outside the window
& asked what went wrong

Hen Party, 2019, screen printing with drawing, acrylic and collage on paper, Deborah Faye Lawrence

[Four triumphant, stalwart female figures stand in opposition to eighty words that mean "bad woman." Adapted by the artist from her original collage on canvas, *Eighty Words*, 2014.]

Rocks on Wheels

Anita Goveas

In the waning days of the summer of 2026, G. Arthur Shale moves permanently into the abandoned Pinocchio movie set behind the derelict Disney-sphere. A landslide has taken out one of his ranches, his hogs walked into a tornado and never returned. He's aware people are struggling with nature because they didn't prepare enough, but he is meticulous and will flourish in a more controlled, less threatening space.

Geppetto's workshop is his main place of occupation. It's sparsely furnished—plywood bench painted to look like mahogany, cardboard shelves, plastic tools, a real metal fireplace with fabric flames. He brought his Vision Emperor Bed, with the built-in storage, some seeds, his high school copy of *Moby Dick* with the annotations. No unnecessary cooking utensils or unreliable refrigeration, he's arranged for food drops. Wagyu beef, Miche bread, the occasional bottle of Châteauneuf-du-Pape—the essentials only.

The days swell in front of him, an infinite resource. He periodically tends his seeds, which he organizes into pots atop the polystyrene carousel on the decaying Pleasure Island. Hardy plants that produce simple vegetables that go well with meat and bread—tomatoes, radishes, lettuce, chillies. Hardy plants that soak up sporadic showers of mildly acidic rain and don't need much tending. The first food drop comes with a newspaper that describes the floods in Kerala, 600 dead, 100 missing. He uses it to make paper swans he floats on the artificial lake that encloses the carbon-fibre Monstro.

He invests in Buckeye chickens intending for fresh meat for spit-roasting but ending up with fresh eggs, unless the chickens die of old age which they seem reluctant to do. With their sleek pea combs, sturdy bodies and scaly yellow dinosaur feet they're survivors, just like him. They nest in the puppet show, spread out across the stage and seats, finding their own roosts and their own food. They're more self-sufficient then he expected.

When the next newspaper arrives, wrapped around a bottle of Laurent-Perrier, he's rearranging the rocks on wheels that flank the Blue Fairy's grotto. He's moved them parallel, in a hexagon, and now to form his initials, a giant G.A.S. that could be seen in space, if the space station hadn't burned up in the dissolving ozone layer. An unexpectedly fierce breeze carries away the page about the drought in the Pampas grains belt of Argentina, affecting corn yields and cattle feed. He doesn't look at the next pages, the cyclone warnings.

He's chasing the chickens away from the disappeared lake when it happens. High enough on fumes from lead-painted acid-burnt fake donkeys and decomposing chicken poop, he hasn't noticed the food parcels have stopped. The chickens scatter, the wind drops, the air stills. Monstro flattens as if stepped on by a giant, and never recovers. 📖

flawed algorithm

Janet Cannon

just so you know
seventy-eight cents
is not equal to one

work place same job
dollar plus we are
not here for corporal

pleasure or disdain
we protest and
suggest you go back

to the element of
the dis functioning
calculator and redo

the equation so that
x equals x and y equals
y are absolute like

a woman is a woman
equals a man is a man
any questions?

really?

Janet Cannon

really? you want less
government but you want to
stuff government into my
uterus like turkey dressing
disguised as compassion

really? you pay for
viagra and cialis but you
won't pay for birth control
like saying *if you work for
me i am your slave master*

really? you say you
want to save babies but
you kill doctors like saying
you are not an addict as
you shoot-up hypocrisy

really? you want to buy
guns without any restrictions
but you don't want your kid
killed by one like a deer in
endless street hunting season

really?

Handmaid Tale, 2019, cartoon/drawing, Tiffany Midge

The Continent of Plastic

Judith Roche

> *. . . turning and turning in the widening gyre*
> —W. B. Yeats

it swirls beneath the surface on ocean currents
massive vortex

new kind of wetland
bobbing and shifting

on no fixed boundaries
roiling reflection of a billion million

stars in the Milky Way
undulating tidewoven flow

swirling and gleaming like Van Gogh's Starry Night,
tooth brushes, plastic bags, fishing nets

shoelace tips, water bottles, broken toys
condoms blasted to bits by sun and waves

this eighth entity kills
inhabitants and visitors alike—

sea-turtles mistake plastic produce bags
for filmy jelly-fish

krill and plankton feeders suck it in
sea birds gorge on fragments—

plastic pearls looking like fish eggs—
and regurgitate

into the waiting mouths
of hungry chicks.

AWAPUHI, 2016, archival pigment print from tintype, Kali Spitzer

V

RESISTANCE

Let us go forth with fear and courage and rage to save the world.
—Grace Paley

Caretaking is the utmost spiritual and physical responsibility of our time . . .
—Linda Hogan

*To tell the truth is to become beautiful, to begin to love yourself, value yourself.
And that's political, in its most profound way.*
—June Jordan

Resist much, obey little.
—Walt Whitman

To oppression . . . we respond with life.
—Gabriel García Márquez

*In a time of destruction, create something: a poem, a parade, a community,
a school, a vow, a moral principle; one peaceful moment.*
—Maxine Hong Kingston

*Hope is the enemy of injustice. Hope is what will get you to stand up
when people tell you to sit down.*
—Bryan G. Stevenson

*People who fight may lose.
People who do not fight have already lost.*
—Bertolt Brecht

The Wall

Anita Endrezze

Build a wall of saguaros,
butterflies, and bones
of those who perished
in the desert. A wall of worn shoes,
dry water bottles, poinsettias.
Construct it of gilded or crazy house
mirrors so some can see their true faces.
Build a wall of revolving doors
or revolutionary abuelas.
Make it as high as the sun, strong as tequila.
Boulders of sugar skulls. Adobe or ghosts.
A Lego wall or bubble wrap. A wall of hands
holding hands, hair braided from one woman
to another, one country to another.
A wall made of Berlin. A wall made for tunneling.
A beautiful wall of taco trucks.
A wall of silent stars and migratory songs.
This wall of solar panels and holy light,
panels of compressed cheetos,
topped not by barbed wire but sprouting
avocado seeds, those Aztec testicles.
A wall to keep Us in and Them out.
It will have faces and heartbeats.
Dreams will be terrorists. The Wall will divide
towns, homes, mountains,
the sky that airplanes fly through
with their potential illegals.
Our wallets will be on life support
to pay for it. Let it be built
of guacamole so we can have a bigly block party.

Mortar it with xocóatl, chocolate. Build it from coyote howls
and wild horses drumming across the plains of Texas,
from the memories
of hummingbird warriors and healers.
Stack it thick as blood, which has mingled
for centuries, la vida. Dig the foundation deep.
Create a 2,000 mile altar, lit with votive candles
for those who have crossed over
defending freedom under spangled stars
and drape it with rebozos,
and sweet grass.
Make it from two-way windows:
the wind will interrogate us,
the rivers will judge us, for they know how to separate
and divide to become whole.
Pink Floyd will inaugurate it.
Ex-Presidente Fox will give it the middle finger salute.
Wiley Coyote will run headlong into it,
and survive long after history forgets us.
Bees will find sand-scoured holes and fill it
with honey. Heroin will cover it in blood.
But it will be a beautiful wall. A huge wall.
Remember to put a rose-strewn doorway in Nogales
where my grandmother crossed over,
pistols on her hips. Make it a gallery of graffiti art,
a refuge for tumbleweeds,
a border of stories we already know by heart.

Berlin Wall, 2017, collage—mixed media, floppy discs, metal, canvas, Sharon M. Carter

dear white america

Danez Smith

i've left Earth in search of darker planets, a solar system revolving too near a black hole. i've left in search of a new God. i do not trust the God you have given us. my grandmother's hallelujah is only outdone by the fear she nurses every time the blood-fat summer swallows another child who used to sing in the choir. take your God back. though his songs are beautiful, his miracles are inconsistent. i want the fate of Lazarus for Renisha, want Chucky, Bo, Meech, Trayvon, Sean & Jonylah risen three days after their entombing, their ghost re-gifted flesh & blood, their flesh & blood re-gifted their children. i've left Earth, i am equal parts sick of your *go back to Africa & i just don't see race*. neither did the poplar tree. we did not build your boats (though we did leave a trail of kin to guide us home). we did not build your prisons (though we did & we fill them too). we did not ask to be part of your America (though are we not America? her joints brittle & dragging a ripped gown through Oakland?). i can't stand your ground. i'm sick of calling your recklessness the law. each night, i count my brothers. & in the morning, when some do not survive to be counted, i count the holes they leave. i reach for black folks & touch only air. your master magic trick, America. now he's breathing, now he don't. abra-cadaver. white bread voodoo. sorcery you claim not to practice, hand my cousin a pistol to do your work. i tried, white people. i tried to love you, but you spent my brother's funeral making plans for brunch, talking too loud next to his bones. you took one look at the river, plump with the body of boy after girl after sweet boi & ask *why does it always have to be about race?* because you made it that way! because you put an asterisk on my sister's gorgeous face! call her pretty (for a black girl)! because black girls go missing without so much as a whisper of where?! because there are no amber alerts for amber-skinned girls! because Jordan boomed. because Emmett whistled. because Huey P. spoke. because Martin preached. because black boys can always be too loud to live. because it's taken my papa's & my grandma's time, my father's time, my mother's time, my aunt's time, my uncle's time, my brother's & my sister's time . . . how much time do you want for your progress? i've left Earth to find a place where my kin can be safe, where black people ain't but people the same color as the good, wet earth, until that means something, until then i bid you well, i bid you war, i bid you our lives to gamble with no more. i've left Earth & i am touching everything you beg your telescopes to show you. i'm giving the stars their right names. & this life, this new story & history you cannot steal or sell or cast overboard or hang or beat or drown or own or redline or shackle or silence or cheat or choke or cover up or jail or shoot or jail or shoot or jail or shoot or ruin

                                        this, if only this one, is ours.

Burnt, 2018, mixed media—photo, newspaper, paint, fire & canvas, Danielle Hark

A Woman Holds a Baby and a Machete

Ronda Piszk Broatch

You wonder what the punchline is,
if there is another way to punctuate,
say, a woman holds a baby, and

a machete was nowhere to be found.
Or maybe the baby was in daycare, sleepy
songs swaddling her while outside, let's say

in a city far away, the woman wields the machete.
She is fighting her way through a dictionary
of neckties. She names her machete #MeToo

and the baby coos as the stars magic themselves
into being. Meanwhile the neckties have no room
for the growing thesaurus of women of any gender,

but so far stop short of the machete. The woman
wonders, if she puts down the machete, picks up
the baby, if she'd have to defend

her choice. The baby sees the woman as nothing less
than the goddess of her womb days, the machete
a natural extension of what she is meant to be.

When I Speak About Gun Control I Wear My Son's Shoes

Stuart Gunter

—for Tom Mauser and Manuel Oliver
In Honor of Daniel Mauser and Joaquin Oliver

When I speak about gun control
I wear my son's shoes. The shoes
he wore when he was gunned down
at his school. All we did was send
him to school. He had a test that day.
When I speak about gun control
I wear my son's shoes. When I
am arrested outside of the NRA
offices five states away, I am unheard
and taunted by a man saying my
fifteen-year-old son should have
carried a gun to school. Our country
has a short memory regarding
school shootings. A short memory.
And when I speak about gun control
I wear my son's shoes.

Taking Action

Ellery Akers

"We live in capitalism. Its power seems inescapable.
So did the divine right of kings. Any human power can be
resisted and changed by human beings."
—Ursula le Guin

It's good to act. To lean into the body of the world.
To know lawyers sit at airports with signs
saying *We Can Help* written in Farsi.

It's good to stop machines—giant needles that drill into the earth—
because what they are stitching is *The End*.

To see soldiers who wear camouflage—
shirts and pants that look like leaves and bark—
kneel in front of the Sioux
and say they're sorry for what's been taken,
even the language for *leaves* and *bark*.

It's good to signal to the others who are shocked,
to know we're not alone in shock,
that when we drive past a house
we know someone is sitting in a chair in front of a TV, shocked.

But the men who want to make us afraid
are afraid.

And my time on earth
is a huge breath:

I can blow that breath into the world.

Take The Knee

F.I. Goldhaber

Red, white, and blue,
a piece of cloth
that represents
subjugation
of Black people,
massacre of
indigenous
nations, abuse
of Latinos,
exploitation
of Asian folk,
persecution
of non-christians
murder of
LGBT
and those who are
other gendered.

You want to sing
an anthem of
war before a
violent game
but take umbrage
when the athletes
who entertain
you take a knee
in memory,
to remind you that

their prowess and
affluence don't
protect them from
cops who slaughter
Black men who dare
to drive, to breathe,
to speak their minds.

You claim to be
a patriot
but deny them rights
enshrined in the
Constitution
you pretend to
honor, revere,
and adhere to,
including rights
to peaceably
assemble and
petition for
a redress of
their grievances,
to speak against
inequality
and injustice.

But you ignore
the amendments
that accord non-
whites the same rights
and privileges
you consider
sacrosanct, and
blamed the victims
of systemic
racism when
they took a knee
to remind the
world that they
risk their lives
just because their
skin has darker
tones than yours.

Resist Hate Map, 2015, Acrylic, collage and varnish on canvas, American flags and recycled paper map, Deborah Faye Lawrence

["This map was inspired by research and activism at The Southern Poverty Law Center, ; it details the astonishing number of extremist hate groups active in the U.S. as of late 2014. The SPLC has been successful in reducing the number of groups and bringing awareness to the issue of intolerance in the U.S.A., but the artist's painstaking arrangement of icons was a two-month exercise in indignation. Icons represent Anti-Islamist, Ku Klux Klan, Neo-Nazi, White Nationalist, Racist Skinhead, Christian Identity, Neo-Confederate, Black Separatist, and General Hate."]

Attack of the Fifty-Foot (Lakota) Woman

Tiffany Midge

In September 2016, a fifty-foot monument bearing the likeness of an unnamed Lakota woman, replete with a blowing-in-the-wind star blanket shawl, was installed upon the banks of the Missouri River in Chamberlain, South Dakota. Her creator titled the giantess sculpture *Dignity*.

At the time of *Dignity*'s launch, if you followed the Missouri river to the north, another launch took place—concussion grenades, water cannons, rubber bullets, dog attacks. A launch of incalculable greed and disregard for life. The NoDAPL [Dakota Access Pipeline protests] demonstration and stand-off was an event on a scale which the world has never seen, and it sparked universal awareness and attention towards the most critically urgent issue of our time.

Protecting the Water. Mni Wiconi. Water is Life.

The Dakota Access Pipeline Project is expected to cover 1,172 miles, and to connect the Bakken and Three Forks production areas in North Dakota to Patoka, Illinois. The pipeline will enable domestically-produced light sweet crude oil to reach major refining markets.

The pipeline cuts straight through ancestral lands sacred to the Standing Rock Nation, and threatens their main water supply, the Missouri River, *Mni Sose*.

LaDonna Brave Bull Allard, Standing Rock Sioux Tribal Preservation Officer, owns the northernmost land of the Standing Rock Reservation. The northern border is the Cannon Ball River. The eastern border is the Missouri River. From her land, you can see the pipeline corridor.

The land she grew up on tells the history of this river back 2,000 years.

When I think of the *Dignity* sculpture and the militarization and stand-offs in the small, otherwise peaceful communities on Standing Rock, where my own mother and grandparents were born, and, specifically, when I think of monsters in regards of the Black Snake Prophecy, I can't help but think of the 1958 creature feature *Attack of the Fifty Foot Woman*.

Counter-Attack of the 50-Foot (Lakota) Woman, 2019, drawing, Jay Dearien

In the movie, a rich socialite encounters an alien life form and is transformed into a giantess, a fifty-foot she-beast. The King Kong-sized woman goes on a rampage after discovering her husband in a bar with a "no-good floozy." Eight industrial-sized hooks, four lengths of chain, forty gallons of plasma, an elephant syringe and electrical fire later, she is finally subdued. The authorities responsible for successfully capturing and bringing her down holler things like, *I can't shoot a lady! Wadda ya want me to do, salt her tail?*

In my reveries, the *Dignity* sculpture breaks from her foundation, secures the blue star quilt firmly around her shoulders, and follows the Missouri River north to Cannonball, up to the Oceti Sakowin—Seven Council Fires—straight into the heart of things, and gets to work killing the black snake.

In my reveries, the authorities do not succeed in bringing her down—(*eight industrial-sized hooks, four lengths of chain, forty gallons of plasma, an elephant syringe and electrical fire*).

In my daydreams she is not defeated, but victorious and freeze-framed eternally (despite concussion grenades and dog attacks, water cannons and rubber bullets).

The land she grew up on tells the history of this river back 2,000 years.
What stories of this river will be told in 2,000 more? 📖

Identity

Keanu Jones

It is acceptable to repel the anthem of the free,
kneel for the souls that rest beneath the unspoken truth.
To have a voice like the echoes of an elk dancing through the autumn leaves.
Float in the streams of colonization but prepare to duel the current.
In the face of fear, you embody your ancestor's prayers,
to reclaim our identity as the warriors and chiefs we once were.

Canadian Anti-Enbridge Oil Campaign, 2012, digital print, Michaela McGuire

Counter-Protest

Stephanie Barbé Hammer

They aren't much to look at, these two white women. One's our age—that is to say 60-ish—and one's younger, but they're just your garden variety progressives, middle class. One is upper. They've both been to college. One's a lawyer of course—one is always a lawyer. Wait—no—she just talks like one. Anyway, the two women get wind of the white supremacists' meeting at the park next to a local winery on our island off the coast.

Our political activism group decides to stay away. "We don't want to give them oxygen," our leader says. Most agree.

But these two women don't. They say, "why should these jokers feel comfortable in our town, in our community?"

The two of them aren't mean about it; they aren't strident.

But they keep on asking that question.

"Confrontation isn't what pacifists do," one of us says, and another says, "besides they are all carrying guns, so forget it!"

"But," says the one woman, D1, "pacifism doesn't mean being passive."

Some of us don't understand that point exactly, and D2 says, "I want to KNOW what they say at that meeting!" Our leader says "that's dangerous!" and D1 says so was Serbia and D2 says so was the army.

We keep on arguing about what to do about the white supremacists.

Some of us just want to stay home and some of us want to stage a rally for love and tolerance in another park in another town nearby, and some of us want to write to the country commissioner and some of us want to write to the newspaper and say, *why are you letting these people hold a rally in our park near the winery?*

Answer: free speech.

Others of us are undecided. We want to stop the rally but we don't know how. We also don't want to get shot. We keep on arguing, although some of us drift off the conversation, do other things, think about Valentine's Day and why our kids never call—they just text and we miss hearing their voices, even though we don't have much to say.

So our activist group goes to the peace and love rally in the other town. And while we're at home reading the newspaper D1 and D2 go to the white supremacy rally. Because they are both white, cisgendered and straight, they get in without a problem, but they raise suspicions because they don't applaud during the speeches. The Q and A happens and D1 asks the question, "If you aren't white supremacists, why do you keep the company you keep and say the things that you say?"

People start yelling at them, calling them cunts. D2 stands next to D1 and they remain steadfast and silent, surrounded by white people with guns screaming at them, while the local police stand on the margins. The cops don't do anything.

Free speech.

"Well," says the white supremacy rally MC, "I can't continue with the Q and A, so come up to the front and I'll take questions privately."

D1 and D2 walk the gauntlet of angry swearing people to their car and drive away.

"Sure, it felt threatening," D1 says later, "but I didn't fear for my life."

"Me neither," says D2.

Our activist group leader says, "Please don't ever do that again."

I sit at home thinking about all the people I know who couldn't even walk into that meeting because of how they look. I think about my own fear, but mostly I think about D1 and D2 standing in the middle of that crowd.

"I'm a veteran," D2 told the screaming white people at the white supremacist rally.

"My father is buried in Arlington National Cemetery," D1 said.

"Your father would be ashamed of you," yelled one of the white supremacists.

I don't know about D1's dad, but I feel proud of them.

"They did this for the wrong reasons," our activist group leader tells me.

What are the right reasons?

I'm not sure, so I talk to my therapist.

"You do what you can," he tells me. So I'm doing what I do best—writing this all down.

Still, I wonder, what should I do the next time the white supremacists come to town? 📖

Lecture to a Girlfriend

Priscilla Long

Why do you refuse love to yourself?
Why fake a smile when others speak?
but so nasty, thinking *You asshole!*
when you yourself stumble or drop a sock.
Girl, it's simple to love your own life.
Imagine pouring dark coffee into your lover's cup,
and pour it dark into your own cup.
Imagine uncorking wine, cooking curry,
spreading cloth and candlelight,
and you are the guest of the house.
Imagine losing yourself in the back roads of a book.
Imagine summer breezes as kisses and caresses,
night's darkness as your own darkness,
and you are the light of the world.
Imagine love. Love does not rush.
Love is kind, love makes allowance.
Love the rain, the street, the college student.
Love the drunk old man, the drug-wasted life.
Love moss and oak leaves.
Love crows, weeds, sparrows, stones.
Love the coots on Green Lake.
Love the newspaper slow-dancing down Brooklyn Street.
That's right: Love a newspaper. Then love yourself.

Lessons

Jennifer deBie

Do not teach
your daughters to fear spiders.
eight-handed sisters,
tricksters with tummies pulled tight,
victims of hubris, a goddess curse,
capable of threading the world together
with nothing but their organs.
Do not teach

your daughters to fear snakes.
Feather-coated carriers of the sky,
bold gardeners who didn't lie,
boneless bodies to encircle
the world, and swallow their tails.
Do not teach

Your daughters to fear the dark.
They were dragged from the night
of your belly, into the sun,
to fly high and be
burned and burned and burned
again. The dark is your nurture,
a vastness of shared heartbeats.
Do not teach

your daughters to fear dirt.
To which they will return,
of which they are made,
built of clay after the animals—
teach your daughters to disobey.
Do not teach

your daughters to fear deep water.
Great mother monster, the first,
before land or light
or god to speak them into being,
alien deeps that gave rise
to the sum. Theater of war,
safe passage promised, chained voyage,
journey to the edge of the world
that does not fall,
doldrums, currents, and reefs uncharted.
Teach your daughters

to sail, swim, and hear whalesong.
To carry the serpent, to free the spider,
to walk by night with dark-crescent smiles
beneath their fingernails.
To unwrite the legends scripted
by chisel and stone. Send
your daughters out
to learn.

Beyond Walls, View from an historic school for African Americans, Maryland, U.S.A., 2017, photograph, Sarah E.N. Kohrs

Migration

Mary Ellen Talley

Raise the wall higher

Monarch butterflies cross the border

every winter without work visas

Free the land for the refugees

Andrew C. Brown

We need love to seed—patch the thatch from roof of truth, shelter helter-skelter and merry-go-round found in dripping sieve of media that gives tributaries of fear where compassion completely disappears into an ugly pool of aggression. Stop, choose which way we want to live, know why to give is only ever the right decision, snuff out the light that ignites fight from those who promote derision, only ever seek sickly heel of fear, do not hear call from those of us who wish to help, to protect the weak, welcome the refugee, those of us, the sum of the embrace, a few true to the pure concept of a working United Nations. Offer salvation, give lie to mask of money manipulation. Display humanity, not depravity, prioritize what values are important in this rich planet, tie empathy to flags, free peoples who are slaves to circumstances capitalist crooks promote. Rescue the boats, dismantle the walls, heed wailing desperate calls. We are just one nation not different states that predicate power, influence —let us be a confluence that streams consciousness understanding that human beings should be banding together in this world being free to throw off their shackles. Silence the cackles of billionaires, liberate their lairs, offer housing that is forever fair, douse homelessness finally. For our children's sake and the generations behind do not be blind to the possibility the ally for our salvation might well be integration of our different positives. Individual traits, individual nationalities, together we can weather stormy times and always be free to accept refugees.

Just Breathe

Susana Praver-Pérez

A solo scrub-jay perched on a wrinkled orange tree
      calls out dawn like nails
           on a chalkboard.

I can still remember mornings like symphonies
      and plump oranges
           on glossy green.

Oakland wakes to a grey brew
      of pollution and soot.
My sister can't stop coughing—
A wheeze planted its rusty roots in her
      once pink lungs.

Pesticides drift,
      settle on a withered hibiscus.
Birds fall, bees die.

Monsanto—Not my saint!
Monsanto dances with the devil
      on a bed of crushed wings,
        dollars jingling in its pockets.

I recycle, reuse, reduce, but what can I do
      to curb corporate cravings
        that shoot up towns and rainforests,
           greenhouse gases spurting
                from exit wounds?

Who would imagine we'd take to the streets and march
        for air to breathe
        for water to drink?

Thousands strong, our chants rising like ravens, we march
        for a future
        for this sacred Earth.

We march in the too hot sun
        so sweetgrass may always grow.

We march lest we leave our children
        a fractured sphere
        and to our grandchildren, nothing
            but prayers.

Rise and Shine, 2019, digital fusion, Meredith Bricken Mills

In Your Face:

Kate Thompson's Portraits of Bold Women

Melissa Kwasny

Her eyes narrow behind thick black frames, a gaze startling in its directness, its cocksure unwillingness to back down. No makeup, no jewelry, no apparent concern for feminine appearance—is this a woman? Her full lips spread in a knowing half-smile. Her short reddish hair blotted with gray. The background is painted with strong burnt-orange brush strokes, the same pigment flickering across her skin. "May I never remember reasons for my spirit's safety," Audre Lorde wrote. It is a gaze hard to return if, well, if you are a man.

The history of portraiture is a social history. Kings, queens, and members of the royal court dominate in the earliest portraits, as do war heroes, gods, and goddesses. The wealthy and powerful chose by their patronage who is worthy of being painted. Even today, traditional portraits are commissioned, whether officially—as in the case of presidents—or unofficially, as an act of monetary speculation: Ralph Wolfe Cowan trimming twenty pounds and years off Donald Trump, dressing him in tennis whites, and titling the portrait "The Visionary," a gambit that worked. The painting now hangs in Mar-a-Lago.

Portraiture, particularly in the field of photography, can function also as a force for social justice, directing our attention to the plight of farm workers during the depression (Dorothea Lange), the AIDS epidemic (Nan Goldin), disabilities (Diane Arbus). In this case, choice of subject is in the hands of the artist, and, if the work is compelling enough, it transforms our view of those whom we have previously ignored into images we can't look away from. Think of Amy Sherald's painting of Michelle Obama in the National Portrait gallery, how little black girls flock to it adoringly, posing in front of it for their own selfies. "I paint things I want to see," says Sherald. "I paint as a way of looking for myself in the world." Think of photographer Jamal Jordan's moving series of black lesbian and gay couples that appeared in *The New York Times* in 2018. As a young, gay, African American man, he says he grew up without images of love between queer men and women of color and sought to remedy that as "a gift to his younger self."

Kate Thompson's recent series shares this revolutionary impulse. "Of the many communities I live in, smart, adventurous, gay women are my floor," she writes in her artist's statement. The show consists of oil portraits of relatively unknown American lesbians over the age of fifty. "What started out as an attempt to become a better painter while not filling up my house with stored canvases became something larger when a good friend passed on," she says. "At the memorial, her portrait—one I had done years earlier—was hung. Who had painted it was fairly irrelevant; what struck me was that it had become a legacy object for an amazing person. Something that helped keep her with us." In a culture obsessed with celebrity, with images of the rich, beautiful, and young, who, we are constantly asked, is worthy of our attention? For most people, I venture, older lesbian women do not immediately come to mind.

* * *

Much has been written about the invisibility of lesbians in American culture. "Lesbian erasure," Adrienne Rich called it in her landmark essay, "Compulsory Heterosexuality and Lesbian Existence," attributing it to systematic erasures in history, politics, and literature, even in feminist analysis. Individual lesbian identity is also often overlooked. Those of us who present as feminine are assumed to be straight. If we present as masculine, we are ignored or disparaged or stereotyped. Within our own queer communities, older lesbians particularly are often shunned as old-fashioned, less hip and transgressive than transgendered or transexual people: the gender fluid, gender expressive, gender queer, nonbinary, pansexual, or even asexual. Like many older women, straight or gay, to the young, lesbians are often indistinguishable from each other: our hair gray, our bodies losing muscle tone, women facing Alzheimer's, back operations, diabetes, things the young do not like to think about. Most older lesbians, unless seen with our lovers, do not really look different from older women in our larger communities, especially so since said communities have appropriated many of the styles of lesbian culture: tattoos, piercings, work boots, short hair. What then, has Thompson made visible (and visibly attractive) here?

Queer people often boast of having the gift of "gaydar," a power that allows us to recognize the one gay person in the crowd through some hard-to-define combination of clothes, hair, gesture, and, especially, eye contact, whether that person is out or not, clues one might not recognize if one isn't gay. Thompson's portraits, most of them painted from photographs she herself has taken, capture this subversive quality. From the looks her subjects return to her, one sees that she is clearly allowed in *as one of their own*. For me, it is a look for which the word "freedom" suddenly springs to mind: freedom from fear of judgment, from shame, from comparison with others, a freedom granted perhaps because of age but also for having lived one's life outside the home rule of men.

Most lesbians have experienced the disassociation of growing up in heteronormative households, the unspoken treaties mandating women be subservient to fathers and brothers, the damage to everyone caused by patriarchy even in the best homes. What enabled us to see that there was not a place for us? Well, family, teachers, and neighbors often pointed out our difference: tomboy, spinster, dyke, dildo, old maid, man-hater, and many other words meant to say that we were not what the world had hoped for. Our own efforts at invisibility, our baggy clothes and neutral colors, our closets—which everyone has entered at one time or another—at work, school, or church, are a result of this. To be able to really see us laughing, playing music, reading, or in intense discussion, is to look past appearance, as Thompson does, to how lesbians "move through their world."

Reddick portrays a woman with a buzz cut and round Marxist spectacles, wearing a blue button-down with a t-shirt underneath, a book under one arm. You might meet her as a salesclerk in a used bookstore; she might point you to Octavia Butler. *Matria*'s long white hair spills in all directions, her glasses fashionable, her pose that of someone holding forth on climate change or the evils of Monsanto. The way she holds her arm high across her waist, as if in a sling, shows us she is fragile, has perhaps broken some limbs, but clearly her political will is undefeated. *Bryher*, her gray bangs poking out of a worker's cap, a peace sign button attached to her army surplus jacket, looks at us with activist intensity and conviction. *Judy Moon*, in a tank top, laughing, is perhaps a carpenter. Note her strong upper arms. Perhaps she spays stray cats; perhaps she spends every dime accompanying a yearly women's delegation to Cuba. We do not know if any of them are partnered, or if they live with others. Each is portrayed alone. Each is the age of parents going or already gone, childhood a distant dream, friends being picked off by death one by one.

Thompson's subjects are her friends, her past and present lovers. Because of this, there is something else made visible in these paintings. It is no surprise, when I think about it, that what makes these portraits inherently lesbian is what, in fact, distinguishes lesbianism, which is a desire for women. *Porter* flexes her androgynous muscles under the rolled sleeves of a black t-shirt, her hip thrust toward the camera, one hand on her knee, showing off a simple wedding band. "I'm married; come hither," she seems to say. There is a sexual confidence in many of these portraits, a look reserved only for other lesbians, that comes across as masculine no matter the length of one's hair or the gender markers of one's clothes because of its *forwardness*. *Michelle* lays her fingers on her biceps, leans in, and smiles. "In Your Face: Portraits of Bold Women" is a show—and a title—that celebrates what queer people are always being accused of: flaunting their sexuality.

You have to love women to love these portraits. Do you? Full disclosure: I am one of the lesbians over fifty whose portrait is included here. After the show closed, Thompson packaged and sent the painting to me as a gift, an act she replicated for each of her subjects, further subverting the hierarchy of patronage. I admit that it took me two months to hang it, too embarrassed to be made visible, or to be seen as too proud. This is what Thompson has so generously proposed to each of us: to dare to be visible. In my portrait, I look straight into your gaze, with a seriousness I recognize in myself. When others see it, will they feel less invisible, too? 📖

Feminismo Mural, Bolivia, 2019, photograph, Susan Deer Cloud

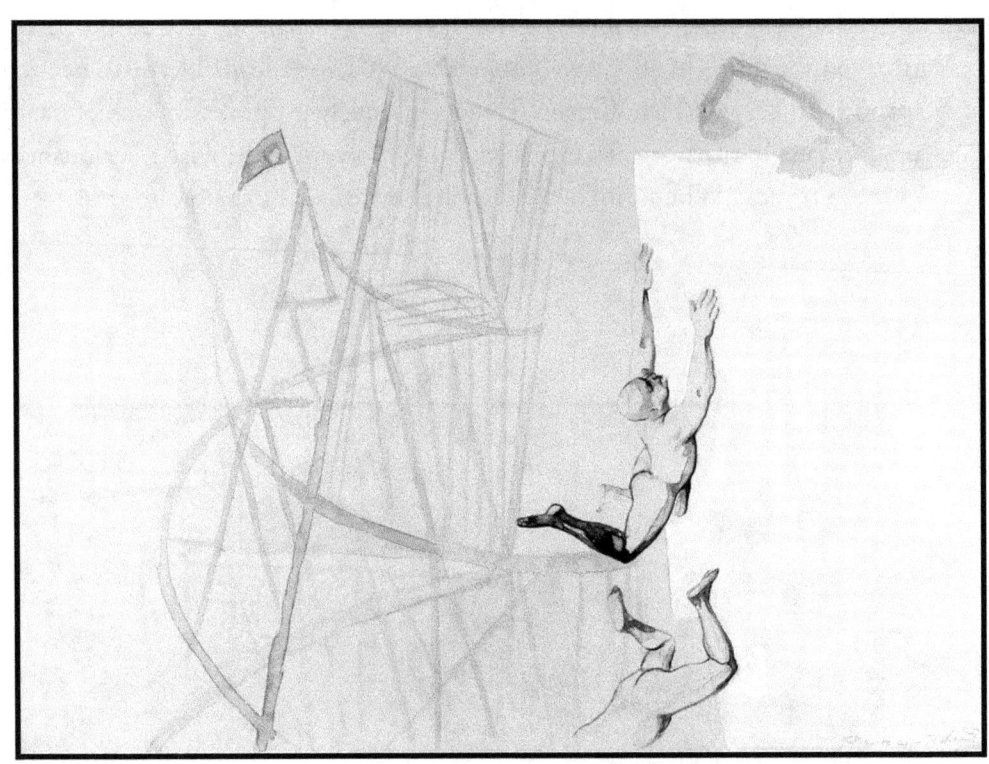

Epic #102 (Rickety Isms Failing Us All), from "Epic Ink Series," 2009, ink, silver marker, gesso on Mylar, Tatiana Garmendia

The Visible Woman

Margaret DeRitter

The visible woman
refuses to lie in pieces
dreaming of being whole,
assembles herself according
to her own directions,
covers her see-through skin
with a suit of armor,
rides wild, visible horses
down marble hallways,
thundering at office doors
and gilded elevators.
She may be vintage but
her voice is unwavering.
Try putting her back
in her cellophane box,
she'll slice her way out—
she's coming for you, Congress.

World Cup 2018

Stuart Stromin

On a green chessboard
acrobats glide
leap and soar,
twenty-two athletes juggling a single round ball
while the planet holds its breath

All war
all politics
reduced to a contest of champions
on a stadium battlefield
elevated to perfection by
young human giants
at the peak of achievement

For a moment
the music of the ballet
like the tranquility of a running stream
drowning out
the yammering, ranting spew
of the orange mouth
on the other channel.

The Coyotes

Gary Copeland Lilley

KRZE Listener Supported Radio: News at Noon

Animal Control officers are searching for a coyote in the area that has been masquerading as a dog. The unidentified suspect has been seen walking the street in broad daylight with his tongue out and wagging his tail. He is described as being the approximate size of a border collie, and appears to be even more intelligent but he does not fetch or catch frisbees. According to Officer Jim Locke, coyote populations are immigrating at an all-time high and modern coyotes have even begun colonizing in cities like Los Angeles, Atlanta, Cleveland, and San Francisco. It is well-established that Washington, D.C. has had a long-time urban coyote problem. Even though coyotes are marginalized they are highly adaptable and will eat just about anything, including rodents, rabbits, fish, livestock, and household pets. Coyotes communicate by singing a primitive song that is apparently more complex than it seems. Authorities have no strategies on stopping their messages, so they gather and usually hunt in packs. The unidentified suspect is unique in that he has a preference for travelling alone, but should still be considered dangerous. Some domestic dogs are starting to form alliances with the coyotes. See something, say something. Presently this coyote is being sought as a "subject of interest" only.

Coyote Incidents from the Daily Police Log

Officers were called at 8:27 a.m., July 7, by a building owner reporting that a transient female coyote was on the Water Street property after being banned and chased away the previous week by law enforcement. The female coyote had been openly copulating with dogs in the parking lot in front of the daycare center as parents were dropping off children. After their arrival, officers did not locate the female coyote in the area.

Officers were called at 10:05 a.m., July 7, by a Sheridan Street business reporting that there was a transient female coyote inside the business knocking wine bottles off the shelves, and devouring French bread and deli meats. The female coyote had left the business before officers arrived. The business has had previous issues with the female coyote's behavior and asked that she be given a trespass admonishment for the store.

Officers were dispatched at 1:38 p.m., July 7, to a possible domestic assault between two sister coyotes on Grant Street. When officers arrived, they found the sisters acting aggressively towards each other: snarling, spitting, and the fur standing on the back of their necks. It was determined that there had been no assault. Officers stood by while one sister coyote gathered her belongings and trotted into the forest to await a friend who was coming to pick her up.

Officers responded at 4:20 p.m., July 7, to an assault in progress involving at least five coyotes near the skateboard park in the 200 block of Monroe Street. When officers arrived, the parties had separated and were found to be nearby at the Maritime Mission. It appeared an argument between two couples began in the skateboard park and rolled into the street. There were no injuries, and none of the subjects involved filed a police report. All the coyotes were warned about possible deportation from the town's parks and forest.

The Smalltown Daily, Metro Section, Page 8, Below the Fold: Police Shooting, Black Lab Mistaken for Coyote

Another fatal shooting of a black lab Tuesday night, August 2, by police officers who had mistaken the congenial family pet for the male coyote being sought as a "subject of interest." Police Officers were responding to an anonymous tip concerning a suspicious animal that was mounting a local champion female border collie on Lawrence Street, and urinating in multiple locations. The animal was engaged in the latter activity when the police officers arrived.

Animal Control Officer Jim Locke, who also responded to the call, stated, "The animal really didn't give the officers a choice; when the officers pulled up with their flashing red and blue lights, and someone had the siren on, the dog tried to bolt. I understand that he was 17 years old, quite elderly, so it was a slow run."

There have been five fatal domestic dog shootings so far this year, as compared to two in the previous year. "This incident is an unfortunate tragedy," stated Police Spokesperson, Sandy Shaw, "The animal refused to obey the officers' commands to stop running and to stop urinating, and fearing for the safety of their fellow officers, and for the safety of the community, the officers then employed deadly force."

The dog, identified as Buster, was struck 17 times. All six officers at the scene discharged their weapons and have been placed on administrative leave.

KSIN TV: The Pulse of the Community

In the wake of the Smalltown police shooting of Buster, who was a victim of mistaken identity and was initially thought to have been a coyote suspect, research reveals that of the five fatal police shootings of domestic dogs this year, four of the victims, including Buster, have been black labs, the fifth victim was a chocolate lab.

Domestic dog owners are nearly 60% of the Smalltown population. This is a place that has an annual Dog Parade, where there are dog bowls of water in the local bars, where people drive with their beloved pets sitting in their laps. Domestic dogs have become part of the fabric of this community. This incident has created tensions between the police and the town's citizens.

Black lab owners have organized several protests, and are demanding to know why their domestic big dogs are targeted and shot. "In 17 years Buster never harmed anyone, and it is very hard for me to believe that he was cavorting like they say, being that he was so old," stated Joan Malone, owner of the late Buster. "Seems like the officers disdain the use of less lethal methods, like Tasers, or sedatives, or dog treats."

According to a credible source who wishes to remain anonymous, not all of Smalltown domestic dog owners agree with the protests, especially owners of the golden members of the breed.

Tiring of the negative attention and the increased scrutiny of domestic big dogs in general as a result of the protests by black lab activists, the golden lab owners have created their own organization, ALL LABS MATTER. Their feeling is that black lab owners need to train their dogs better, and they state that there are several very good affordable private schools in the area, where this can be done.

"Any dog that does not sit and roll over when told dies."

Police Spokesperson Sandy Shaw on department directive concerning domestic big dogs in the expanding threat of coyote terrorism

Domestic big dogs have the ability to ward off coyote attacks and now appear to have formed a cooperative, but wary, coexistence with the coyote colony which continues to terrorize the Smalltown community with rampages through restaurants and grocery stores, and by the kidnapping of cats, pet rabbits, and baby goats from the organic farms. Investigators believe that some domestic big dogs may have become the first line in the coyote's defense alert systems, and bark mayday warnings on the approaches of police and animal control officers. The coyote behaviors that domestic big dogs are adopting include the unabashed copulation with multiple partners, staying in the shadows when shifting locations, and refusing to obey any human command.

Raven and Salmon Woman, 1997, wood engraving on Japanese rice paper, Caroline Orr

those boys

Brynn McCall

when the boys who love to talk about
the ways they'd like to kill me
follow through for once in their lives,
i think we'll all learn a valuable lesson.

when they set the date and stencil
an expiration label across my stomach.
when they fuck me because why shouldn't
they, because that's what boys do, isn't it?

when they spill their saliva across my bruises
and drool over my painted skin. when they
finally leave me for dead, maybe then they
will realize that they should have listened
to their mothers.

when they look through what's left of me,
their fingers tracing a victory lap through
my lungs, when they read these words.
maybe then they'll understand that i
won't let them forget.

i will haunt them in 12 point times new roman.
i will bury myself in their collective conscience.
i will carve the words into their thick skulls.

i will take
my time

so that they feel each letter in the dips and ridges, the way
their hands slipped over my hips. feel it the way i did.

remind them
again and
again and
again that
dead and gone
are two different things.

Strategies for Outlasting Trumplandia

Gail Tremblay

Lately, each day I wake to a world where the sun seems
to rise over the eastern edge of this whirling planet,
that for millennia has made life possible, and I find
things in chaos. I watch beautiful beings becoming
extinct, forests burning, hurricanes destroying cities
and islands, water polluted by chemicals, oil,
and pesticides, polar ice melting, and coastal land
consumed by the sea, all while a man who, like me,
is seventy-three and old enough to know better
makes policies to harm the earth and the circle of things
that supports life, so he and his friends can become richer
by stripping the land of resources we should never use
if we are to sustain life for our grandchildren.
The older I get, the harder it becomes to understand greed,
the lack of grace, and insatiable desire to devour that makes
life bearable. I long to join with humans who every day thank
plants for transforming the carbon dioxide we exhale
and the light of the sun into the air we inhale and the food
we eat. How, living among a million natural miracles, can
any of us forget the delicate balancing act required to protect
the systems that make survival possible. Each one of us
needs to remember to give back to earth more than we take,
needs to whisper into the ear of our mysterious universe
and work ceaselessly to transform everyone's consciousness,
so we can celebrate together the shift to a new way of living
in harmony with this spinning orb we ride for thousands
of miles in a great spiral path through the vastness of a space
that even in our dreams, we have barely come to know.

The Way to Rainbow Mountain

Susan Deer Cloud

We saved the new year for finding our way
to Peru's Rainbow Mountain . . . January 9th,
my roving companion John's 69th birthday.
What better celebration than to seek that peak
of many colors concealed until four years ago,
climate change freeing the mountain's
thick poncho of ice. Ever since I first saw
a picture of Vinicunca, "seven colored mountain,"
I dreamed in its direction, my heart beating
to whatever awaited me in Incan Andes,

my soul frozen by the Ice Age of *loco*
Estados Unidos, by all the hate and crazy
and then the breast cancer that hit two Mays ago.
Sí, I dreamed of ascending to Rainbow Mountain
and maybe thaw to the woman of color
I once was. Chile, Argentina, Bolivia,
lastly Peru . . . wandering through desert,
altiplano, along ocean and over cloud-touching
passes down into pueblos and cities looking
bombed out except in the *turista* areas, and John

on his birthday driving us ever higher on road
winding to the base camp of his birthday gift,
steep drops from crumbling dirt edges
reminding us why people pray to whatever gods
or goddesses they hope exist. How close we came
to plummeting off cliffs where vultures keep watch.
Then we made it to the trail's beginning,

hail pelting down, mists like shape-shifters
swirling down a vast valley and snaking around
mountainsides. Two Indian guides led us up
on their horses, I in three layers of clothes
marveling at my guide seemingly gliding

in bare feet and sandals through hail stones,
patches of snow, puddles and streams. When
my mare, gentle and reddish brown, stopped,
the guide talked low and kind to her until we
continued on. John's horse, a stallion, whinnied
and pranced sometimes while I patted my mare
on her neck as softly as the guide spoke. We had to
disembark and trudge up the final vertical of path.
Despite the Diamox I took, I could barely
breathe, feared I might have to crawl to reach
that place I needed to go. John grabbed
my hand, gripped it tight and helped pull me
to the mountaintop facing Rainbow Mountain,
the *mirador*, for no human was allowed to step on
the mineral-made sacred rainbow. I knelt

by a stone wall, refuge from winds 16,000 feet high,
gazed as llamas, alpacas, vicuñas, and descendants
of Incas gazed in their ur-language of silence.
"O beautiful holy Rainbow Mountain, we greet you
and we thank you." And your *"De nada"*? Sun blazing
in to part the clouds, just as we met an indigenous family
celebrating their matriarch's 60th birthday, everyone
in traditional clothes, grandmother vivid like the gift
of the Mountain. "Happy Birthday, *Feliz Cumpleaños!*"
We smiled, talked, laughed, took photographs
of each other, of our two Americas coming together,
warming me back to a woman of color.

Indigenous Family Near Rainbow Mountain, Peru, January 2019, photograph, Susan Deer Cloud

#4

Brendan Connolly

in the west village we saw a man kneeling on the sidewalk, resting the weight of his upper body on his knuckles, his face almost touching the concrete

in front of him was a soft red mylar balloon with arabic words in black, anchored by a large pile of wrapped flowers and candles and photographs

the curbs of the sidewalk were lined with guardrails for pride week and people crouched against them, openly weeping in the sun

the sign on the building reminded me of something and i asked jackie if this was that place? where that riot happened? where the police came in and found people unwilling to take it anymore?

a man next to me said yes, this is where the gay rights movement started

we stood there in the sounds of traffic until the kneeling man stood up and walked away, past police officers with machineguns resting on their hips

There Will Be No Revolution

Sherry Rind

*With words from "The Revolution Has Ended"
by Adam Zagajewski*

All day, explosions rumble from the gun range.

Hunters honing their scopes for deer season
shatter paper silhouettes.

The leashed dogs and pedestrians march
up the street, inured to the crash and rumble
of transport trucks charging over the hills.

The wind has shifted, blowing off wildfire smoke

and bringing rain like pebbles on children
peeved as always, shouldering each other
at the bus stop, the mothers changed
from summer dresses to hoodies,

the victory of loading children each day into school
and packing them home safe.

They believe life has restrained
its tendency to darken with the season;
they stop listening to shrieking headlines.

No weapons can leave us victors or vanquished.
Down the street, an old woman sits in the café and cries.

Women's March, Seattle, 2017, photograph, Anna Bálint

Tender

Alice Derry

When the men drift away, the women begin
to speak their pain. How it keeps them awake nights,
that their doctors have prescribed this and that.
They don't complain—as if suffering rose
without cause and infused them,
sun soaking this pasture after rain,
releasing scent. Around these words,

we hover near Sara's tailgate set with snacks,
hands warming on tea cups. A pair of ravens tramps
through air like solid ground.
Eagles building a nest this spring
pushed them farther along the hogback.
They're still objecting.

Volunteers, we've only known each other
these summer weeks, but as we amble back to weed,
daylighting the newly-planted oak trees,
the women's talk, like allowance,
frees your story, Rachel—

losing your brother when he was eight,
losing your mother's listening then too.
Put my ashes there—she told you on your last visit,
pointing to the big cedar at the field's edge—
where his play was happiest—
although you steadied her across the field.

No matter how high you hold it,
the black salamander you've found,
green stripe down its two-inch back,
tries to jump from your hand
to its grasses and seeps, its familiar.

Something allows the hidden
to surface in us, a strike of light or the distraction
of small animals. Nothing contiguous, except
that we guard these moments against indifference,
and they pile in jumbled groups, waiting.

No child of the six in my family died,
but our mother left us as surely as yours,
her attention fixed elsewhere.

What a close family we have, our parents said,
annulling any words for absence.
The salamander tips from your hand into the grass.

I don't tell you that story when you turn for my answer
because all morning a woman's hand has been
in front of me—from last night's TV.
I tell you that a person can refuse to pass on depravity,
that tenderness, like the assertion
of sun into a field, takes substance
at that very moment—

tender, I say, how, her body still immobile from injury,
the woman reaches her hand
to cup the curled head of her toddler
clutching to her blanket—their eyes locked together.
How her tenderness to him never ends.
Two days ago acid was thrown on her.
I feel like a corpse, she says through the translator,
but for my child I have to keep on.

Love, Long Beach, California, 2011, photograph, Kathleen Gunton

When the Patriarchy Crumbles: Instructions for Men

T. Clear

Look both ways
before stepping out of your car
in the parking garage. Look both ways
when you return. Check that the pepper spray
is still in your pocket. Line up the trigger.

Clutch your keys like a weapon, the tips
extended between the fingers of your fist.
Did you remember to lock the car?
Check your back seat.
Lock it now, as soon as you get in.

Look both ways when you step onto the sidewalk.
Look behind you, look over your shoulder.
Be wary of shrubs, parked cars, cars that slow down,
unlit corners. Avoid alleys.
Listen for footsteps.

Walk with a purpose, walk with power.
Walk like you're seventeen again
and can outrun everyone in your class.
Even when you're old and haven't run for years—
walk like you can.

Don't forget any of this, don't
become lax, don't ever think you're immune.
Don't question what you've been taught,
don't think you're the only one that's ever done this
because women have done this forever

to stay safe, to remain alive.
It will become as routine
as brushing your teeth, so automatic
you won't even think of the keys
jutting from your fist like daggers.

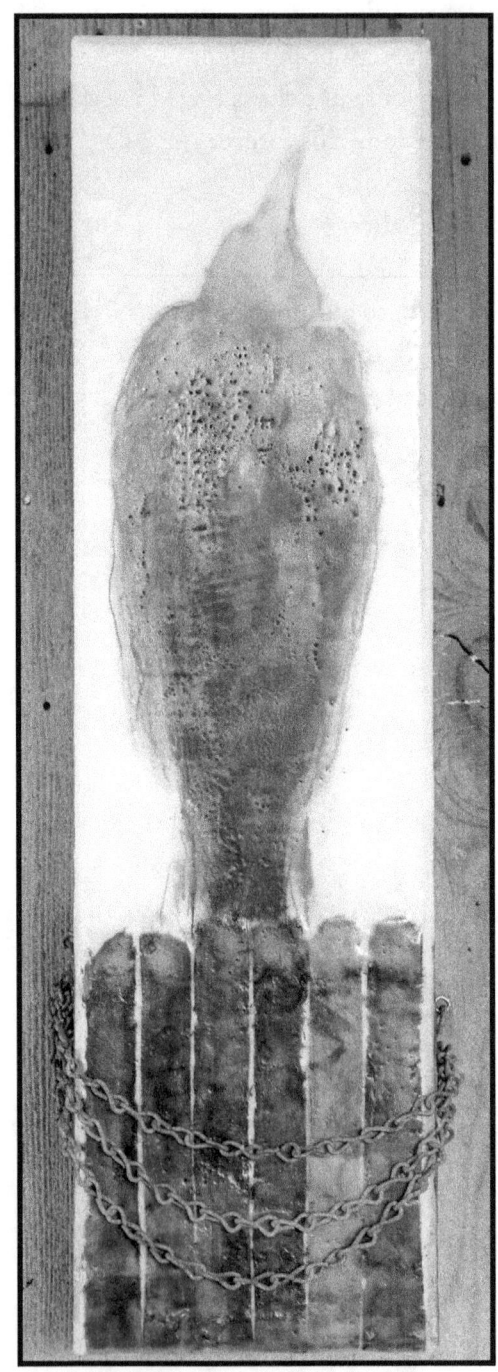

Illumination I, 2019, mixed media,
Catherine E. Skinner

The Word of the Day

Penina Ava Taesali

Every day is Earth Day

The word of the day could be dreadful or atrocious or lost for the roses root deeper for cleaner water to survive this August. Their petals pealing to blossom our eyes open so we may protect the wild green dawn   so we could stop   let the unexpected tributaries off 14th Street & Madras stream for the mallard and her drake with her seven ducklings paddling through narrow brook of the First Peoples lands mourning for Mother Earth

and the word of the day tomorrow? Let it not be brutality or money or rifle or my religion or yours   let it be leopard or rhinoceros or red abalone or blue whale or Yangtze River dolphin or let the word be African talking drum or Fijian canoe drum or Pilipino kulingtang or Appalachian dulcimer or ukulele or slack-key guitar or let it be trombone carried on the confident shoulders of a ten-year-old girl—let us think the where and how and why

we pick up and play and write and sing and dance so that the Honduran emerald hummingbird the leatherback sea turtle the mountain guerilla the tiger salamander the fender blue butterfly the honeybees the living coral reefs the breathing rainforests in Brazil in Guinea and there in the Sacramento Delta where river otters fish and breed let our word be bigger as in humility as in mountain water tree food sun moon stars for them for them for them

Rest As Resistance, 2019, ink on bristol, Noel Franklin

Rest As Resistance, 2019, ink on bristol, Noel Franklin

Why Whales Are Back in New York City

Rajiv Mohabir

After a century, humpbacks migrate
again to Queens. They left
due to sewage and white froth

banking the shores from polychlorinated-
biphenyl-dumping into the Hudson
and winnowing menhaden schools.

But now grace, dark bodies of song
return. Go to the seaside—

Hold your breath. Submerge.
A black fluke silhouetted
against the Manhattan skyline.

Now ICE beats doors
down on Liberty Avenue
to deport. I sit alone on orange

A train seats, mouth sparkling
from Singh's, no matter how
white supremacy gathers

at the sidewalks, flows down
the streets, we still beat our drums
wild. Watch their false-god statues

prostrate to black and brown hands.
They won't keep us out
though they send us back.

Our songs will pierce the dark
fathoms. Behold the miracle:

what was once lost
now leaps before you.

Families Belong Together, Protest at Sea-Tac Federal Detention Center, 2018, photograph, Anna Bálint

At Any Moment, There Could be a Swerve in a Different Direction

Ellery Akers

There was a moment when shooting egrets for feathers became wrong.
There was a moment when the Wilderness Act
changed the lives of billions of blades of grass.

I remember the moment when a river that used to catch fire
turned from flammable to swimmable.

A swerve smells astringent, like the wind off the sea;
it tastes red, the way Red Hot peppermints burn in your mouth;
it's heavy, the way the weight of letters are heavy,
arriving in sacks at the Senate;
it sounds like the click of knitting needles
as hundreds of thousands of women knit pink hats;
it looks like a coyote, crossing the freeway to go home.

Represent 98118 Project, Hillman City, Seattle, 2011, photograph, Anna Bálint

Ravens, drawing, Kree Arvanitas

VI

RAVEN NOTES

NOTES, PERMISSIONS AND PUBLICATION CREDITS

Edward Ahern: "An Apology for Hate." First published in *The Garfield Lake Review*, 2018. Copyright © by Edward Ahern. Reprinted by permission of the author.

Maryna Ajaja: Her photograph "Wat (temple) Lao Dhammacetiyaram, #5," appeared in *Raven Chronicles Magazine, Vol. 17, No. 1-2, A Sense of Place*, 2012, and, initially, in the "Represent 98118: a Self Portrait of a Culturally Rich Community" project, Seattle, October 2011. Ajaja has lived in Seattle's zip code 98118, "the most diverse zip code in America," since 2004.

Ellery Akers: "At any Moment, There Could be a Swerve in a Different Direction." First published online in *Rise Up Review*, www.riseupreview, spring 2019. Copyright © 2019 by Ellery Akers. Reprinted by permission of the author.

Carrie Albert: "Angela of Liberty." First published in *Up the Staircase Quarterly #38, The Audio/Visual Issue*, 2017. Copyright © 2017 by Carrie Albert. Reprinted by permission of the author.

Kathleen Alcalá: "El Paso del Norte." First published in *The Seattle Times Op-Eds*, https://www.seattletimes.com/author/kathleen-alcala/, August 16, 2019. Copyright © 2019 by Kathleen Alcalá. Reprinted by permission of the author.

Kathleen Alcalá: "What Tahlequah Said" first appeared online at https://uwpressblog.com/2019/03/25/tahlequah-orca-global-warming/. Copyright © 2019 by Kathleen Alcalá. Reprinted by permission of the author.

Eneida P. Alcalde: "Roulette." First published in *Parentheses Journal*, 2018. Copyright © 2018 by Eneida P. Alcalde. Reprinted by permission of the author.

Anna Bálint: "Journeys." First published, in a different version, in *Raven Chronicles Journal, Vol. 24, Home*, 2017. Copyright © 2017 by Anna Bálint. Reprinted by permission of the author.

Karen Bonaudi: "Exiles," from *Editing a Vapor Trail* (Pudding House Publications, 2010). Copyright © 2010 by Karen Bonaudi. Reprinted by permission of the author.

Andrew C. Brown: "Free the land for the refugees." First published in a different form as "Sonnet to Free Benefit" in *Militant Thistles*, 2015; then published in online mag *I am not a Silent Poet*, 2016. Copyright © 2015 by Andrew C. Brown. Reprinted by permission of the author.

Jericho Brown: "Bullet Points" and "Riddle," from *The Tradition* (Copper Canyon Press, 2019). Copyright © 2019 by Jericho Brown. Reprinted with the permission of The Permissions Company, LLC, on behalf of Copper Canyon Press, www.coppercanyonpress.org.

Janet Cannon: "flawed algorithm." First published in *Poetry South Issue # 9*, Mississippi University for Women, December 2017. Copyright © 2017 by Janet Cannon. Reprinted by permission of the author.

Janet Cannon: "really?" First published in *Overthrowing Capitalism Volume 2: Beyond Endless War, Racist Police, Sexist Elites*, Revolutionary Poets Brigade, Kallatumba Press, 2015. Copyright © 2015 by Janet Cannon. Reprinted by permission of the author.

Catalína Maríe Cantú: "Back Home." First published in *The Jack Straw Anthology, Vol. 21*, 2017. Copyright © 2017 by Catalína Maríe Cantú. Reprinted by permission of the author.

Sharon M. Carter: "Un Boton Rojo." Used by permission of the author.

Lucille Clifton: "slaveships," from *The Collected Poems of Lucille Clifton, 1965-2010* (BOA, Editions LTD, 2012). Copyright © 1996 by Lucille Clifton. Reprinted with the permission of The Permissions Company, LLC, on behalf of BOA Editions Ltd., www.boaeditions.org.

Keats Conley: "The God of Vaquitas." First published online in *The Ecological Citizen: A Peer-Reviewed Ecocentric Journal*, https://www.ecologicalcitizen.net/issue.php?i=Vol+3+No+1, July 2019. Copyright © 2019 by Keats Conley. Reprinted by permission of the author.

Beth Copeland: "Valentine's Day, 2018." First published online in *Rise Up Review*, www.riseupreview, Issue # 15, March 2019. Copyright © 2019 by Beth Copeland. Reprinted by permission of the author.

Risa Denenberg: "Yellow Star." First published in *Lavender Review: Lesbian Poetry & Art*, 2011. Copyright © 2011 by Risa Denenberg. Reprinted by permission of the author.

Alice Derry: "Tender," from *Hunger* (MoonPath Press, 2018). Copyright © 2018 by Alice Derry. Reprinted by permission of the author.

Anita Endrezze: "The Wall." First published in *Raven Chronicles Journal, Vol. 24, Home*, 2017. Reprinted in *Enigma* (Press 53, Silver Concho Poetry Series, 2019). Copyright © 2017 by Anita Endrezze. Reprinted by permission of the author.

Anita Endrezze: "The Daily News." First published in *Raven Chronicles Journal, Vol. 25, Balancing Acts*, 2018. Copyright © 2018 by Anita Endrezze. Reprinted by permission of the author.

Jeannine Hall Gailey: "Every Child is a Legend." First published online, in a slightly different version, in *Rise Up Review*, www.riseupreview, early 2019. Copyright © 2019 by Jeannine Hall Gailey. Reprinted by permission of the author.

Ray Gonzalez: "The Border Is a Line," from *Cutting The Wire, Photographs and Poetry from the US-Mexico Border* (University of New Mexico Press, 2018). Copyright © 2018 by Ray Gonzalez. Reprinted by permission of the author.

Anita Goveas: "Rocks on Wheels." First published online in *Hypnopomp, A Literary Magazine*, https://hypnopompblog.wordpress.com, April 20, 2019. Copyright © 2019 by Anita Goveas. Reprinted by permission of the author.

Edward Harkness: "Union Creek in Winter." First published online in *Terrain.org*, https://www.terrain.org/2017/poetry/letter-to-america-harkness/, January 17, 2017. Reprinted in *The Law of the Unforeseen* (Pleasure Boat Studio: A Literary Press, 2018). Copyright © 2017 by Edward Harkness. Reprinted by permission of the author.

Janis Butler Holm: "Memo To Barbie: Re the Breakup." First published in *Tessera* (Canada), 2005; reprinted in *This Poem Is Sponsored by...: Poems in the Face of Corporate Power* (Corporate Watch, 2007). Copyright © 2005 by Janis Butler Holm. Reprinted by permission of the author.

Tamam Kahn: "Nurse's Day." First published in *Antiphon Issue 19*, 2017. Copyright © 2017 by Tamam Kahn. Reprinted by permission of the author.

Ilya Kaminsky: "We Lived Happily During the War" and "In a Time of Peace," from *Deaf Republic* (Graywolf Press, 2018). Copyright © 2018 by Ilya Kaminsky. Reprinted with the permission of The Permissions Company, LLC, on behalf of Graywolf Press, Minneapolis, Minnesota, www.graywolfpress.org.

Mercedes Lawry: "At the Drop-In Center." First published in *Spillway, Poetry Magazine # 26*, June 2018. Copyright © 2018 by Mercedes Lawry. Reprinted by permission of the author.

Chip Livingston: "52 Hawks." First published in *Kestrel, A Journal of Literature and Art*, Issue 36, Fall 2016. Copyright © 2016 by Chip Livingston. Reprinted by permission of the author.

Claudia Castro Luna: "I see myself, and courage and hope, in the faces of the caravan." First published in *The Seattle Times Op-Eds*, https://www.seattletimes.com/opinion/i-see-myself-and-courage-and-hope-in-the-faces-of-the-caravan/, November 9, 2018. Copyright © 2018 by Claudia Castro Luna. Reprinted by permission of the author.

Michaela McGuire: "Anti-Enbridge Oil Campaign," Canada, 2012, digital print. Published in *Raven Chronicles Journal, Vol. 19, Race—Under Our Skin*, 2014, with an essay by Susan Noyes Platt, "Haida Gwaii, Tradition Resurrected." Copyright © 2012 by Michaela McGuire.

Lawrence Matsuda: "The Noble Thing," from *A Cold Wind from Idaho* (Black Lawrence Press, 2010). Copyright © 2010 by Lawrence Matsuda. Reprinted by permission of the author.

Lawrence Matsuda: "Just a Short Note to Say Something You Already Know." First appeared on *Raven Chronicles'* website, https://www.ravenchronicles.org/poets-against-hate-lawrence-matsuda/, 2016; reprinted in *Writers Resist: The Anthology 2018* (Running Wild Press, 2018). Copyright © 2016 by Lawrence Matsuda. Reprinted by permission of the author.

Tiffany Midge: "When White People Talk About their Country Being Stolen (I Throw Up in My Mouth a Little Bit)." First published in *Transmotion, Vol 4, No 1*, https://journals.kent.ac.uk/index.php/transmotion/article/view/501/1192, 2018. Copyright © 2018 by Tiffany Midge. Reprinted by permission of the author.

Tiffany Midge: "Attack of the Fifty-Foot (Lakota) Woman." First published in *Indian Country Today, Digital Indigenous News*, March 9, 2017. Also published in *Bury My Heart at Chuck E. Cheese's* (University of Nebraska Press, 2019). Copyright © 2017 by Tiffany Midge. Reprinted by permission of the author.

Dunya Mikhail, translated by Elizabeth Winslow: "The War Works Hard," from *The War Works Hard* (New Directions Publishing Corp, 2005). Copyright © 2005 by Dunya Mikhail. Reprinted by permission of New Directions Publishing Corp.

Rajiv Mohabir: "Why Whales Are Back in New York City." Originally published in Poem-a-Day, https://poets.org/poem/why-whales-are-back-new-york-city, October 16, 2017, by the Academy of American Poets. Copyright © 2017 by Rajiv Mohabir. Reprinted by permission of the author.

Jeanne Morel: "It's Happening Here, It's Happening There." First published, as "Push Me-Pull Me Gentrification," in *Raven Chronicles Journal, Vol. 19, Race—Under Our Skin*, 2014. Copyright © 2014 by Jeanne Morel. Reprinted by permission of the author.

Jed Myers: "Lost Crossing." First appeared online in *Poets Reading the News, Journalism in Verse*, December 16, 2018. Copyright © 2018 by Jed Myers. Reprinted by permission of the author.

Shankar Narayan: "*The Times* Asks Poets to Describe the Haze Over Seattle." First appeared online, https://wapoetlaureate.org/, on Washington State Poet Laureate Claudia Castro Luna's blog. Copyright © 2018-2019 by Shankar Narayan. Reprinted by permission of the author.

Susana Praver-Pérez: "Just Breathe." First published in *Still Point Arts Quarterly*, June 1, 2019. Also published in *Civil Liberties United: Diverse Voices from the San Francisco Bay Area* (Pease Press Books, 2019). Copyright © 2019 by Susana Praver-Pérez. Reprinted by permission of the author.

dan raphael: "Whose Hand Between my Head and the Door Frame." First published in *Calibanonline, Literary and Arts Magazine*, https://www.calibanonline.com, April, 2018. Copyright © 2018 by dan raphael. Reprinted by permission of the author.

Susan Rich: "For the first time I am afraid." First published in *3rd Wednesday, A Quarterly Journal of Literary & Visual Arts*, fall 2018 (not available online). Copyright © 2018 by Susan Rich. Reprinted by permission of the author.

Sherry Rind: "There Will Be No Revolution." To be published in *Between States of Matter* (The Poetry Box Select, 2020). Copyright © 2019 by Sherry Rind. Used by permission of the author.

Judith Roche: "The Continent of Plastic," from *All Fire All Water* (Black Heron Press, 2015). Copyright © 2015 by Judith Roche. Reprinted by permission of the publisher.

Morgan Russell: "Promised Land." First published in *Cabildo Quarterly Online*, https://cabildoquarterly.tumblr.com/post/182453583620/new-poetry-morgan-russell, January 31, 2019. Copyright © 2019 by Morgan Russell. Reprinted by permission of the author.

Nancy Scott: "A Kid Called Diamond." First published in a slightly different form in *One Stands Guard, One Sleeps* (Plain View Press, 2009). Copyright © 2009 and 2019 by Nancy Scott. Reprinted by permission of the author.

Dave Seter: "Jackhammer." First published in *Paterson Literary Review, Issue #43*, 2015-2016. Copyright © 2015-2016 by Dave Seter. Reprinted by permission of the author.

Danez Smith: "dear white america" and "dinosaurs in the hood," from *Don't Call Us Dead* (Graywolf Press, 2017). Copyright © 2017 by Danez Smith. Reprinted with the permission of The Permissions Company, LLC, on behalf of Graywolf Press, Minneapolis, Minnesota, www.graywolfpress.org.

Scott T. Starbuck: "What I Can't Say at My Neighbor's Party Looking at a Map of the United States." First appeared, in a different form, online in *Rivet: The Journal of Writing That Risks*, September 2, 2014, and in *Industrial Oz: Ecopoems* (Fomite Press, 2015). Copyright © 2014 by Scott T. Starbuck. Reprinted by permission of the author.

Stuart Stromin: "World Cup 2018." First published in *Conceit Magazine*, 2019. Copyright © 2019 by Stuart Stromin. Reprinted by permission of the author.

Tim White Eagle: "Sister Hellfire." Ancestor painting from his project AIDS Memorial Pathway, "There Comes A Time When You Have to Give Them Back," 2019.

Richard Widerkehr: "At The Grace Café." First published in *Arts & Letters, Issue 34,* Spring 2017. Copyright © 2017 by Richard Widerkehr. Reprinted by permission of the author.

Carletta Carrington Wilson: "letter to a laundress," in the form of a poem and sculpture, was part of the exhibit, *Open Sesame! The Magic of Artist's Books Revealed*, March 1-June 9, 2019, Bainbridge Island Museum of Art. Co-Curator Catherine Alice Michaelis wrote: "Carletta C. Wilson honors the historically invisible black women laundresses, descendants of slaves, in *Letter to a Laundress,* made from photographs sewn onto textile pieces pinned on a laundry line." Copyright © 2019 by Carletta Carrington Wilson. Reprinted by permission of the author.

Tanaya Winder: "Love Lessons in a Time of Settler Colonialism." First published in *Poetry Magazine*, June 2018. Copyright © 2018 by Tanaya Winder. Reprinted by permission of the author.

Carolyne Wright: "Ghazal for Emilie Parker." First published in *North American Review, Vol. 299, No. 2,* Spring 2014. Awarded the 2014 James Hearst Poetry Prize (Third Place). Reprinted in *This Dream the World: New & Selected Poems* (Lost Horse Press, 2017). Copyright © 2014 by Carolyne Wright. Reprinted by permission of the author.

Elaine Zimmerman: "Echo of Stone." First published in *Connecticut (CT) River Review*, 2016. Recipient of CT 2016 Poetry Award. Copyright © 2016 by Elaine Zimmerman Reprinted by permission of the author. 📖

BIOGRAPHICAL NOTES
Artists/Illustrators

Niel Abston, born in Jackson, Mississippi, is a college student currently majoring in studio arts. She often experiments with mediums such as charcoal, oil, and acrylic paint. She strives to represent the lives and experiences of women of color, especially black women in her own community and beyond, through the use of her art. Through her endeavors, she hopes to inspire other women of color who are artists to continue to create and to make themselves known. Her piece in this anthology, *You Can't Take This From Me* (2019), which is also a self-portrait, shines a light on the realities of racism and how, for centuries, black people are constantly stripped of their culture. Although the connotation of this is dark, the piece brings forth a form of hope claiming that no matter how much trauma is inflicted upon us, we can never lose our strong African, ancestral, and cultural connection.

Maryna Ajaja is a writer and a film programmer for the Seattle International Film Festival and specializes in Eastern, Central European, and Russian films. Ajaja has lived in Seattle's zip code 98118, the most diverse zip code in America, since 2004. In 2011, she was introduced to the "Represent 98118: a Self Portrait of a Culturally Rich Community" project by American Book Award-winning author Nancy Rawles, also a resident of 98118. The idea behind the project was to record what that diversity looks like. They discovered that collecting photos of faces and scenes from their neighborhood changed the way they look at people. Whether the journey to 98118 was arduous, accidental, intentional or circumstantial, the result made our zip code a rich one. The project coincided with the Laotian celebration of Boun That Laung, so Ajaja accompanied her neighbor, Bounpone Keolouangkhoth, a Laotian American, to her local wat (temple), Wat Lao Dhammacetiyaram, located on Kenyon Street in South Seattle. Boun That Laung is a holiday when people of the community help each other plan and raise needed funds and items for their local temples. Ajaja was warmly welcomed, generously allowed access to photograph, and fed a traditional meal.

Carrie Albert is a multifaceted artist and poet who lives in Seattle. Her drawings, collage and poems are featured at Four Corners Art, and her visual art and poems have been published and/or featured in many diverse journals, such as *cahoodaloodaling*, *Grey Sparrow*, *Foliate Oak*, *Earth's Daughters*, *Up the Staircase Quarterly*, and *Gargoyle*. More of her work can be viewed at Penhead Press online, where she is a Poet-Artist in Residence.

Seattle-based artist **Alfredo Arreguín** has exhibited his work internationally, recently at the Museo de Cadiz in Spain (2015). He has exhibited solo shows at Linda Hodges Gallery since 2001. In 1980, he received a fellowship from the National Endowment for the Arts. In 1988, Arreguín won the commission to design the poster for the Centennial Celebration of the State of Washington (the image was his painting *Washingtonia*); that same year he was invited to design the White House Easter Egg. Perhaps the climatic moment of his success came in 1994, when the Smithsonian Institution acquired his triptych, *Sueño (Dream: Eve Before Adam)*, for inclusion in the collection of the National Museum of American Art. Arreguín's work is now in the permanent collections of two Smithsonian Museums: The National Museum of American Art and the National Portrait Gallery. http://www.alfredoarreguin.com.

Kree Arvanitas is a mixed-media artist based in Seattle, with cultural roots in Greece and Western Europe (Netherlands). An autodidact, she has been illustrating or drawing since childhood. Currently she is focusing on acrylic, altered photos, mixed-media, and collage as her "weapons of choice" under the name RebelDog Studio. She co-curated the exhibit *Artful Henna* in 2010 (with artist Jeanie Lewis), which featured henna-inspired art on and off the human body from internationally acclaimed body artists. She also curated *Tesseract: 4 Artists, 4 Dimensions* in 2015, featuring three other artists (Matthew Potter, Lesley Rialto, and Jeanie Lewis). Kree is Art Director for the online magazine, *Enzyme Arts Magazine* (https://www.facebook.com/enzymemag/), and is a member of CoCA Seattle (Center On Contemporary Art) and A/NT Gallery in Seattle, Washington.

Jasmine Iona Brown: "My paintings, photography and illustrations usually focus on the face. I paint portraits, masks and icons or take photographs that highlight individual beings. I use facial expressions and words that convey messages, illustrate a stream of thought, or give voice to the private thoughts of marginalized individuals. I incorporate poetry, symbols, or landscapes that represent the persona of the models I have encountered during my travels around the world. I am influenced by the sacred art of several world religions. African masks, Voodoo textiles, Buddhist thangkas, Native American carvings, as well as Russian and Ethiopian icons, have ceremonial significance and spiritual potency that I strive to embody in my work. I currently live in Tacoma, Washington. I earned my BFA. from Howard University and MA from UCLA. My work is in the collections of the Wing Luke Museum, the municipal collections of both Seattle and Tacoma, and the Trayvon Martin Foundation." https://jasmineiona.artstation.com/projects/RzdND."

Jane Caminos is a narrative painter of women. Born in Brooklyn, raised in Jersey, with a 1969 BFA in illustration from RISD, Jane switched her focus from illustration to narrative painting in the mid-70s when she began a series of paintings featuring unsung women. The series grew and she built her artistic reputation by telling their stories. In 2012, Jane saw a PBS documentary about the horrific gang rape in Dehli, India of twenty-three-year-old Jyoti Singh that resulted in her death. Enraged and saddened, Jane. vowed to create art that explored and helped raise awareness of violence against women and girls across all cultures. This was the beginning of a series of paintings: *On Women Bound*. Jane's piece in this anthology, *FollowU*, is one of the twenty-four paintings currently in the series. The work is ongoing.

Sharon M. Carter is a poet, visual artist, and retired physician. Originally from the UK, she has lived in the Pacific Northwest for many years. Her work has been published online and in many small presses. A manuscript entitled "Quiver" is currently with an editor for consideration.

In February 2020, she will be one of four poets to take over running the Northwinds Reading series in Port Townsend, Washington.

Manit Chaotragoongit was born September 30, 1983, in Bangkok, Thailand, where he still lives. He has received many photography awards from the Globalhunt Foundation and the Berggruen Institute, in India and the U.S. Photography is a passion for him. Streets and alleys are the places he journeys to for inspiration.

Daniel J. Combs hails from Waterford, New York. He attended Hope College in Holland, Michigan, earning a BA in English and Communication. His passion, which has developed over the years, is photography. After several years living in Vermont, Seattle, Washington, and New York City, he is back in western Michigan. Recently, Daniel has exhibited his work at the following venues: ArtPrize 2018, the Muskegon Museum of Art, Frederick Meijer Garden, The Crooked Tree Gallery in Petoskey, Michigan, and at LowellArts 33rd Annual Competition, February 23-March 30, 2019. www.danielcombsphotography.com.

Lisa Dailey is a Montana native and third-generation photographer living in the Pacific Northwest. Writer by day and reader by night, she loves creating—writing, photography, silversmithing, and cooking. Most recently, her photographs were featured in the inaugural publication of *Montana Mouthful*, an online literary journal, and on the cover of *True Stories, The Narrative Project Volume 1*. Along with her husband and two teenage sons, Lisa spent seven months traveling around the world, exploring thirteen countries and more than eighty locations. Seeing so much of the world rendered her a travel addict and photography junkie. The world serves as the backdrop for her memoir, "Square Up," which tells the story of her journey through grief into peace. http://lisa-dailey.com.

Jay Dearien is a reformed Tokyoite, poetaster, social critic, board game inventor, certified massage therapist, Japanese permanent resident, science groupie, terpa conjurer, trekkie, wannabe pseudo-intellectual, world traveler, recovering ne'er-do-well, comic/manga artist, pretty kosher for a goy boy, freedom-liker, stand-up comedian, and a Carnegie Mellon/École Polytechnique Fédérale de Lausanne (BS-EE) and University of Idaho (MA-Linguistics) grad.

Sarah Deckro is a writer, teacher, and visual artist with a passion for stories. She received a bachelor's degree in history from Connecticut College and has studied storytelling in a variety of venues. Sarah is a preschool teacher in Boston, Massachusetts, where she works to support the development of self-esteem and empathy in young children. Sarah's photographs and poetry have appeared in a number of publications including *The Esthetic Apostle, Camas Magazine, Kaaterskill Basin Literary Journal, Curating Alexandria*, and the anthologies *An Outbreak of Peace* (Arachne Press Limited, 2018) and *The Dreamers Anthology* (Social Justice Anthologies, (publication affiliate of Beautiful Cadaver Project Pittsburgh, 2019).

Andrew Drawbaugh has been a photographer of one kind or another in Seattle (and elsewhere) for more than twenty years. He studied at The Photography Center Northwest and is a daily shooter who just can't help himself. Film to digital, darkroom to Photoshop, the method makes the madness confined in the frame. Press the shutter.

Noel Franklin is a cartoonist best known for her short-form comics journalism and heavy-hitting auto-bio work. Noel's first published work was *Memorex Masochism*, which ran in *The Stranger* newspaper on June 29, 2014, but her stories soon exploded onto the pages of international anthologies such as *Outre* (Norway), *Skulptura* (Serbia), *The Strumpet* (UK), and *Not My Small Diary* (United States). Her comics have been awarded grants from Seattle's major arts funders, and a 2017 Cartoonist Northwest Toonie Award. She recently completed work that you can see online (*Hollow Kingdom*—debut novel by Kira Jane Buxton—Trailer: https://www.youtube.com/watch?time_continue=28&v=Drmb-0e78oc&feature=emb_title), currently in print (*Drawing Power*, Diane Noomin's brilliantly edited anthology of women cartoonists' stories of surviving sexual aggression) and soon-to-be-in-print (*Not My Small Diary*). She is actively working on a graphic novel about suicide and addiction, and recently moved back to Seattle from Arizona. More will be revealed. http://ww.noelfranklinart.com/Home.html.

Tatiana Garmendia was born in Cuba at the height of the Cold War, and moved to the U.S.A. as a young girl. She teaches painting and drawing at Seattle Central College. Garmendia has exhibited her work at The Bronx Museum of Arts, Art In General, and Stux Gallery in New York. Among the European galleries where Garmendia has shown are The Milan Art Center in Italy, Castfield Gallery in England, and the Galeria Riesa Efau in Germany. Her works are in public collections in New York, Miami, Illinois, California, Ohio, and the Dominican Republic. The artist is the recipient of a Washington State Artist Fellowship, a Pollock-Krasner Grant, and a CityArtists Project Grant (Seattle Arts Commission). The drawing here is from the *Epic Ink Series* that explore our wars, bi-partisan skirmishes, and social conflicts on the abstract stage of the mylar and ink. Secret titles encased in parenthesis function like the comments the audience members whisper to each other during the gruesome plays. http://tatianagarmendia.com.

Jan Gosnell received his BFA from the University of Texas and his MFA from the University of Arkansas. His professional background includes that of picture painter, university art instructor, gallery owner, commercial art director, movie sketch artist, editorial cartoonist, and author/illustrator. He has had numerous solo exhibitions and shown competitively in such regional exhibitions as *The Mid-South* in Memphis and *The Delta* in Little Rock. At present, Jan makes his home in Fayetteville, Arkansas, where he continues to pursue his life as a working artist. https://www.fenixfayettevilleart.com/jan-gosnell.

Lindsey Morrison Grant is an award-winning poet, screenwriter, journalist, photographer, ceramic and mixed-media artist from Portland, Oregon. She is a Storyteller and, as such, adheres to the truth ascribed to Charles Dickens' illustrator, Fred R. Barnard, who's quoted as saying, "A picture is worth ten thousand words." Her works, therefore, reflect the qualities of a good story. They're colorful, textured, and actively engage the imagination of those who choose to engage with them. Although her works may use traditional canvas/paint, Grant chooses to incorporate other sensory stimuli in the form of auditory augmentation and illumination. Additionally, atypical "canvases" have included a vintage fruit crate, an ironing board, masks, and even felt hats.

Kathleen Gunton is a poet/photographer who believes one art feeds another. She is completing, "If In This Sleep," her second collection of poems with photos. In addition to appearances in *Raven Chronicles Magazine*, her images appear on the cover of *Arts & Letters*, *Thema*, *Flint Hills Review*, and *The Potomac Review*—to name a few. Regarding her photo *Love* in this book: "Only love fills the empty spaces caused by evil"—Pope Francis.

Ethar Hamid is an aspiring writer and artist from Khartoum, Sudan. She writes poetry and essays, and creates illustrations and comics. Some themes she gravitates towards in her writing are spirituality (in its many definitions and manifestations), adversity (like poverty and illness), and breaking away from tradition—questioning the order of things. The themes she uses in her visual art are mainly social and cultural issues, like advocacy for certain causes, and societal resistance towards certain people or ideas, as well as personal issues, like isolation and family problems. Ethar has lived in Sudan (from birth to age two), Malaysia, the United States, the United Arab Emirates, and Qatar, though she has spent the majority of her life in northern Virginia. She studied English and creative writing in college. She blogs at https://findingapeacefulplace.wordpress.com/about/.

Danielle Hark is a writer and artist who lives with PTSD and bipolar disorder. She is the founder of the non-profit Broken Light Collective that empowers people with mental health challenges using photography. Danielle lives and creates in New Jersey with her husband, two sassy young daughters, two and a half ukuleles, a Samoyed pup, a Scottish Fold cat, and a typewriter named Cori Blue. www.daniellehark.com; IG/twitter: @daniellehark.

Hank Hobby was born in Charlotte, North Carolina. He has two children's picture books, *Where You Belong* (MacLaren-Cochrane Publishing) and *Paper Wings* (Native Ink Press) that are in development and will be released in the coming months. He is also the creator and writer of the comic book series *Ruwans* (Keenspot Entertainment). "My work is inspired by the complex world that surrounds me and the inescapable experience of the human condition. I find art serves as an organic remedy for the illusory feeling of powerlessness I tend to encounter. Although each project varies, they're all derived from a source of hope for a better future I so relentlessly dream of."

Doug Johnson, the founding editor of Cave Moon Press, has appeared in multiple journals with his art and poetry. He also has a focus on music and collaboration, helping to organize a benefit for AIDS orphans, "Keys around the World." He published an anthology of Kenyan folk tunes arranged for band with Dr. David Akombo of Jackson State University. Please reach out to collaborate at cavemoonpress@gmail.com.

Tom Kiefer: Born in Wichita, Kansas, fine art photographer Kiefer was raised primarily in the Seattle area and worked in Los Angeles as a graphic designer. Kiefer moved to Ajo, Arizona, in Dec-ember 2001 to fully develop and concentrate his efforts in studying and photographing the urban and rural landscape and the related cultural infrastructure. Kiefer's first project, *Journey West Exhibit* (2001-2011), was created during his process of discovering and documenting the natural and man-made landscape between towns and cities in his adopted state of Arizona. Kiefer's current project, *El Sueño Americano—The American Dream* (2007-present), features the personal effects and belongings of people apprehended in the desert by U.S. Border Patrol agents that were subsequently seized, surrendered, or forfeited as they were processed at a U.S. Customs and Border Patrol facility in southern Arizona. These personal effects and belongings represented their choice of what was important for them to bring as they crossed the border to either start or continue their life in the U.S. http://www.tomkiefer.com.

Sarah E. N. Kohrs is an artist and writer, whose poetry has been published in *Adelaide Literary Magazine, Colere, Crosswinds Poetry Journal, From the Depths, Gone Lawn, Horn & Ivory, Poetry From The Valley Of Virginia, Rattle, Scintilla*; her photography in *Blueline Literary Magazine, Columbia College Literary Review, Esthetic Apostle*, and 3*Elements*. She has a BA in Classical Languages and Archaeology from The College of Wooster in Ohio, as well as a Virginia state teaching licensure endorsed in Latin and Visual Arts. Life experiences that bolster her artistic pursuits include home schooling three young sons, creating pottery for local Empty Bowl soup suppers, and serving in other altruistic roles, such as managing editor of *The Sow's Ear Poetry Review*, director of The Corhaven Graveyard (a preserved burial ground for African Americans enslaved on an antebellum plantation in Virginia), and helping with Nasaruni Academy (a non-profit Maasai girls school in Kenya). http://senkohrs.com.

Deborah Faye Lawrence: "I was raised by American radicals in the 1950s-70s, and my mother brought home the first *Ms. Magazine* in 1972. Since then, as a collagist I have refrained from cutting up that publication, but I have eviscerated the American flag, gun catalogs, the US Constitution, *the Bible, Artforum, Vogue*, and other documents with which I clash. My artwork has been honored by awards from Creative Capital Foundation, Pollock-Krasner Foundation, Puffin Foundation, Adolph Gottlieb Foundation, Washington State Arts Council, WESTAF, National Endowment for the Arts, Seattle Office of Arts & Cultural Affairs, and Los Angeles Department of Cultural Affairs. A native of California, I earned a MFA degree from Claremont Graduate University, and have lived with my husband in Seattle since 1993. See more of my artwork at http://www.deedeeworks.com/."

Russell Lee: (1903-1986) His image with Carletta Carrington Wilson's poem, "letter to a laundress," was titled, "Wife of FSA client former sharecropper, washing on back porch of old home on Southeast Missouri farms, May 1938." Lee first worked as a chemist but became a painter. His process included making photographs before painting and, soon, he abandoned painting for the creation of photographs of friends, family, and the public. He joined the FSA (Farm Security Administration project) in 1936. The FSA was created in 1935 as part of the

New Deal as an effort to combat poverty in rural America during the Depression. The FSA is noted for its photograph program, 1935-1941, that focused on the challenges of rural poverty.

Mario Loprete: From online *PIF Magazine,* 2018: "artist Mario Loprete has found a unique niche. Marrying his love of hip-hop iconography with the enduring medium of concrete, he has cultivated a portfolio of truly distinctive pieces. He's worked with all manner of tools and canvases, but says he has found his voice in the form of concrete canvas." He lives in Catanzaro, Italy. "The new series of works on concrete—it's the one that is giving me more personal and professional satisfactions. The reinforced cement, the concrete, was created two thousand years ago by the Romans. It has a millenary story, made of amphitheaters, bridges and roads that have conquered the ancient and modern world. Now it's a synonym of modernity. Everywhere you go and you find a concrete wall, there's the modern man in there. From Sidney to Vancouver, from Oslo to Pretoria, the reinforced cement is present. For my Concrete Sculptures I use my personal clothing., plaster, resin and cement. My memory, my DNA, my memories, remain concreted inside, transforming the person that looks at the artworks, [making them] a type of post-modern archeologist that studies my work as if they were urban artefacts."

Meredith Bricken Mills: "I am 'retired' in West Seattle after careers in teaching, Virtual Reality development, and hospice nursing. Now I'm focused on learning how to speak with images. I've been experimenting with digital image manipulation since 1990, when Photoshop was first released, and I began to explore what I think of as Digital Fusion, in which many layers of photographic and hand-drawn elements are filtered and merged. The image 'Rise and Shine' was inspired by our Democrat Congresswomen at the State of Union Address on February 5, 2019. When these new members of the House were formally welcomed, they broke into a spontaneous victory dance—it brought me great joy watching these diverse women (first Native American, Black, Black/Indian, Latina, etc.), dressed in suffragette white, standing and celebrating together directly in the face of misogyny and ethnic prejudice. My recent work can be seen in three galleries at the online Museum of Computer Art (MOCA), most recently at http://moca.virtual.museum/autogallery2019/autogallery_mills/index.asp."

Nuansi is a Seattle doodler and mural artist whose visual stories speak for her. She loves travel, and has been deeply influenced by the artistic traditions, plants, and animals of Thailand, where she grew up. Nuansi enjoys using pen and colored pencils to tell her stories. She hopes her work will inspire others to recognize their own beauty. Her drawings share her joy in nature, its infinite diversity and respect for each unique life. Nuansi also enjoys learning the Southern Lushootseed language and carving. She prepares each year for the Tribal Canoe Journey with her Canoe Family, Carvers' Camp. She is a puller in their Umiak [open skin boat] named *sqəlǝč*—"octopus" in Southern Lushootseed.

Caroline Orr has tribal affiliations with the Confederated Tribes of the Colville Reservation, Washington State, and the Lillooet, Okanagan and Arrow Lakes Bands, British Columbia, Canada. She has a BA (Art) and a BFA (Painting) from the University of Washington. Her work has been exhibited in San Francisco, Hood River, Oregon, and the Burke Museum, Seattle. She has worked in oils, glass, and printmaking—pulling monoprints from paintings on plexiglass. "Growing up on the reservation, the immense landscape and its creatures formed my imagination, fed by the stories of my ancestors. For fifty years, the spirits of native myths have haunted my artistic efforts: the charismatic and crafty Coyote, the mystical magnetism of Merman, the sustaining return of Salmon Woman, the comforting refuge of Caribou, the empowering flight of Man with the Eagles. Blue Jay and Magpie together form the sky, while Snake carries the daily light. I've tried to capture these fleeting images in paint, print, glass, sculpture, and photography. *Raven and Salmon Woman* was created as part of an exhibit at Daybreak Star Gallery in Seattle, in 1997. It is a wood engraving printed on Japanese rice paper."

J. Ray Paradiso: A confessed outsider, Chicago's Paradiso is a recovering academic in the process of refreshing himself as an experiMENTAL writer and street photographer. His work has appeared in dozens of publications, both online and in print. Equipped with cRaZy quilt graduate degrees in both Business Administration and Philosophy, he labors to fill temporal-spatial, psycho-social holes and, on good days, to enjoy the flow. All of his work is dedicated to his true love, sweet muse and body guard: Suzi Skoski Wosker Doski.

Willie Pugh is a long time Seattle photographer and an Alabama native, who attended an all black high school in Selma, Alabama, during the height of the Civil Rights Movement. At age fifteen he took part in the Selma to Montgomery Marches. It was during this period that he first became interested in photography as a way of recording and remembering the world in which he lived. To him photography is more than seeing. It is paying attention, remembering, and sharing. His compositions capture moments from everyday life, found objects, landscapes, and people being themselves. His works have appeared in such diverse places as *Ebony Magazine*, *Beacon Hill Times* and *Raven Chronicles Magazine*.

Ana Rodriguez is a graphic artist and illustrator exploring ideas through line work and water techniques. It all started as a way to speak her mind, and she found analog work refreshing after years working in the television industry, exclusively in digital mediums. Her main interest is in the conceptualization of raw emotion and exploring the environment (both physical and relational)—talking about the journey that we seem to be tuned into as the world grows closer together. Born in Bogota, Colombia, 'Nita came to the states in 1996, and graduated in Graphic Design from the Art Institute of Fort Lauderdale. She has spent the length of her career mainly as a broadcast designer and more recently creating large scale artworks for participatory painting events and murals.

Tonya Russell is a poet and photographer of color. She has a BS degree in Sociology from Texas Woman's University in Denton, Texas. Her work has been published in numerous literary journals.

Mona Nicole Sfeir is poet and visual artist and holds an MFA from the California College of Arts, an MA in Children's Literature and Illustration from San Jose State University, and a

BA from the University of Colorado, Boulder. On her work, *Building Babel*, a 24" x 24" acrylic collage on canvas: "Today over 6,500 languages are spoken on earth, each language embodying its own unique cultural history. Geneticists have also discovered that we all carry the genes of a common ancestor. This painting carries in it the hope that we can learn to appreciate our differences, as our numerous cultures are linked through historical exchanges, while honoring and respecting the fact that we are all genetically related."

Dave Sims was born in Pittsburgh, earned his MFA in Fairbanks, Alaska, and spent over thirty years teaching writing and literature to thousands of diverse students in places ranging from the Arctic Slope to the bayous of Louisiana. Since emerging from the trenches of academe, he now dwells and creates in the mountains of central Pennsylvania. A multi-genre artist, his words and images appear on the covers and inside the pages of *The Raw Art Review, Talking Writing, Freezeray, Burningword, The Nashville Review, Nunum* and *Arkana*, with more comics and paintings forthcoming in *Silver Needle, RiversEdge,* and *Stonecoast Review*. He can be reached at tincansims@gmail.com.

Catherine Eaton Skinner divides her time between studios in Seattle and Santa Fe, working full-time as a multidisciplinary artist: painting, encaustic, printmaking and photography. Her sculptures, cast glass and bronze, depict the transformation between man and raven/hawk. Skinner's work centers on a balance of opposites, exploring concepts in many cultures, as well as investigating how methods of numerical systems and patterning have been used to construct an order to our often unstable and ever delicate world. *108*, Skinner's latest book, was published by Radius Books, Santa Fe, 2017. *Unleashed* was published in 2008 by the University of Washington Press, in conjunction with Woodland Park Zoo, Seattle. Skinner's work is included in numerous poetry anthologies, often using her poetry for statements for over thirty-six solo exhibitions in her fifty-year professional art career.

Kali Spitzer is Kaska Dena from Daylu (Lower Post, British Columbia) on her father's side and Jewish from Transylvania, Romania, on her mother's side. She is from the Yukon and grew up on the West Coast of British Columbia in Canada on unceded Coast Salish Territory. At the age of twenty, Kali moved back north to spend time with her Elders, and to learn how to hunt, fish, trap, tan moose and caribou hides, and bead. Kali documents these practices with a sense of urgency, highlighting their vital cultural significance. She is a trans-disciplinary artist who mainly works with film—35mm, 120 and wet plate collodion process using an 8 x 10 camera. Her work includes portraits, figure studies, and photographs of her people, ceremonies, and culture, and has been exhibited and recognized internationally. Spitzer recently received a Reveal Indigenous Art Award from the Hnatyshyn Foundation in Canada, and was featured in *National Geographic* and *Photo Life* magazines in 2018.

Nico Vassilakis is the author of several books of poetry. He co-edited *The Last Vispo Anthology: Visual Poetry 1998-2008* (Fantagraphics Books, 2012) with Crag Hill. He was also a founder of Seattle's long-running Subtext reading series. His text-based work concerns the visual phenomenology of experiencing text, and his visual work pushes the outer limits of text's possibility within words. Nico's website is Staring Poetics: https://staringpoetics.weebly.com/. He lives in New York City.

Votan (Cover artist), a Los Angeles native who is of Maya and Nahua roots, blends the knowledge of his ancestry, graphic design, street art, and awareness of the issues facing native peoples today. He expresses his voice primarily on city streets in the form of large-scale murals and street art, to create artworks which include blending contemporary art techniques with old Mayan symbology and Native American imagery. He is also the owner and founder of NSRGNTS, a collective and brand that uses indigenous oral tradition, resistance and Native accomplishments to add strength to indigenous resilience. He's had the opportunity to do artist in residences in Germany, Ecuador, United Arab Emirates, and throughout the U.S. His murals of resistance have created dialogue and broadened the conversations of indigenous peoples right to exist, thrive, and practice self-determination. He is featured in the permanent exhibition at the Natural History Museum of Los Angeles as a contributor to shaping L.A.'s art history. He has also been awarded (with NSRGNTS) a proclamation by the city of Duluth, Minnesota. The proclamation honors the mural painted on the American Indian Community Housing Organization's (AICHO) building. This four story mural has positively and profoundly affected the Native community.

Timothy White Eagle is a Native American artist based in Seattle. He earned a BFA from the University of Utah. He crafts objects, photographs, performances and spaces, and his art and performances have been presented on three continents. Timothy currently works as an artistic director with MacArthur Genius Taylor Mac on his Pulitzer Prize finalist project, "A 24-Decade History of Popular Music." In 2014, his book, *The Return*, with collaborator Adrain Chesser, was published by Daylight Books. In 2019 he received two major commissions to create public work. In 2020, Timothy will premiere his performance, "The Violet Symphony," at On the Boards in Seattle, and at LaMama in New York City.

Matika Wilbur: (Swinomish and Tulalip) is one of the nation's leading photographers, based in the Pacific Northwest. She earned her BFA from Brooks Institute of Photography where she double majored in Advertising and Digital Imaging. Her most recent endeavor, *Project 562*, has brought Matika to over 500 tribal nations dispersed throughout all fifty U.S. states where she has taken thousands of portraits, and collected hundreds of contemporary narratives from the breadth of Indian Country all in the pursuit of one goal: *To Change The Way We See Native America*. As a former educator, she realized that the representation of Native peoples in media and in learning materials as "leathered and feathered" dying peoples deeply affected the identity and perceived potential of her students. Thus began *Project 562*, the mission of which is to photograph and collect stories of Native Americans from each federally-recognized tribe in the United States. Through her lens, we are able to see the vibrancy and diversity of

Indian Country and, in seeing, we challenge stereotypical representations and begin shifting consciousness about contemporary Native America.

Christopher Woods is a writer, teacher and photographer who lives in Chappell Hill, Texas. His published works include a novel, *The Dream Patch*, a prose collection, *Under a Riverbed Sky*, and a book of stage monologues for actors, *Heart Speak*. His short fiction has appeared in many journals, including *The Southern Review*, *New Orleans Review* and *Glimmer Train*. His photography prompt book for writers and journal keepers, *From Vision To Text*, is forthcoming from Propertius Press. He conducts private creative writing workshops in Houston. His photography can be seen in his gallery http://christopherwoods.zenfolio.com/.

Angel Ybarra has been clean and sober for many years now. A vital part of her recovery was discovering herself as an artist, something that made her feel alive and made peace with the traumas of her past. But she hasn't forgotten what it's like to struggle with mental illness and addiction while living on the streets. She enjoys taking photos and writing stories that help build compassion and awareness for those still suffering and in need of help. The photograph included in this anthology is part of an ongoing project titled "The Homeless, Addicted, and the Mentally Ill." A longtime member of Safe Place Writing Circle at Seattle's Recovery Café, Angel is a featured writer in the anthology *Words From the Café*. She works at Catholic Community Services, where she also enjoys giving back to others in recovery.

Lawrence Paul Yuxweluptun: Born in Kamloops, British Columbia in 1957, Yuxweluptun grew up in Vancouver, British Columbia. His father belongs to the Cowichan Tribes, a Coast Salish First Nation, and his mother is Syilx, part of the Okanagan Nation Alliance. Both of his parents were politically active. His father was a member of the North American Native Brotherhood, and a founder of the Union of British Columbia Indian Chiefs, while his mother led the Indian Homemakers Association of British Columbia. His name means "man of many masks," and was given to him in his adolescence by the Sxwaixwe Society. Yuxweluptun attended the Emily Carr Institute of Art and Design in the late 1970s and early 1980s, and graduated in 1983 with an honours degree in painting. Yuxweluptun works primarily in painting but has also created multimedia and sculptural works. Many of his pieces show elements of Surrealism, including similarities to the melting objects in Salvador Dali's paintings. His work incorporates traditional elements from Northwest First Nations art, as well as evocations of the Canadian landscape painting tradition, such as the Group of Seven. 📖

BIOGRAPHICAL NOTES
Writers

Ed Ahern (p.141) resumed writing after fort- odd years in foreign intelligence and international sales. He's had over two hundred and fifty stories and poems published so far, and four books. Ed works the other side of writing at *Bewildering Stories*, where he sits on the review board and manages a posse of five review editors.

Ellery Akers (p.267, 319) is the author of three poetry collections: *Practicing the Truth*, which won the Autumn House Poetry Prize, the San Francisco Book Festival Poetry Award, and an Independent Publisher Award; *Knocking on the Earth*, which was named a Best Book of the Year by the *San Jose Mercury News*; and *Swerve: Environmentalism, Feminism, and Resistance*. She is also the author of a children's novel, *Sarah's Waterfall*. Akers has won thirteen national awards, including the Poetry International Prize, the John Masefield Award, the Paumanok Poetry Award, and *Sierra Magazine*'s Nature Writing Award. Her poetry has been featured on National Public Radio and on *American Life in Poetry*, and has appeared in such journals as *The American Poetry Review, Poetry*, and *The Sun*. She is a writer, artist, and naturalist living on the Northern California coast and teaches private poetry workshops.

Carrie Albert (p.87) is a multifaceted artist and poet based in Seattle. Her works have been published in many diverse journals and anthologies, including *Grey Sparrow Journal, Foliate Oak, Earth's Daughters, ink, sweat & tears*, and upcoming in Beautiful Cadaver Project Pittsburgh—*The Dreamers Anthology: Writing Inspired by Martin Luther King, Jr. and Anne Frank*. She is a fixture as Poet-Artist-in-Residence at Penhead Press.

Kathleen Alcalá (p.90, 233), a founding editor of *The Raven Chronicles*, has degrees from Stanford University, the University of Washington, and the University of New Orleans. A graduate of the Clarion West Science Fiction and Fantasy program, her work embraces both traditional and innovative storytelling. She is the author of six books that include a collection of stories, three novels, a book of essays, and, most recently, *The Deepest Roots: Finding Food and Community on a Pacific Northwest Island* (University of Washington Press, 2016). Recognition includes the Western States Book Award, the Governor's Writers Award, and two Artist Trust Fellowships. She lives near Seattle, Washington, and is a member of Los Norteños Writers Group.

Eneida P. Alcalde's (p.211) Chilean-Puerto Rican background fuels her writing, which seeks to ask questions, explore mysteries, and elevate the underrepresented. Her stories and poems have appeared in literary outlets such as the *Stoneboat Literary Journal, As/Us Journal*, and *The Acentos Review*. You may learn more about her work at www.eneidapatricia.com.

Ibrahim Al-Masri (p.162) is an Egyptian poet and writer, member of The Egyptian Writers Union, and Chief News Editor on TV. He covered events as a television correspondent in Kosovo in 1999, in Iraq in 2003 and 2004, in Darfur in 2007, and in Libya and Tunisia in 2011. He has written over thirty books, including: *Poetry is a Being Without . . . Work* (Bideyet House, 2010), *The Game of Paper Boats* (Department of Culture and Information, Sharjah, 1998), *Dream Smugglers* (Dar Al-Adham, 2012), and *Water Meal . . . Amber Meal* (Dar Al-Nassim, 2013). He received the Kathak Literary Award from Bangladesh in 2018.

Anna Bálint (p.117): See editors bios.

Miriam Bassuk (p.150) treasures the Northwest not only for its beauty and thriving literary community, but also because her grandson lives here. She has been published in *The Journal of Sacred Feminine Wisdom*, *Between the Lines*, *PoetsWest Literary Journal*, and *3 Elements Review*. She is one of the featured poets in the digital/online portion of the *WA 129* project created by Tod Marshall, the 2016-2018 Washington State Poet Laureate.

Marc Beaudin (p.37, 40) is a poet, theatre artist, and bookseller living in Livingston, Montana, dubbed "America's finest open-air asylum" for multiple reasons. His work has been anthologized in *We Take Our Stand* (edited by Rick Bass), *Poems Across the Big Sky Volume II*, and *Unearthing Paradise: Montana Writers in Defense of Greater Yellowstone* (of which he is a co-editor). His latest book, *Vagabond Song: Neo-Haibun from the Peregrine Journals*, was called "a jazzy, free-wheeling, rollicking road trip into the beating heart of the Eternal Now," by *Montana Quarterly*. A frequent performer of poetry and spoken word, Beaudin has worked and recorded with a variety of jazz and rock musicians at venues across the country, as well as on several public and independent radio stations. He believes the *Brahms' Violin Concerto in D* is more powerful than all the guns, smokestacks and coal trains in the world.

Sara Beckmann (p.95) experienced six and a half years of homelessness related to mental illness and addiction. Now, after "a ton of recovery work" and a long wait (due to the shortage of affordable housing), Sara has finally moved into safe permanent housing. She joined Safe Place Writing Circle at Recovery Café in 2018 with no prior writing experience but with a love of words, images, and trying new things. Much of Sara's writing explores homelessness and "sleeping rough," sometimes in ways that finds humor even in dark circumstances.

Karen Bonaudi (p.248), author of *Editing a Vapor Trail* (Pudding House Publications, 2010), has taught writing in schools and workshops and now publishes others' books. Her poetry has appeared in *The Bellingham Review*, *South Dakota Review*, *Pontoon 2*, *Salal Review*, *Snow Monkey* and King County Metro's *Poetry on the Buses*. A former president of the Washington Poets Association, she lives and works as a private contractor in Renton, Washington.

Anita K. Boyle (p.127) is an artist and poet whose works are inspired by the natural and man-made landscape of the Pacific Northwest. Her poetry books include *What the Alder Told Me* (MoonPath Press, 2011), *The Drenched*, *Bamboo Equals Loon* (Egress Studio Press, 2001 2014); another is forthcoming from MoonPath Press in 2020. Her poems appear in anthologies such as *WA 129* (Sage Hill Press, 2017), *Last Call* and *Ice Cream Poems* (World Enough Writers, 2018, 2017); and in literary magazines including *Clover*, *The Raven Chronicles* and *Crab Creek Review*.

Ronda Piszk Broatch (p.265), poet and photographer, is the author of *Lake of Fallen Constellations* (MoonPath Press, 2015). Ronda was a finalist for the Four Way Books Prize, and her poems have been nominated several times for the Pushcart prize. Her journal publications include *Blackbird, Prairie Schooner, Sycamore Review, Mid-American Review, Puerto del Sol*, and Public Radio KUOW's *All Things Considered*, among others.

Andrew C. Brown (p.282) has had poems published on three continents. His words draw on experiences as an addict, a prisoner, and living on one of the most deprived estates in the UK. When his head was straight, he achieved a community regeneration award for his work with offenders and their families in South Bristol, as well as a Highly Commended Award in the national Koestler competition.

Jericho Brown (p.36, 184) is the recipient of a Whiting Writers Award, and fellowships from the Radcliffe Institute for Advanced Study at Harvard University and the National Endowment for the Arts. His poems have appeared in *The New York Times*, *The New Yorker*, and *The Best American Poetry*. His first book, *Please* (New Issues, 2008), won the American Book Award. His second book, *The New Testament* (Copper Canyon Press, 2014), won the Anisfield-Wolf Book Award and the Thom Gunn Award. His recent book is *The Tradition* (Copper Canyon Press, 2019), A Lannan Literary Selection and finalist for the 2019 National Book Award in Poetry. He is an associate professor of English and Creative Writing and Director of the Creative Writing Program at Emory University in Atlanta.

Gabriel Castilloux Calderón (p.98) (they/them) is nij-manidowag (two spirit) Mi'kmaq, Algonquin, Scottish and French Canadian. They currently thrive in Cree/Blackfoot/Salteaux/Nakota Sioux Treaty 6 territory (Edmonton, Canada). Gabriel is actively involved in several different forms of traditional indigenous culture and ceremony, as a drummer and a grass, jingle and buffalo dancer, and proudly celebrates an addiction free life. Gabriel is a first-time author of the short story "Andwànikàdjigan, forthcoming in the anthology *Love After the End*, Bedside Press, Canada. This collection of stories showcases a variety of stories by Indigenous authors imagining different possible futures of our world, told through the lens of the 2SQ (Two-Spirit & queer) heroes in the lead roles.

Janet Cannon's (p.253, 254) poems have been published in many literary journals, including *Berkeley Poetry Review* (University of California), *The Midwest Quarterly* (Pittsburgh State University), *Texas Review* (Sam Houston State University), and *G.W. Review* (George

Washington University)—among others. She has received awards from ASCAP, the Rio Grande Writers Association, and Bless Me Anima. Cannon is a graduate of the University of Iowa where she also did graduate work. She has taught oral history writing workshops at the NYC Public Library, Chelsea Branch, and English as a Second Language (ESL) at The New School in NYC. She is the author of three chapbooks—*Day Laborers* (Plan B Press), *The Last Night in New York* (Homeward Press), and *Percipience* (Cross Cut Saw Press). Janet has read her poems and performed via singing the spoken word all over the United States.

Catalína Maríe Cantú (p.93) is a multi-genre writer, interdisciplinary artist, and 2017 Jack Straw Fellow. Her writing has been published in *La Bloga*, King County Metro's *Poetry on Buses*, *Seattle Poetic Grid*, *Raven Chronicles*, and *The Inspired Poet*. She is a co-founding member and current President of La Sala: Latinx Artists' Network.

Nancy Canyon's (p.217) writing is published in *Last Call*, *Nature's Healing Spirit*, *Ice Cream Poems*, *Songs of Ourselves*, *Raven Chronicles*, *Water~Stone Review*, *Fourth Genre*, *Main Street Rag*, *Floating Bridge Review*, *Clover: A Literary Rag*, and more. She holds an MFA in Creative Writing from Pacific Lutheran University, a Certificate in Fiction from the University of Washington, and studied with Natalie Goldberg in Taos, New Mexico. Canyon works for The Narrative Project as a writing coach, and teaches art and writing privately in Historic Fairhaven, a quaint village overlooking Bellingham Bay in Washington State. Her novel, *Celia's Heaven*, is forthcoming from Penchant Press. Her poetry book, *Saltwater*, is available on Amazon. https://nancycanyon.com.

Sharon M. Carter (p.175) is a poet, visual artist, and retired physician. Originally from the UK, she has lived in the Pacific Northwest for many years. Her work has been published online and in many small presses. A manuscript entitled "Quiver" is currently with an editor for consideration. In February 2020, she will be one of four poets to take over running the Northwinds Reading series in Port Townsend, Washington.

T. Clear (p.310) A co-founder of Floating Bridge Press, her poetry has appeared in many magazines and anthologies, most recently in *Bracken Anthology*, *Red Earth Review* and *Sheila-Na-Gig*. Her work has been nominated for both a Pushcart Award and the Independent Best American Poetry Award. She is a lifelong resident of Seattle, facilitates the Easy Speak Seattle critique group Re/Write, and, in September 2020, will host Poets at Carrowholly, a six-day poetry workshop and retreat in the West of Ireland.

Lucille Clifton (p.29) was born in 1937 in DePew, New York, and grew up in Buffalo. She studied at Howard University, before transferring to SUNY Fredonia, near her hometown. She was discovered as a poet by Langston Hughes (via friend Ishmael Reed, who shared her poems), and Hughes published Clifton's poetry in his highly influential anthology, *The Poetry of the Negro* (1970). A prolific and widely respected poet, Lucille Clifton's work emphasizes endurance and strength through adversity, focusing particularly on the African American experience and family life. Awarding the prestigious Ruth Lilly Poetry Prize to Clifton in 2007, the judges remarked that "One always feels the looming humaneness around Lucille Clifton's poems—it is a moral quality that some poets have and some don't." In addition to the Ruth Lilly prize, Clifton was the first author to have two books of poetry chosen as finalists for the Pulitzer Prize, *Good Woman: Poems and a Memoir, 1969-1980* (1987) and *Next: New Poems* (1987). Her collection *Two-Headed Woman* (1980) was also a Pulitzer nominee and won the Juniper Prize from the University of Massachusetts. She served as the state of Maryland's Poet Laureate from 1974 until 1985, and won the prestigious National Book Award for *Blessing the Boats: New and Selected Poems, 1988-2000*. In addition to her numerous poetry collections, she wrote many children's books. Clifton was a Distinguished Professor of Humanities at St. Mary's College of Maryland and a Chancellor of the Academy of American Poets.

Keats Conley (p.241) lives and writes in southern Idaho. A marine biologist, she earned graduate degrees at the University of Oregon, then returned home to work on salmon recovery amid Idaho's sage-brush seas. She enjoys writing poetry as a means of sharing science with a broader audience, particularly to help cultivate a sense of urgency about global biodiversity loss. Her recent work has been published in journals such as *The Ecological Citizen*, *Animal Magazine*, and *Arkana*. The two poems included in this anthology stem from her forthcoming book titled *Guidance from the God of Seahorses*, published by Green Writers Press. The poems are framed as short "advice columns" from the God of threatened or endangered species. The intent of co-opting God's voice is to interrupt the purely human narrative and instill the reader with a renewed sense of urgency about the quiet decline of our cohabitants of planet Earth.

Brendan Connolly's (p.304) work has been featured in *Genre: Urban Arts*, *OPEN: Journal of Arts & Letters*, and *Breathe Free Press*. He lives and writes in New York City.

Nancy Cook (p.25) only recently joined the ranks of full-time writers after twenty years of single-handedly raising an adopted daughter. A Minnesota State Arts Board grantee, Nancy runs the "Witness Project," a series of free community writing workshops in Minneapolis designed to enable creative work by underrepresented voices. Nancy spent the early part of 2019 in Northern Ireland doing some community-building writing projects there. Her latest work can be found in *The Tangerine*, *Existere*, *Litbreak*, *Stoneboat*, and *Third Wednesday*.

Beth Copeland (p.212) is the author of three full-length poetry books: *Blue Honey*, recipient of the 2017 Dogfish Head Poetry Prize; *Transcendental Telemarketer*; and *Traveling through Glass*, recipient of the 1999 Bright Hill Press Poetry Book Award. Her poems have been published in literary magazines and anthologies, and have been featured on international poetry websites. She was profiled as Poet of the Week on the *PBS NewsHour* website. Beth lives in the Blue Ridge Mountains where she owns and runs Tiny Cabin, Big Ideas™, a retreat for poets, writers, and artists.

Jennifer deBie (p.278) is a native Texan and current PhD candidate at University College Cork in Cork, Ireland. She obtained an MA in Creative Writing from the same institution in

2017. She has published an essay on Mary Shelley with *LittleAtoms*, poetry on refugees with *PactPress*, and has a novel about superheroes forthcoming from Dreaming Big Publications. She enjoys muscadine wine, good poetry, and opera as long as there's a pee break in the middle.

Susan Deer Cloud (p.26, 301), a Catskill Native, is the recipient of a National Endowment for the Arts Literature Fellowship, two New York State Foundation for the Arts Poetry Fellowships, and an Elizabeth George Foundation Grant. Published in numerous journals and anthologies, her most recent books are *The Way to Rainbow Mountain* (Shabda Press, 2019), *Before Language* (Shabda Press, 2016), and *Hunger Moon: Poems* (Shabda Press, 2014). She also edited the anthologies *I Was Indian (Before Being Indian Was Cool), Volumes I & II* (Foothills Publishing 2009, 2012). Currently Deer Cloud balances her life Libra-like between her mountain home and roving afar, her rambling naturally becoming an interior journey resulting in visions, stories, essays, and poems. For more: https://sites.google.com/site/susandeercloud/.

Tom A. (TA) Delmore (p.105) lives in Bellevue, Washington. His books of poetry include *Eclipsing F Crow Poems* (Little Letterhead Press, 1996); *Child is working to Capacity* (Moon Pie Press, 2006); *A Poultice for Belief* (March Street Press, 2009); *Tell them that you saw me but you didn't see me saw* (Moon Pie Press, 2011). Individual poems have been published in *Raven Chronicles* and *Seattle M.E.N. Magazine*.

Risa Denenberg (p.69) lives on the Olympic peninsula and is co-founder and editor at Headmistress Press, publisher of lesbian/bi/trans poetry. She publishes poetry book reviews at *the Rumpus* and other venues, and curates *The Poetry Café*, an online meeting place where poetry chapbooks are reviewed. She has published three full-length collections of poetry, most recently, *slight faith* (MoonPath Press, 2018). Visit: https://thepoetrycafe.online/ and https://risadenenberg.com/.

Margaret DeRitter (p.291) was one of the winners of Kalamazoo Friends of Poetry's 2018 Celery City Chapbook Contest for her chapbook *Fly Me to Heaven By Way of New Jersey*. She also has a full-length poetry collection, *Singing Back to the Sirens*, due out in March 2020 from Unsolicited Press, Portland, Oregon. She is the copy editor and poetry editor of *Encore*, a feature magazine for Southwest Michigan, and a former editor and reporter at the *Kalamazoo Gazette*. Her poetry has appeared in numerous journals and anthologies. She lives in Kalamazoo, Michigan.

Alice Derry (p.307) was educated in Washington, Montana, Washington, D.C., and Germany. She holds an MFA from Goddard College (now Warren Wilson). Her latest volume of poems is *Hunger* (MoonPath Press, 2018). She has published four other volumes, and three chapbooks. She lives and works on Washington States' Olympic Peninsula.

Mike Dillon (p.134), retired publisher of Pacific Publishing Co., grew up on Bainbridge Island. As publisher of a half-dozen community newspapers in Seattle and environs, he won numerous awards for his feature and column writing, including a first place in the social issues category from the Society of Professional Journalists for a three-part series on sexual abuse. Bellowing Ark Press has published four books of his poetry; three books of his haiku have been published by Red Moon Press. Several of his haiku were included in *Haiku in English: The First Hundred Years* (W. W. Norton, 2013). His most recent book is *Departures: Poetry and Prose on the Removal of Bainbridge Island's Japanese Americans After Pearl Harbor* (Unsolicited Press, April 2019). His poetry, essays, and feature writing have appeared in numerous journals in this country, including *Raven Chronicles*, and abroad.

Patrick Dixon (p.204) is a writer/photographer retired from careers in teaching and commercial fishing. A board member of the Olympia Poetry Network, he has been published in *Cirque Literary Journal, Panoplyzine, Oberon, The Tishman Review,* and the anthologies *FISH 2015* and *WA 129*. He is the poetry editor of *National Fisherman Magazine*'s quarterly, *North Pacific Focus*. Dixon received an Artist Trust Grant for Artists to edit *Anchored in Deep Water: The FisherPoets Anthology,* published in 2014. His chapbook, *Arc of Visibility,* won the 2015 Alabama State Poetry Morris Memorial Award.

Anita Endrezze (p.196, 260) is an author and artist. She was inspired to write the poem "The Wall" to protest in a literal and symbolic way—her grandmother came from Mexico a hundred years ago. Her latest collection of poems is *Enigma* (Press 53, 2019). Her short story collection, *Butterfly Moon,* was published in 2012 by the University of Arizona Press. Anita's Red Bird Press Chapbooks include *Breaking Edges* (2012) and *A Thousand Branches* (2014). Her work has been translated into ten languages and taught around the world. She won the Bumbershoot/Weyerhaeuser Award, a Washington State Governor's Writing Award, and a GAP Award for her poetry. She collaborates on art projects with a small group of women. An altered book project on the value of art in Latin America is archived at the Smithsonian. She is half-European (Slovenian, German, and Italian) and half Yaqui (a nation native to Mexico). She has MS and is housebound.

Chris Espenshade (p.190) An archaeologist, Chris branched into creative writing in 2017. He's had political commentary and satire published by *Poached Hare, The Paragon Journal, Write Launch, Thrice Fiction, Fewer Than 500,* and *Chachalaca Review*. This is his third work to appear in *The Raven Chronicles*. Chris lives in Wellsboro, Pennsylvania.

Jeannine Hall Gailey (p.155) served as the second Poet Laureate of Redmond, Washington. She's the author of five books of poetry: *Becoming the Villainess* (Steel Toe Books), *She Returns to the Floating World* (Two Sylvias Press, re-issue), *Unexplained Fevers* (New Binary Press, March 2013), *The Robot Scientist's Daughter* (Mayapple Press, 2015), and *Field Guide to the End of the World* (Moon City Press, 2016)—winner of the Moon City Press Book Prize and the SFPA's Elgin Award. She's also the author of *PR for Poets: A Guidebook to Publicity and Marketing*. Her work appeared in journals such as *American Poetry Review, Notre Dame Review,* and *Prairie Schooner*. Her web site is www.webbish6.com. Twitter and Instagram: @webbish6.

Tess Gallagher's (p.236) eleventh volume of poetry, *Is, Is Not* (Graywolf Press, 2019), received a Best Book of 2020 from the Pacific Northwest Booksellers Association. Other books published by Graywolf: *Midnight Lantern: New and Selected Poems* (2011) and *The Man from Kenvara: Selected Stories* (fiction, 2009). She companioned the productions of the film *Birdman* and *The Revenant*, directed by Mexican director Alejandro González Iñárritu. *Birdman* uses a story and a poem written by her late husband Raymond Carver. She writes in a cottage on Lough Arrow in the West of Ireland where many of the poems from her latest book are set. Her volume of poetry, *Boogie-Woogie Crisscross*, written in collaboration with Lawrence Matsuda (Madhat, Inc. / Plume Editions, 2016), was composed in her chair at this cottage. She writes and lives also in her hometown of Port Angeles, Washington.

F.I. Goldhaber's (they/them) (p.268) words capture people, places, and politics with a photographer's eye and a poet's soul. As a reporter, editor, business writer, and marketing communications consultant, they produced news stories, feature articles, editorial columns, and reviews for newspapers, corporations, governments, and non-profits in five states. Currently, electronic and audio magazines, books, newspapers, calendars, street signs and origami display Goldhaber's poetry, fiction, and essays. More than one hundred of their poems appear in fifty-plus publications. Their fourth collection, *Food ♦ Family ♦ Friends* (Political Poetry Publishing, 2017), explores how those three things send us feasting, flinching, and/or frolicking through life. Visit http://www.goldhaber.net/.

Ray Gonzalez (p.160) Poet, essayist, and editor, his work is inextricably linked to his Mexican ancestry and American upbringing in the deserts of the Southwest. Gonzalez is the author of numerous books of poetry, including *The Heat of Arrivals* (1997), which won the PEN/Oakland Josephine Miles Book Award; *Cabato Sentora* (2000), a Minnesota Book Award Finalist; *The Hawk Temple at Tierra Grande* (2003), winner of the Minnesota Book Award for Poetry; *Cool Auditor* (2009); *Faith Run* (2009); and *Beautiful Wall* (2015). With Lawrence Welsh and Bruce Berman he collaborated on the book *Cutting the Wire: Poetry and Photography from the US-Mexico Border* (University of New Mexico Press, 2018). His poems have appeared in *The Best American Poetry* and *The Pushcart Prize: Best of the Small Presses 2000*. He has served as Poetry Editor of the *Bloomsbury Review* for twenty-five years, and founded *LUNA, A Journal of Poetry and Translation*, in 1998. He is a professor in the MFA Creative Writing Program at the University of Minnesota-Minneapolis.

Rebecca Ruth Gould's (p.193) poems and translations have appeared in *Nimrod*, *Kenyon Review*, *Tin House*, *The Hudson Review*, *Salt Hill*, and *The Atlantic Review*. She translates from Persian, Russian, and Georgian, and has translated books such as *After Tomorrow the Days Disappear: Ghazals and Other Poems of Hasan Sijzi of Delhi* (Northwestern University Press, 2016) and *The Death of Bagrat Zakharych and other Stories by Vazha-Pshavela* (Paper & Ink, 2019). Her literary translations have earned comparison with the world's greatest poets, with a reviewer in *The Calvert Journal* recently noting, "With her new translation, Rebecca Ruth Gould follows in the footsteps of Russian literature luminaries like Osip Mandelstam and Marina Tsvetaeva."

Her poem "Grocery Shopping" was a finalist for the Luminaire Award for Best Poetry in 2017, and she is a Pushcart Prize nominee.

Anita Goveas (p.251) is of British-Asian ancestry, based in London, and fueled by strong coffee and paneer jalfrezi. She was first published in the *2016 London Short Story Prize Anthology*, and most recently in *Okay Donkey*, *X-Ray lit* and *New Mag*. She's on the editorial team at *Flashback Fiction*, an editor at *Mythic Picnic's* Twitter zine, and tweets erratically @coffeeandpaneer. Links to her stories can be found at https://coffeeandpaneer.wordpress.com.

Stuart Gunter (p.266) is working toward a Master's Degree in Mental Health Counseling, and lives in Schuyler, Virginia. He likes to paddle the Rockfish River and play drums in obscure rock bands. His poems have been published in *Sow's Ear Poetry Review*, *Streetlight*, *Gravel*, *Deep South*, and *New Plains Review*, among others.

Stephanie Barbé Hammer (p.275) is a five-time Pushcart Prize nominee, with work in the *Bellevue Literary Review*, *Pearl*, *Hayden's Ferry*, *the James Franco Review*, *the Gold Man Review*, and *the Chiron Review*, among other places. She is the author of a magical realist novel, *The Puppet Turners of Narrow Interior*, a prose poem chapbook, *Sex with Buildings*, a full-length poetry collection, *How Formal?*, and a how-to-write-magical-realism craft book, *Delicious Strangeness*. Stephanie currently resides in rural Washington State and is a founding member of Indivisible Whidbey Island and Teachers Against Child Detention. She is managing editor of *Shark Reef Literary Magazine*.

Edward Harkness (p.153) is the author of three full-length poetry collections, *Saying the Necessary*, *Beautiful Passing Lives*, and, most recently, *The Law of the Unforeseen* (Pleasure Boat Studio Press, 2018). His poems can be found online in *2River*, *Atticus Review*, *Cascadia Review*, *The Good Men Project*, *Hinchas de Poesia*, *The Humanist*, *Rat's Ass Journal*, *Raven Chronicles*, *Salt River Review*, *Split Lip Magazine*, *Switched-On Gutenberg* and *Terrain.Org.*, as well as in print journals including *Chariton Review* and *Miramar*. His chapbook, *Ice Children*, was published by Split Lip Press in 2014. He lives in Shoreline, Washington. To hear Ed read selected poems from *The Law of the Unforeseen*, including "Tying a Tie" and "Airborne," the two winning poems of *Terrain.org's* 8th Annual Contest in Poetry (2018), go to https://www.terrain.org/2018/poetry/edward-harkness-2/.

Matthew E. Henry (MEH) (p.79) is a multiple Pushcart and Best of the Net-nominated poet and short story writer. His works are appearing or forthcoming in various publications, including *The Raven Chronicles*, *Longleaf Review*, *Poetry East*, *The Radical Teacher*, *Rhino*, *Rise Up Review*, *Rigorous*, *Spillway*, *Tahoma Literary Review* and *3Elements Literary Review*. MEH is an educator who received his MFA from Seattle Pacific University, yet continued to spend money he didn't have completing an MA in theology and a PhD in education. His first collection of poetry—*Teaching While Black*—is forthcoming from Main Street Rag Publishing Co. His work can be found on MEHPoeting.com.

Janis Butler Holm (p.62) has served as Associate Editor for *Wide Angle*, the film journal. Her prose, poems, and performance pieces have appeared in small press, national, and international magazines, including *the Berkeley Poetry Review, Copper Nickel, Diagram, the Gay and Lesbian Review, Iowa Review, LIT, the Montreal Review*, and *Permafrost*. Her plays have been produced in the U.S., Canada, and the U.K.

Thomas Hubbard (p.106): See editors bios.

Paul Hunter's (p.136) poems have appeared in numerous journals, as well as in seven full-length books and three chapbooks. His first collection of farming poems, *Breaking Ground* (Silverfish Review Press, 2004), was reviewed in *The New York Times*, and received the 2004 Washington State Book Award. A second volume of farming poems, *Ripening*, was published in 2007, a third companion volume, *Come the Harvest*, appeared in 2008, and the fourth, *Stubble Field*, from the same publisher, appeared in 2012. He has been a featured poet on *The News Hour*, and has a prose book on small-scale, sustainable farming, *One Seed to Another: The New Small Farming* (Small Farmer's Journal, 2010). His book of prose poetry, *Clownery, In lieu of a life spent in harness*, was published by Davila Art & Books (2017), Sisters, Oregon. His book of eighteen contemporary cowhand stories, *Sit a Tall Horse*, was published in January 2020.

Rob Jacques (p.229) resides on a rural island in Washington State's Puget Sound, and his poetry appears in literary journals, including *Atlanta Review, Prairie Schooner, Amsterdam Quarterly, Poet Lore, The Healing Muse*, and *Assaracus*. A collection of his poems, *War Poet*, was published by Sibling Rivalry Press in 2017, and a second collection, *Adagio for Su Tung-p'o*, was published by Fernwood Press in 2019.

Erin Jamieson (p.249) holds an MFA in Creative Writing from Miami University of Ohio. Her work has been published or is forthcoming in *After the Pause, Into the Void, Flash Frontier*, and *Foliate Oak Literary Magazine*, among others. Jamieson's fiction has been nominated for a Pushcart Prize, and she currently teaches English Composition at the University of Cincinnati-Blue Ash College and works as a freelance writer.

Ashley Jenkins (aka L.L. Asher) (p.219) has a BA in Psychology and is working on a second degree in English with a concentration in Writing. Jenkins is a member of Sigma Tau Delta, a #FWContest winner, and has published over twenty short stories in *TL;DR Press, Constant Readers, Manqué, Zimbell House Publishing, Medusepod, Bewildering Stories, Castabout Art & Literature, The Raven Chronicles, Blood Moon Rising, Things in the Well, Fantasia Divinity Publishing, Bending Genres, Writer's Club* and the *Cygnet*. https://www.facebook.com/lilu.asher.5.

Keanu Jones (p.273) is a member of the Navajo Nation, originally from Grand Falls, Arizona. He is a student at Navajo Technical University studying Creative Writing and New Media. He's had one piece published and is seeking opportunities to grow as a writer. He is not only a beginning writer, but he enjoys creating films and taking photographs of nature. Writing is a skill he is continuously trying to improve and he draws inspiration from his Navajo culture and unique Indigenous perspective of the world.

Tamam Kahn (p.206) is the author two books on the women of early Islam: *Untold, A History of the Wives of Prophet Muhammad* (Monkfish Books, 2010), was awarded an International Book Award in 2011, and translated into Indonesian; and *Fatima's Touch, Poems and Stories of the Prophet's Daughter* (Ruhaniat Press, 2016). Tamam has traveled to sacred sites in Morocco, Syria, Jordan, Andalusia, and India, and spent two decades researching early Islamic history. In 2009, she was invited by the Royal Ministry of Morocco to read her poetry at a world-wide Sufi conference in Marrakesh. She continues to travel and teach from her books about the women at the dawn of Islam. Website: https://completeword.wordpress.com.

Ilya Kaminsky (p.81, 130) was born in the former Soviet Union City of Odessa. He lost most of his hearing at the age of four after a doctor misdiagnosed mumps as a cold; his family was granted political asylum by the United States in 1993, settling in Rochester, New York. After his father's death in 1994, Kaminsky began to write poems in English. He explained in an interview with the *Adirondack Review*, "I chose English because no one in my family or friends knew it—no one I spoke to could read what I wrote. I myself did not know the language. It was a parallel reality, an insanely beautiful freedom. It still is." Kaminsky went on to earn a BA in Political Science at Georgetown University, and a JD at the University of California's Hastings College of Law. With Paloma Capanna, he co-founded Poets for Peace, which sponsors poetry readings across the globe to support relief work. Kaminsky's honors include a Whiting Writers' Award, the Milton Center's Award for Excellence in Writing, *Poetry Magazine's* Levinson Prize as well as their Ruth Lilly Fellowship, and a Lannan Foundation fellowship. Kaminsky is the author of *Dancing in Odessa* (Tupelo Press, 2004), which won the Tupelo Press Dorset Prize, the American Academy of Arts and Letters' Metcalf Award, and *ForeWord Magazine's* Best Poetry Book of the Year Award. His most recent collection, *Deaf Republic* (Graywolf Press, 2019), was a Finalist for the National Book Award for Poetry.

J.I. Kleinberg (p.129) is a poet, freelance writer, and a Best of the Net and Pushcart nominee. Her poetry has appeared in *One, Diagram, Otoliths, Raven Chronicles, Psaltery & Lyre*, and elsewhere. She lives in Bellingham, Washington, and posts most days at https://chocolateisaverb.wordpress.com and https://thepoetrydepartment.wordpress.com.

Melissa Kwasny (p.286) is the author of six books of poetry, most recently *Where Outside the Body is the Soul Today* (University of Washington Press Pacific Northwest Poetry Series, 2017), and *Pictograph* (Milkweed Editions, 2015), as well as a collection of prose writings, *Earth Recitals: Essays on Image and Vision* (Lynx House Press, 2013). She is the editor of *Toward the Open Field: Poets on the Art of Poetry 1800–1950* (Wesleyan University Press, 2004), and co-editor, with M.L. Smoker, of the anthology *I Go to the Ruined Place: Contemporary Poets in Defense of Global Human Rights* (Lost Horse Press, 2009). *Putting on the Dog: The Animal Origins of What We Wear*, her first book of nonfiction, was published by Trinity University Press in 2019.

Rosalie Lander (p.42) is a part-time poet, full-time storyteller, and recent graduate of Western Washington University. Her current goal is to become a full-time author, but copyediting looks promising as well. When she isn't cursing a blue streak at verb tense, she can be found petting dogs, and reading good books—preferably ones with wizards in them.

Sheree La Puma (p.85) is an award-winning writer whose personal essays, fiction, and poetry have appeared in or are forthcoming in *O:JA&L*, *Burningword Literary Journal*, *I-70 Review*, *Inflectionist Review*, *Levee*, *Crack The Spine*, *Mad Swirl*, *The London Reader*, Bordighera Press: *VIA: Voices in Italian Americana*, *Gravel*, *Foliate Oak*, *PacificReview*, *Westwind* and *Ginosko Literary Review*, among others. She received an MFA in Writing from the California Institute of the Arts and taught poetry to former gang members. Born in Los Angeles, she now resides in Valencia, California, with her rescues, Bello the cat and Jack the dog.

Mercedes Lawry (p.103) has previously published poems in such journals as *Poetry*, *Natural Bridge*, *Nimrod*, and *Prairie Schooner*. She's had three chapbooks published—*There are Crows in My Blood*, *Happy Darkness*, and *In the Early Garden With Reason*, which was selected by Molly Peacock for the 2018 WaterSedge Poetry Chapbook Contest. Mercedes received the Vachel Lindsay Poetry Prize from Twelve Winters Press and her manuscript, *Small Measures*, is forthcoming. She's received honors from the Seattle Arts Commission, Jack Straw Foundation, Artist Trust and Richard Hugo House, been a five-time Pushcart Prize nominee, and was a Writers in Residence at Hedgebrook.

Gary Copeland Lilley (p.293) is the author of seven books of poetry, the most recent being *The Bushman's Medicine Show* (Lost Horse Press (2017). He is originally from North Carolina and now lives in the Pacific Northwest. He has received the Washington, D.C. Commission on the Arts Fellowship for Poetry, and was a finalist for 2018-2020 Washington State Poet Laureate. He is published in numerous anthologies and journals, including *Best American Poetry 2014*, *Willow Springs*, *Waxwing*, the *Taos International Journal of Poetry & Art*, and the *African American Review (AAR)*. He is usually seen attached to a guitar. He is a Cave Canem Fellow.

Anna Odessa Linzer (p.242) is the author of the award-winning novel, *Ghost Dancing*, and of *A River Story*, that was adapted into a two-person performance piece. Her home waters are the Salish Sea, where she is a long distance, cold-water swimmer. *Home Waters*, a trilogy of three novels, *Blind Virgil*, *Dancing on Waters*, and *A River Story*, was published as a limited edition by Marquand Books. Her stories, poems, and essays have been published in anthologies and literary magazines, including *Kenyon Review*, *Carolina Quarterly*, *Paris LA*, *Raven Chronicles*, *NW Ethnic News*, and *Caliban*.

Chip Livingston (p.221) is the author of the novel, *Owls Don't Have to Mean Death*; a collection of essays and stories, *Naming Ceremony*; and two poetry collections, *Crow-blue, Crow-black* and *Museum of False Starts*. His writing has appeared in *Ploughshares*, *Prairie Schooner*, *New American Writing*, on the Academy of American Poets and the Poetry Academy websites, and other journals and anthologies. Chip teaches in the low-rez MFA program at the Institute of American Indian Arts in Santa Fe, New Mexico. He lives in Montevideo, Uruguay.

Priscilla Long (p.188, 277) is a Seattle-based writer of poetry, essays, creative nonfictions, fictions, science, and history. She has an MFA degree from the University of Washington and teaches writing. Her guide to writing is *The Writer's Portable Mentor: A Guide to Art, Craft, and the Writing Life* (University of New Mexico Press, second edition, 2018). Her book of poems is *Crossing Over: Poems* (University of New Mexico Press, 2015). Her collection of linked literary nonfictions is *Fire and Stone: Where Do We Come From? What Are We? Where Are We Going?* (University of Georgia Press, 2016). Her handbook for artists of all kinds is *Minding the Muse: A Handbook for Painters, Composers, Writers, and Other Creators*. Her scholarly history book is *Where the Sun Never Shines: A History of America's Bloody Coal Industry*. Priscilla serves as Founding and Consulting Editor of HistoryLink.org, the free online encyclopedia of Washington State history, https://www.historylink.org. Visit her website https://www.priscillalong.net.

Claudia Castro Luna (p.176) served as Seattle's first Civic Poet from 2015-2017, and was appointed the fifth Washington State Poet Laureate for 2018-2020. She is the author of *Killing Marías* (Two Sylvias Press), short-listed for Washington State 2018 Book Award in Poetry, and *This City* (Floating Bridge Press). She is the creator of the acclaimed Seattle Poetic Grid (http://www.seattlepoeticgrid.com). Castro Luna is the recipient of an Academy of American Poets Laureate Fellowship, the recipient of individual artist grants from King County/4Culture and Seattle's Office of Arts and Culture, a Hedgebrook and VONA alumna, and a 2014 Jack Straw fellow. Born in El Salvador, she came to the United States in 1981. She has an MA in Urban Planning, a teaching certificate, and an MFA in poetry. Her poems have been featured in *PBS Newshour*, KQED San Francisco, KUOW Seattle, and have appeared in *Poetry Northwest*, *La Bloga*, *Dialogo*, and *Psychological Perspectives*, among others. Her non-fiction work can be read in several anthologies, among them *This Is The Place: Women Writing About Home* (Seal Press). Living in English and Spanish, she writes and teaches in Seattle, where she gardens and keeps chickens with her husband and their three children. Visit: http://www.castroluna.com.

Eve Lyons (p.151, 209) is a poet and fiction writer who also dabbles in writing creative nonfiction. Her work has appeared in *Lilith*, *Hip Mama*, *Mutha Magazine*, *Word Riot*, *Dead Mule of Southern Literature*, as well as other magazines and several anthologies. Her first book of poetry, *Tikkun Olam: Repairing the World*, is due out in May 2020 from WordTech Communications.

Brynn McCall (p.298) is a high school student from Denver, Colorado. Her work has been featured in *Syntax & Salt Magazine*, and she is somehow incredibly hopeful for the future.

Stephani E. D. McDow (p.114, 180) has recently been published in *Still Point Arts Quarterly*, *Genre: Urban Arts No. 7*, *Femme Literati: Mixtape Anthology By Women of Color*, *Edify Fiction* and *armarolla*. Formerly a contributing author at *Woman Around Town*, freelance writer/editor McDow is a nonprofit professional, member of RAINN's Speakers Bureau, and an advocate of justice. A native D.C. Washingtonian, and graduate of Duke Ellington School of the Arts, she is currently pursuing an MA in English at Bowie State University, working on completing her first novel, and building a collection of poetry. Visit: http://stephanimcdow.com.

Lawrence Matsuda (p.45, 76) was born in the Minidoka WRA Center, which was a concentration camp for Japanese and Japanese Americans during WWII. He is a regional Emmy award-winning writer and author of two books of poetry: *A Cold Wind from Idaho* (Black Lawrence Press, 2010), and *Glimpses of a Forever Foreigner*, in collaboration with artist Roger Shimomura (CreateSpace Independent Publishing Platform , 2014). Recently he and poet Tess Gallagher collaborated on a book of poetry, *Boogie-Woogie Crisscross* (Madhat, Inc. / Plume Editions, 2016). A chapter from his graphic novel, *Fighting for America: Nisei Soldiers*, was animated and won a 2016 regional Emmy.

Tiffany Midge (p.112, 270), a citizen of the Standing Rock Sioux Nation, is the author of *Bury My Heart at Chuck E. Cheese's* (Bison Books, University of Nebraska Press, 2019). She's the recipient of a Pushcart Prize, the Simons Public Humanities Fellowship, the Kenyon Review Earthworks Indigenous Poetry Prize, and a Western Heritage Award. Midge resides in the Inland Northwest and aspires to be the first Distinguished Writer-in-Residence in Seattle's Space Needle.

Dunya Mikhail (p.202) was born in Iraq (Baghdad), and is renowned in the Arab world for her subversive, innovative, and satirical poetry. New Directions publishes her books in English: *The War Works Hard* (translated by Elizabeth Winslow), short-listed for the Griffin Poetry Prize; *Diary of A Wave Outside the Sea* (co-translated with Elisabeth Winslow), winner of the Arab American Book Award; *The Iraqi Nights* (translated by Kareem James Abu-Zeid); and *The Beekeeper: Rescuing the Stolen Women of Iraq* (co-translated with Max Weiss), finalist for PEN/John Kenneth Galbraith award in non-fiction and long-listed for the National Book Award. *In Her Feminine Sign* (New Directions, 2019), is a "brilliant poetic exploration of language and gender, place, and time, seen through the mirror of exile." She is the co-founder of Michigan-community-based Mesopotamian Forum for Art and Culture. She currently works as a special lecturer of Arabic at Oakland University in Michigan.

Jesse Minkert (p.159) lives in Seattle. In 2008, Wood Works Press published his collection of flash fiction, *Shortness of Breath & Other Symptoms*. His work appears in over seventy journals, including *Confrontation*, *Floating Bridge Review*, *Poetry Northwest*, and *Harpur Palate*. In 2017, Finishing Line Press released Minkert's poetry chapbook, *Rookland*.

Rajiv Mohabir (p.316) is the award-winning author of the poetry collections *The Taxidermist's Cut* (Four Way Books, 2016), and *The Cowherd's Son* (Tupelo Press, 2017). His awards include the Kundiman Poetry Prize, the 2015 AWP Intro Journal award, and a PEN/Heim Translation Fund Grant. His poetry and translations appear internationally in *Best American Poetry 2015*, *Quarterly West*, *Guernica*, *Prairie Schooner*, *Crab Orchard Review*, *Drunken Boat*, *Poetry Magazine*, and many other places. He received his MFA in Poetry and Translation from Queens College, CUNY, and a PhD in English from the University of Hawai'i. He is an Assistant Professor of poetry in the MFA program at Emerson College in Boston, Massachusetts

Jeanne Morel (p.231) is the author of two chapbooks: *That Crossing Is Not Automatic* (Tarpaulin Sky Press) and *Jackpot* (Bottlecap Press). Recent poems have appeared in *Bone Bouquet, december magazine*, and *Dunes Review*. Jeanne holds an MFA from Pacific University, and is a three-time Pushcart nominee—in both poetry and fiction. She has taught writing workshops in community colleges, arts organizations, prisons, and retirement centers. She lives in Seattle and is a gallery guide at the Frye Art Museum.

Jed Myers (p.172) is author of *Watching the Perseids* (winner of the Sacramento Poetry Center Book Award), *The Marriage of Space and Time* (MoonPath Press), and four chapbooks, including *Dark's Channels* (winner of the *Iron Horse Literary Review* Chapbook Award), and *Love's Test* (winner of the Grayson Books Chapbook Competition). He's winner of *The Briar Cliff Review*'s 2019 Poetry Contest. Other recent recognitions include the *Prime Number Magazine* Award for Poetry, *The Southeast Review*'s Gearhart Poetry Prize, and *The Tishman Review*'s Edna St. Vincent Millay Poetry Prize. Recent poems appear in *Rattle, Poetry Northwest, The American Journal of Poetry, Southern Poetry Review, Tinderbox Poetry Journal, Ruminate*, and elsewhere. He is Poetry Editor for the journal *Bracken*.

Shankar Narayan (p.47, 197) explores identity, power, mythology, and technology in a world where the body is flung across borders yet possesses unrivaled power to transcend them. Shankar is a four-time Pushcart Prize nominee, winner of the 2017 Flyway Sweet Corn Poetry Prize, and has been a fellow at Kundiman, Jack Straw, and Richard Hugo House. He is a 4Culture grant recipient for "Claiming Space," a project to lift the voices of writers of color, and his chapbook, *Postcards From the New World*, won the Paper Nautilus Debut Series Chapbook Prize. Shankar draws strength from his global upbringing and from his work as a civil rights attorney for the ACLU. In Seattle, he awakens to the wonders of Cascadia every day, but his heart yearns east to his other hometown, Delhi. Connect with him at ShankarNarayan.net.

Cynthia Neely (p.239) is the winner of Bright Hill Press's chapbook contest for *Passing Through Blue Earth* (2016), and the winner of *Flyway: Journal of Writing and Environment*'s chapbook contest for *Broken Water* (2011). Her poems appear in numerous journals, including *Pontoon* (2016 Paula Jones Gardiner Memorial Award-Floating Bridge Press), *Bellevue Literary Review* (runner up for the Jan and Marica Vilcek prize), *Crab Creek Review, Raven Chronicles, Terrain.org*, and in several anthologies. Her full-length book, *Flight Path* (2014), was a finalist in the Aldrich Press book contest. Her chapbook, *Hopewell Bay* (2017), a single, long hybrid poem, is available from Seven Kitchens Press. Her essay and creative non-fiction work appear in *The Writers' Chronicle, Cutthroat Journal* (runner up for the Barry Lopez Prize), and *Terrain.org*. Neely earned her MFA in creative writing from Pacific University.

Larry C. Nichols (p.67) is a retired long-time college and university writing teacher and writing center director, now focusing more on his own writing. "My poem 'Just Being a Friendly Guy' arose from my increasing awareness of random violence against people of color and the deep chill I feel knowing how my middle-class life and whiteness insulate me from being a target of that violence."

Valin Paige (p.58) is a butch-trans-woman, poet, and essayist who started her writing career bathed in small town Iowa folk punk. Her work can be found in *FreezeRay Poetry*, *Crab Fat Magazine*, *VASTARIEN*, *Coffin Bell*, and on *Button Poetry*. She is currently an MFA student in creative writing at Hamline University in Saint Paul, Minnesota.

Carl "Papa" Palmer (p.195) of Old Mill Road in Ridgeway, Virginia, lives in University Place, Washington. He is retired from the military and Federal Aviation Administration (FAA), enjoying life now as "Papa" to his grand descendants and being a Franciscan Hospice volunteer. Carl is a Pushcart Prize and Micro Award nominee. His Motto: Long Weekends Forever!

Marge Piercy (p.70, 142) is an American poet, novelist, and social activist. She is the author of the *New York Times* bestseller, *Gone to Soldiers* (1987), a sweeping historical novel set during World War II. She is author of nineteen volumes of poems, among them *The Moon is Always Female* (1980, considered a feminist classic), and *The Art of Blessing the Day* (1999), as well as fifteen novels, one play, *The Last White Class*, co-authored with her husband Ira Wood, one collection of essays, *Parti-Colored Blocks for a Quilt* (1982), one non-fiction book, and one memoir, *Sleeping with Cats: A Memoir* (2001). Her work has been included in more than two hundred anthologies, and has been translated into sixteen languages. Her 20th book of poems, *On the Way Out, Turn Off the Light*, will be out from Knopf in September 2020. Her manuscripts are housed at the University of Michigan's Harlan Hatcher Graduate Library.

Kenneth Pobo (p.66) has a new book out from Duck Lake Books, *Dindi Expecting Snow*. Forthcoming from The Poetry Society of Alabama, is his chapbook *Your Place Or Mine*. His work appears in: *Nimrod*, *Mudfish*, *Atlanta Review*, *Hawaii Review*, and elsewhere.

Susana Praver-Pérez (p.283) is an Oakland-based poet, memoirist, and co-founder of La Tertulia Boricua, a monthly cultural salon that has been bringing creative community together since 2011. To date, her work has appeared in *The Acentos Review, La Respuesta, Milvia Street Arts and Literary Journal, Still Point Arts Quarterly, Civil Liberties United* (an anthology), and now in *Raven Chronicles*. Although Susana is passionate about writing, she's not ready to give up her day job at La Clínica de la Raza in Oakland, California, where she has worked for over three decades as a Physician Assistant and, currently, as Associate Medical Director.

dan raphael (p.245) For over four decades raphael has been active in the Northwest as poet, performer, editor, and reading host. *Manything*, his 21st book, was published in 2019 by Unlikely Books. Other collections include *Everyone in This Movie Gets Paid* (Last Word Press), and

Impulse & Warp: The Selected 20th Century Poems (Wordcraft of Oregon.) Raphael is known for the energy of his performances of his highly imaginative and driven poetry in places like Bumbershoot, Cascadia Poetry Festival, Powell's Books, Wordstock, Red Sky Poetry Theatre, Reed College, and the Portland Jazz Festival. Most Wednesday's dan writes and records a current events poem for the KBOO Evening News.

henry 7. reneau, jr. (p.144, 185) writes words of conflagration to awaken the world ablaze, an inferno of free verse illuminated by his affinity for disobedience, like a discharged bullet that commits a felony every day, a spontaneous combustion that blazes from his heart, phoenix-fluxed red & gold, exploding through change is gonna come to implement the fire next time. He is the author of the poetry collection, *freedomland blues* (Transcendent Zero Press), and the e-chapbook, *physiography of the fittest* (Kind of a Hurricane Press), available from their respective publishers. Additionally, he has self-published a chapbook entitled *13hirteen Levels of Resistance*, and his collection, *The Book Of Blue(s) : Tryin' To Make A Dollar Outta' Fifteen Cents*, was a finalist for the 2018 Digging Press Chapbook Series. His work has also been nominated for the Pushcart Prize and Best of the Net.

Susan Rich (p.135) is the author of five books, most recently, *Cloud Pharmacy*, short-listed for the Julie Suk prize, honoring poetry books from independent presses. She is the winner of the PEN USA Award for Poetry and *The Times Literary Supplement* Award, London. Her poems appear in places such as *the Academy of American Poets Poem-a-Day, New England Review, Southern Review*, and *World Literature Today*. She is cofounder of Poets on the Coast, a yearly writing retreat that takes place in La Conner, Washington. Recently, she has learned how to change the battery in her car's FOB. The poem in this anthology, "For the first time I am afraid," will be included in her upcoming book, *Gallery of Postcards and Maps: New and Selected Poems*, due out in 2022 from Salmon Press.

Sherry Rind's (p.305) previous books are *The Hawk in the Back Yard* (Anhinga Award), and *A Fall Out the Door* (King County Arts Award, Confluence Press). Chapbooks are *The Whooping Crane Dance* and *A Natural History of Grief*. She has received grants and awards from the Seattle and King County Arts Commissions, Pacific Northwest Writers, National Endowment for the Arts, and Artist Trust. Her poem in this anthology, "There Will Be No Revolution," appears in her book, *Between States of Matter*, published by The Poetry Box Select Series in March 2020.

Katelyn Durst Rivas (p.50) is a poet, community artist, and youth organizer living in Detroit. She has been working in youth development and community organizing for over ten years. As a teaching artist, she loves creating environments for young authors to discover and unleash their voice. She is the Chapter Founder and Director of The Free Black Women's Library-Detroit, a mobile pop-up black feminist library housing books written by black women and femmes. In her spare time, she values restorative self care practices, and thinking up names for their future dog with her husband.

Rayn Roberts (p.68, 227) says, "I'm more a puppeteer than a poet. I dangle figures on stage to share insights and poke fun. I don't expect to enlighten anyone, but it could happen. He toured Ireland and England in 2018, where he was invited to read for the Dylan Thomas House by Geoff Haden in Swansea, Wales. He supports the reading series at Seattle's Green Lake Branch Public Library for PoetsWest. More info: https://www.pw.org/content/rayn_roberts.

Judith Roche (p.256) [1941-2019] won two American Book Awards and published four collections of poetry: *GHOSTS* (Empty Bowl, 1984); *Myrrh: My Life as a Screamer* (Black Heron Press, 1993); *Wisdom of the Body* (Black Heron Press, 2007), winner of an American Book Award; and *All Fire All Water* (Black Heron Press, 2015). She was also co-editor, with Meg McHutchison, of *First Fish, First People: Salmon Tales of the North Pacific Rim* (University of Washington Press, 2003), which also won an American Book Award. Roche was a founding member of Red Sky Poetry Theatre in Seattle. She taught at all levels, from elementary school to university, including at Antioch Seattle, Seattle University, Cornish College for the Arts, the Richard Hugo House, and poetry workshops in universities and poetry centers throughout the country. The Literary Arts Director for Bumbershoot between 1986 and 2005, she was the recipient of the Golden Umbrella Award for Lifetime Achievement in the Arts in September 2007. She has poems installed in several Seattle-area public art installations, including an installation about salmon at the Chittenden Locks in Ballard. Judith died in Seattle, on November 14, 2019.

James Rodgers (p.224) is a prolific poet living in Pacific, Washington for more than two decades. James has three self-published chapbooks, and has had poems published by *Prism Magazine, Ha!, Poets of the Kent Canterbury Faire, Fly By Night Press, WPA Members Anthology, Wrist, Washington English Journal*, and many more. He was the winner of the WPA Charles Proctor Award for Humor in 2005. His book of poems, *They Were Called Records, Kids*, was published by MoonPath Press in 2018. He lives with his very patient wife and two very psychotic cats. He has created his own humorous style of haiku that he calls Haikooky, and you can see his blog at jamesrodgershaikooky.blogspot.com.

Frank Rossini (p.32) grew up in New York City and moved to Eugene, Oregon, in 1972. He taught at the University of Oregon and Lane Community College for thirty-eight years. He has published work in various journals, including *The Seattle Review, Chiron Review, Clackamas Review, Raven Chronicles, Más Tequila Review* and *Paterson Literary Review*. Silverfish Review Press published his poetry chapbook, *sparking the rain*. In 2012, sight|for|sight books published a book of his poems, *midnight the blues*.

Morgan Russell (p.232) (she/her) is a rhetorician and poet, and her work can be found in a number of places, mostly logged at linktr.ee/morgankrussell. She is the Creative Writing Editor for the online literary magazine, *Marías at Sampaguitas*, and spends far too much time drinking wine with her aunt at her local indie bookstore. When she's not reading or writing, she can be found mainlining coffee, babysitting, or toiling away at her cubical job in Corporate America—dreaming of the day she becomes a professor of rhetoric and communication who also writes poetry (because this is a dream).

Nancy Scott (p.183) has been the managing editor of *US1 Worksheets* (https://us1poets.com) for more than a decade. She is the author of nine collections of poetry, numerous short stories, a novella, and an upcoming novel, *Shattered*, which addresses PTSD and romantic involvement in the life of a young Marine returning from Korea in 1952. Scott frequently writes about social justice, poverty and homelessness based on decades of street experience as a social worker for the State of New Jersey, and also as a volunteer in an Innocence Project in New Jersey. Visit: www.nancyscott.net.

Dave Seter (p.102) is a civil engineer and poet. Originally from Chicago, he currently lives in Sonoma County, California. His poetry and critical works have recently appeared in *Paterson Literary Review, Evansville Review, Palaver, Confluence*, and other journals. He received his undergraduate degree from Princeton University and his graduate degree from the Dominican University of California, where he studied Ecopoetics. His poetry chapbook, *Night Duty*, was published in 2010 by Main Street Rag Publishing Company.

Mona Nicole Sfeir (p.199) is the child of two refugees, and a first generation American born in New York City and raised in five countries. She received her MFA in Textiles from California College of the Arts (CCA) in San Francisco, and is both a poet and a visual artist. Her poems have been published in journals like *World Literature Today, Hawai'i Review, About Place Journal, WSQ/The Feminist Press CUNY*, and, most recently, in the anthology, *America, We Call Your Name*, from Sixteen Rivers Press. Her artwork has been exhibited both in the United States and abroad and, like her poetry, addresses political, social and environmental issues.

Judith Skillman (p.133) is the recipient of awards from the Academy of American Poets and Artist Trust. Her recent collection is *Came Home to Winter* (Deerbrook Editions, 2019). Work has appeared in *Poetry, The Iowa Review, The Southern Review, Zyzzyva, Nasty Women Poets*, and elsewhere. She is a faculty member at Richard Hugo House in Seattle, Washington. Visit www.judithskillman.com.

Danez Smith (p.88, 263) is a Black, queer, poz writer and performer from St. Paul, Minnesota. Danez is the author of *[insert] boy* (YesYes Books, 2014), winner of the Kate Tufts Discovery Award and the Lambda Literary Award for Gay Poetry, and *Don't Call Us Dead* (Graywolf Press, 2017). Latest collection is *Homie: poems* (Graywolf Press, 2020). Danez is also the author of two chapbooks, *hands on your knees* (Penmanship Books, 2013) and *black movie* (Button Poetry, 2015), winner of the Button Poetry Prize. They are the recipient of fellowships from the Poetry Foundation, the McKnight Foundation, and was a 2017 National Endowment for the Arts Fellow. Danez's work has been featured widely, including on *Buzzfeed, Blavity, PBS NewsHour*, and on *the Late Show with Stephen Colbert*. They are a two-time Individual World

Poetry Slam finalist, three-time Rustbelt Poetry Slam Champion, a founding member of the multi-genre, multicultural Dark Noise Collective, and the youngest winner of the Forward Prize. Visit http://www.danezsmithpoet.com.

Kathleen Stancik (p.178) is a Northwest poet whose work has appeared in *Cirque, Windfall, Twenty-Fourth, Shrub-Steppe Poetry Journal, WA 129+3 Digital Chapbook, Poets Unite!, The LiTFUSE @10 Anthology*, and others. She was a featured poet at the Inland Poetry Prowl in 2017. She enjoys singing, acting, baking and dachshunds.

Scott T. Starbuck's (p.44) *Hawk on Wire: Ecopoems* (Fomite, 2017) was a July 2017 "Editor's Pick" (along with *The Collected Stories of Ray Bradbury*) at *Newpages.com*, and selected from over 1,500 books as a 2018 Montaigne Medal Finalist at Eric Hoffer Awards for "the most thought-provoking books." *Industrial Oz* was published by Fomite Press in 2015. His latest book, *Carbonfish Blues: Ecopoems* (Fomite Press, 2018), features twelve artworks by Guy Denning, whose pieces of activism, refugees, human vulnerability, and realism are known throughout Europe. Starbuck's site, *Trees, Fish, and Dreams Climateblog* (riverseek.blogspot.com), has 58,000 views from 104 countries.

Stuart Stromin (p.292) is a South African-American writer and filmmaker, living in Los Angeles. He was educated at Rhodes University, South Africa, the Alliance Francaise de Paris, and UCLA. His work has appeared in *Sheila-na-gig* online, *River River, 500 miles, The Cynic, Blood Puddles, Rigorous, Alternating Current*, and other publications. Visit: https://stuartstromin.wordpress.com/.

Faiza Sultan (p.156) is originally from the Kurdistan region of Iraq. In 1996, she fled Iraq after working as an interpreter with American NGOs and settled in Seattle; she lives in California now. She is the President and CEO of Translation4all, Inc., and the Publisher/Editor of DARSAFI, LLC. She published two poetry books: *Let Us Give War a Chance* and *I Am a Visitor on this Earth*; and translated two books of poetry from Arabic to English: *It took Place in this House*, by Amal Gamal, and *The Coffee of War*, by Osama Ali Ahmad Suliman.

Penina Ava Taesali (p.165, 313) is a Samoan poet, educator, and cultural arts activist. She is the author of *Sourcing Siapo* (University of Hawaii, Ala Press, 2016), a full-length book of poetry about lost family stories. Her chapbook *SUMMONS: Love Letters for the People*, was published by *Hawai'i Review* in April 2018. For nine years, Ms. Taesali worked as artistic director for the Oakland Asian Cultural Center (OACC) in Oakland, California, where she founded the Asian Pacific Islander Youth Promoting Advocacy and Leadership, Talking Roots Art Collective. AYPAL TRAC is a youth arts education program that serves 150 to 200 low-income high school and middle school students annually. Presently, she teaches creative writing and drama to middle school students in Keizer, Oregon. Ms. Taesali earned an MFA in writing from Mills College in 2012, and lives and writes in Salem, Oregon.

Mary Ellen Talley's (p.281) poems have recently been published in *Raven Chronicles, U City Review* and *Ekphrastic Review*, as well as in anthologies, *All We Can Hold* and *Ice Cream Poems*. Her poetry has received two Pushcart Nominations. A chapbook, *Postcards from the Lilac City*, is forthcoming from Finishing Line Press.

Vanessa Taylor (p.64) is a writer based out of Philadelphia who explores Black Muslim womanhood and technology through various narrative forms. Her articles, essays, fiction, and more have appeared in outlets such as *Barren Magazine, Belt Magazine, Catapult, The Intercept*, and other publications. She is a 2019 Echoing Ida cohort member, and the Editor-in-Chief of *The Drinking Gourd*, a Black Muslim literary magazine.

Gail Tremblay (p.300) is an Onondaga/Mi'Kmaq poet, writer, teacher, and artist born in Buffalo, New York. After graduating from the University of New Hampshire with a BA in drama, she earned an MFA in creative writing from the University of Oregon. She has been a member of the faculty at The Evergreen State College in Washington State since 1980, where she has mentored students in the fields of visual arts, writing, Native American and cultural studies. She shares her unique vision through her multi-media visual works, art installations, her writing on Native American Art, and her poetry. Tremblay is the author of four books of poetry: *Night Gives Women the Word* (1979), *Close to Home* (1981), *Indian Singing in 20th Century America* (1990), and *Indian Singing* (revised edition, 1998) from Calyx Books, and *Farther From and Too Close to Home* (Lone Willow Press, 2014). Her poetry is widely anthologized and poems have been translated into French, German, Spanish, and Japanese.

Terra Trevor (p.108) is the author of a diverse body of work and a contributor to fifteen books, including *Children of the Dragonfly: Native American Voices On Child Custody and Education* (University of Arizona Press) and *The People Who Stayed: Southeastern Indian Writing After Removal* (University of Oklahoma Press). Her memoir, *Pushing up the Sky*, is widely anthologized. Her work and portrait is featured in *Tending the Fire: Native Voices and Portraits* (University of New Mexico Press). Her work also has appeared previously in *The Raven Chronicles, News From Native California* (Heyday), *Voices Confronting Pediatric Brain Tumors* (Johns Hopkins University Press), and in numerous magazines, anthologies, and literary journals.

Angelina Villalobos (p.171) (aka pseudonym 179), grew up in Seattle, Washington, within a mosaic of cultures and ideas. Inspired by folklore, stories humans have created and collected to explain the unknown, Angelina crosses tales about animals and their wit with current events and religion. In combining these elements, Angelina creates a fairytale land filtered through the eyes of an anime and comic book lover. This union, influenced by being raised in the Pacific Northwest in the 90s, is an intimate exemplification of her personal pursuit of understanding the world around her. The poem in this anthology, "For the Man Who is Half of Me," was written when Angelina was eighteen, in 2001, as a student of Anna Bálint at El Centro de la Raza.

Richard Widerkehr (p.75, 111) earned his MA from Columbia University, and won two Hopwood first prizes for poetry at the University of Michigan. He has two books of poems, *In The Presence Of Absence* (MoonPath Press) and *The Way Home* (Plain View Press), along with three chapbooks and a novel, *Sedimental Journey*. Recent work have appeared in *Verse Daily, Writer's Almanac, Crab Creek Review, Raven Chronicles,* and others.

Carletta Carrington Wilson (p. 30, 52) is a literary and visual artist. Her poems and literary works have appeared in a number of publications, including *African American Review, Calyx Journal, Make It True: Poems from Cascadia, Cimarron Review, Obsidian III, The Seattle Review, Raven Chronicles, Beyond the Frontier: African American Poetry for the 21st Century, The Journal: Book Club of Washington, Pilgrimage, Uncommon Waters: Women Write About Fishing,* and *Seattle Poets and Photographers: A Millennium Reflection*; and online in *Rattapallax: Innovative Northwest Poets* and *Torch*. Recent poems were published in *African American Review, Raven Chronicles' Last Call,* and *Stealing Light: A Raven Chronicles Anthology, Selected Work, 1991-1996*. Her installation, *letter to a laundress*, was exhibited at the Bainbridge Island Museum of Art, the University of Puget Sound's Kittredge Gallery, and Seattle's King Street Station.

Tanaya Winder (p.24) is a poet, vocalist, writer, educator, and motivational speaker from the Southern Ute, Duckwater Shoshone, and Pyramid Lake Paiute Nations. She received a BA in English from Stanford University and, after completing her MFA in creative writing from the University of New Mexico, she co-founded *As/Us: A Space for Women of the World*, a literary magazine publishing works by Indigenous women and women of color. In 2015, she co-founded the *Sing Our Rivers Red* traveling earring exhibit to raise awareness about murdered and missing Indigenous women and girls. Her advocacy also includes working with Native youth and reservation communities as the Director of the University of Colorado at Boulder's Upward Bound program, which serves approximately 103 Native youth from across the country. Her debut poetry collection, *Words Like Love*, was published in 2015, and her chapbook, *Why Storms Are Named After People and Bullets Remain Nameless*, was released in 2017. Learn more about her work at https://tanayawinder.com.

Katelyn Winter (p.55, 56) is growing roots in Philadelphia after graduating in 2018 from Muhlenberg College in Pennsylvania. There, she completed a thesis on the language of murder, "Narration, Sensation, and Responsibility in the True Crime Story," and continues to explore themes of danger, the body, and untruths in her work today.

Carolyne Wright's (p.214) most recent books are *This Dream the World: New & Selected Poems* (Lost Horse Press, 2017), whose title poem received a Pushcart Prize and was included in *The Best American Poetry 2009*; and the bilingual volume of Seattle-based Chilean poet Eugenia Toledo, *Trazas de mapa, trazas de sangre / Map Traces, Blood Traces* (Mayapple Press, 2017), a Finalist for the 2018 Washington State Book Award in Poetry, and also for the 2018 PEN Los Angeles Award in Translation. Wright co-edited the ground-breaking anthology, *Raising*

Lilly Ledbetter: Women Poets Occupy the Workspace (Lost Horse Press, 2015) that received ten Pushcart Prize nominations. She teaches for Richard Hugo House and for national and international literary conferences and festivals. A Contributing Editor for the Pushcart Prizes, Wright has received grants from the NEA, 4Culture, and Seattle's Office of Arts & Culture.

Hannah Yoest (p.243) is an art director based in Washington D.C. Her poetry is seen in several literary magazines, including *Columbia Journal, Atlanta Review, Barely South, Aperion Review*, and others. She is a graduate of the University of Virginia where she studied fine art. She studied poetry at the Iowa Writers Workshop summer course, attended the *VQR* writers' conference, and the Kenyon Writers' Workshop. She is also an artist in residence at the ceramics studio KUZEH Pottery. You can find her on instagram: https://www.instagram.com/avecruth/ and twitter: https://twitter.com/ruthyoest.

Dr. Shahed Yousaf (p.210) is a British writer and artist of Pakistani heritage. He is a GP who works in prisons and with the homeless community, and is interested in the therapeutic potential of literature and the arts. Shahed is the author of two medical books. He is a writer of flash fiction, short stories and plays, and is working on a novel—a medical thriller set in a prison. His writing has been described as "shocking, electric and full of the most incredible anecdotes." He was short-listed for the Bath Flash Fiction Prize 2016, and commended for the Faber & Faber FAB Prize 2017. Shahed won a place on the Middle Way Mentoring Project 2018 for writers based in the Midlands, UK, and chaired the Stirling Publishing "Colours of Madness" event at Waterstones, Birmingham, England, in October 2018. He follows a long and illustrious tradition of writers who are doctors.

Nicole Yurcaba (p.72) is a Ukrainian-American English instructor, goth (yes, with a lowercase "g"), novelist, essayist, and poet. She teaches at Bridgewater College in Virginia, and she recently graduated from Lindenwood University's MFA program.

Elaine Zimmerman (p.215) is a policy leader for children, an essayist and poet. Publications include poetry in journals and newspapers such as *The Hartford Courant, Lascaux Review, Americana, Coal Hill Review, CT River Review, Lilith, Adanna Literary Journal—Women and War, New Millennium, The New Guard Literary Review*, and anthologies including *All We Can Hold, Jewish Poetry in the Third Millennium, Forgotten Women*, and *Worlds in Our Words: Contemporary American Women Writers*. Honors include Connecticut Poetry, William Stafford, and a Pushcart nomination.

BIOGRAPHICAL NOTES
Foreword

Diane Glancy: Proficient in numerous genres—fiction, nonfiction, poetry, and playwriting—Glancy often creates work that reflects her Native American heritage. Part Cherokee, and of English and German descent, Glancy was born in Kansas City, Missouri. She has served as artist-in-residence for the Oklahoma State Arts Council (traveling around the state to teach poetry to Native American students) and has taught Native American literature and creative writing at Macalester College in St. Paul, Minnesota. "Writing is a conversation," she states on her Macalester webpage.

Reviewers have noted her ability to combine genres, to portray both Native American and non-Native characters, and to depict Native American beliefs and Christianity in her writing. Adept at writing free verse as well as prose poems, she often portrays the intersections of new and old worlds, reporting on history, religion, and the loss of Native traditions. Glancy has explored Native American history in depth in her novels *Pushing the Bear: A Novel of the Trail of Tears* (1996) and *Stone Heart: A Novel of Sacajawea* (2003).

Glancy's collection of poems, *Primer of the Obsolete*, won the 2003 Juniper Prize for Poetry. She has also received the Five Civilized Tribes Playwriting Laureate Prize; the Oklahoma Book Award; the Cherokee Medal of Honor, Cherokee Honor Society, Tahlequah, Oklahoma; the Pablo Neruda Prize for Poetry; grants from the National Endowment for the Arts; and a Sundance Screenwriting Fellowship. See her work at http://www.dianeglancy.com.

BIOGRAPHICAL NOTES
Editors

Anna Bálint is the author of *Horse Thief*, Curbstone Press, 2004, a collection of short fiction spanning cultures and continents that was a finalist for the Pacific Northwest Book Award. Two earlier books of poetry are *Out of the Box* and *spread them crimson sleeves like wings*; her poems, stories and essays have appeared in numerous journals and magazines. She edited *Words From the Café*, Raven Chronicles Press, 2016, an anthology of writing by people in recovery; and was a contributing editor for *Raven Chronicles Journal* for many years. In response to the 9/11 attack, invasion of Afghanistan, and increased Islamophobia, she organized "Evidence of Compassion: A Reading of Middle Eastern and Central Asian Poetry & Literature" (Elliott Bay Book Company), uniting a culturally diverse group of established and emerging writers as presenters. An alumna of Hedgebrook Writers Retreat and the Jack Straw Writers Program, Anna has also taught creative writing for many years, including at Washington State prisons, El Centro de la Raza, Writers in the Schools, Antioch University, Richard Hugo House, and Path With Art (all in Seattle). Currently, she teaches adults in recovery from trauma, addiction, mental illness, and homelessness at Seattle's Recovery Café, where she founded Safe Place Writing Circle.

Phoebe Bosché is a cultural activist, and has been managing editor of The Raven Chronicles literary organization/Raven Chronicles Press since 1991. Since 1984, she has organized literary events and readings in the Pacific Northwest. In 1985, she co-founded, along with poet Roberto Valenza, "Alternative To Loud Boats," a literary and musical festival which ran for ten years in various venues in Seattle. She was co-editor of *Swale Magazine* (with Valenza), and *SkyViews* (with Jim Maloney, et al), a monthly literary publication of Red Sky Poetry Theater, in the mid-1980s to early 1990s. Her spoken word poems appear in various publications, including the anthology *Durable Breath, Contemporary Native American Poetry*, Salmon Run Publishing Co., Anchorage, Alaska, and *Open Sky*. She is a full-time editor and book designer. Her favorite poet is Archy, the cockroach, whose muse is Mehitabel, the alley cat.

Thomas Hubbard, a retired writing instructor and spoken word performer, authored *Nail and other hardworking poems*, Year of the Dragon Press, 1994; *Junkyard Dogz* (also available on audio CD); and *Injunz*, a chapbook. He designed and published *Children Remember Their Fathers* (an anthology), and books by seven other authors. His book reviews have appeared in *Square Lake, Raven Chronicles, New Pages* and *The Cartier Street Review*. Publication credits include poems in *Yellow Medicine Review*, spring 2010, *I Was Indian*, editor Susan Deer Cloud (Foothills Publishing, 2010), and *Florida Review*; and short stories in *Red Ink* and *Yellow Medicine Review*. 📖

ACKNOWLEDGMENTS

Raven Chronicles is indebted to our 2019-2020 co-sponsors for partial funding of our programs: the City of Seattle Office of Arts & Culture (Civic Partners); 4Culture/King County Lodging Tax (Arts Sustained Support Program); the Washington State Arts Commission/ArtsWA, with National Endowment (NEA) funding for project support. Thanks to Esther Altshul Helfgott for her early emotional support. Special thanks to Anonymous, Alfredo M. Arrequín, Kathleen Alcalá, Anna Bálint, Stesha Brandon, Lawrence Eickstaedt, Kathleen Figetakis, Cammie Hall, Larry Laurence, Loreen Lilyn Lee, Anna Odessa Linzer, Lawrence Matsuda, Susan Pace (in memory of Keith Pace), Joan Rabinowitz, Carol Sunde, Scott T. Starbuck, and Carletta Carrington Wilson—for their generous donations in support of Raven publications and programs in 2019 and into 2020. Thanks to GiveBig 2019 and 501 Commons for their support of regional non-profit organizations during a successful 2019 donation campaign.

We are the originators, makers and sole distributors of National Waffle Association products. Visit our Headquarters at www.nationalwaffleassociation.com for a look at our full line.

The intrepid little sticker that launched our brand back in 1999 still delights folk from Tulsa to Tibet.

Guaranteed to produce many rear view smiles per mile. You won't be disappointed! Sticker comes in stunning full-color. Shown at 25% size.

Become an NWA Member

- Gain Instant Social Status
- Be the Envy of Your Peers
- Get Member Only Promos
- Membership for Life
- No Annual Dues
- Laminated Member Card

For details visit:www.nationalwaffleassociation.com

All images © 1999 - 2018 Tin Hat Novelties

PUBLISHER
Raven Chronicles Press

MANAGING DIRECTOR
Phoebe Bosché, Seattle

FOUNDING EDITORS
Kathleen Alcalá
Phoebe Bosché
Philip Red Eagle

ANTHOLOGY EDITORS
Anna Bálint
Phoebe Bosché
Thomas Hubbard

COPY EDITORS
Phoebe Bosché
Anne Frantilla
Paul Hunter

ALL QUERIES
The Raven Chronicles

Office Address:
4131 Greenwood Avenue North
Seattle, Washington 98103

Mailing Address:
15528 12th Avenue Northeast
Shoreline, Washington 98155-6226

Tel: 206.941.2955
https://www.ravenchronicles.org
editors@ravenchronicles.org

© 2019-2020 The Raven Chronicles
a non-profit, 501(c)(3) organization
Founded in 1991

www.ingramcontent.com/pod-product-compliance
Lightning Source LLC
Chambersburg PA
CBHW060457010526
44118CB00018B/2444